D1285485

*Lucrezia Tornabuoni
de' Medici*

SACRED
NARRATIVES

᪣

*Edited and Translated
by Jane Tylus*

THE UNIVERSITY OF CHICAGO PRESS
Chicago & London

Jane Tylus is professor of Italian and associate dean for the humanities in the College of Letters and Science, University of Wisconsin, Madison. Her books include *Writing and Vulnerability in the Late Renaissance* and *Epic Traditions in the Contemporary World: The Poetics of Community*, coedited with Margaret Beissinger and Susanne Wofford.

The University of Chicago Press, Chicago 60637
The University of Chicago Press, Ltd., London
© 2001 by The University of Chicago
All rights reserved. Published 2001
Printed in the United States of America
10 09 08 07 06 05 04 03 02 01   1 2 3 4 5

ISBN: 0-226-80852-1 (cloth)
ISBN: 0-226-80854-8 (paper)

Library of Congress Cataloging-in-Publication Data

Tornabuoni, Lucrezia, 1425–1482.
    [Poemetti sacri. English]
    Sacred narratives / Lucrezia Tornabuoni de' Medici ;
    edited and translated by Jane Tylus.
        p. cm.
    Includes bibliographical references and index.
    ISBN 0-226-80852-1 (cloth : alk. paper) — ISBN 0-226-80854-8 (pbk. :
alk. paper)
        1. Tornabuoni, Lucrezia, 1425–1482—Translations into English. 2.
Religious poetry, Italian—Translations into English. I. Tylus, Jane, 1956–
II. Title.
PQ4664.T59 P613 2001
851'.2—dc21

                                                          00-048840

To Bill, Alex, and Nathan

CONTENTS

ACKNOWLEDGMENTS

M any people have generously helped bring this book into being. From the very beginning of the project Albert Rabil Jr. was the most industrious and encouraging of editors, and I appreciate his and Margaret King's conviction that Lucrezia Tornabuoni's poetry deserved an English translation. My thanks to the Vilas Trust of the University of Wisconsin for funding my visit to Italy in 1998; to Silvia, Roberto, and Stefano Fanciullacci, Anna Grilli, and Helen Burroughs, my hosts in Sesto Fiorentino; and to the courteous staff in the Sala dei Manoscritti of the Biblioteca Nazionale, Florence, and at the Biblioteca Riccardiana. I am also grateful to Paul Bucklin for his efforts in procuring a microfilm version of Magliabechiano VII, 338 that allowed me to take Lucrezia home to Wisconsin.

Natalie Tomas provided assistance from afar, sending me materials from Australia that inexplicably could not be found in Florence and turning a critical eye on the introduction. Gail Geiger, William Klein, and Joseph Tylus also read the introduction and gave me many useful suggestions. Toma Longinovic kindly invited me to give a paper on Tornabuoni for his forum on cultural translation, and I appreciate the feedback I received from my colleagues and students at Madison. Jodie Rogers Mariotti provided invaluable assistance on art historical matters. For help with notes and difficulties in translation, I thank Maria Galli Stampino, Barbara Martellini, Deborah Gillette, Tom Cravens, Chris Kleinhenz, Ernesto Livorni, Graziella Menechella, and Francesco Benvenuti; any errors are of course my own. The Graduate School of the University of Wisconsin gave me summer funding in 1999 to complete the manuscript and supplied a wonderful editorial assistant, Nhora Serrano, to help prepare the book for publication. David Marsh carefully read the manuscript for the University of Chicago Press, and I am grateful for his many suggestions. Alice Bennett and Anthony Burton at the Press saw the book through publication, and my father spent his Thanksgiving vacation reading page proofs; I greatly appreciate the time and attention they gave to Lucrezia.

Finally, thanks to Bill for his constant support and to Alex and Nathan for allowing me not only to work on this volume when I should have been spending time with them but to substitute one version of the translation after another for the usual bedtime stories.

THE OTHER VOICE IN EARLY MODERN EUROPE: INTRODUCTION TO THE SERIES

Margaret L. King and Albert Rabil Jr.

THE OLD VOICE AND THE OTHER VOICE

In western Europe and the United States women are nearing equality in the professions, in business, and in politics. Most enjoy access to education, reproductive rights, and autonomy in financial affairs. Issues vital to women are on the public agenda: equal pay, child care, domestic abuse, breast cancer research, and curricular revision with an eye to the inclusion of women.

These recent achievements have their origins in things women (and some male supporters) said for the first time about six hundred years ago. Theirs is the "other voice," in contradistinction to the "first voice," the voice of the educated men who created Western culture. Coincident with a general reshaping of European culture in the period 1300–1700 (called the Renaissance or early modern period), questions of female equality and opportunity were raised that still resound and are still unresolved.

The "other voice" emerged against the backdrop of a three-thousand-year history of the derogation of women rooted in the civilizations related to Western culture: Hebrew, Greek, Roman, and Christian. Negative attitudes toward women inherited from these traditions pervaded the intellectual, medical, legal, religious, and social systems that developed during the European Middle Ages.

The following pages describe the traditional, overwhelmingly male views of women's nature inherited by early modern Europeans and the new tradition that the "other voice" called into being to challenge reigning assumptions. This review should serve as a framework for understanding the texts published in the series "The Other Voice in Early Modern Europe." Introductions specific to each text and author follow this essay in all the volumes of the series.

TRADITIONAL VIEWS OF WOMEN, 500 B.C.E.–1500 C.E.

Embedded in the philosophical and medical theories of the ancient Greeks were perceptions of the female as inferior to the male in both mind and body. Similarly, the structure of civil legislation inherited from the ancient Romans was biased against women, and the views on women developed by Christian thinkers out of the Hebrew Bible and the Christian New Testament were negative and disabling. Literary works composed in the vernacular of ordinary people, and widely recited or read, conveyed these negative assumptions. The social networks within which most women lived—those of the family and the institutions of the Roman Catholic Church—were shaped by this negative tradition and sharply limited the areas in which women might act in and upon the world.

GREEK PHILOSOPHY AND FEMALE NATURE. Greek biology assumed that women were inferior to men and defined them as merely childbearers and housekeepers. This view was authoritatively expressed in the works of the philosopher Aristotle.

Aristotle thought in dualities. He considered action superior to inaction, form (the inner design or structure of any object) superior to matter, completion to incompletion, possession to deprivation. In each of these dualities he associated the male principle with the superior quality and the female with the inferior. "The male principle in nature," he argued, "is associated with active, formative and perfected characteristics, while the female is passive, material and deprived, desiring the male in order to become complete."[1] Men are always identified with virile qualities, such as judgment, courage, and stamina, and women with their opposites—irrationality, cowardice, and weakness.

The masculine principle was considered to be superior even in the womb. The man's semen, Aristotle believed, created the form of a new human creature, while the female body contributed only matter. (The existence of the ovum, and the other facts of human embryology, was not established until the seventeenth century.) Although the later Greek physician Galen believed there was a female component in generation, contributed by "female semen," the followers of both Aristotle and Galen saw the male role in human generation as more active and more important.

In the Aristotelian view, the male principle sought to reproduce itself. The creation of a female was always a mistake, therefore, resulting from

---

1. Aristotle, *Physics* 1.9 192a20–24 (*The Complete Works of Aristotle*, ed. Jonathan Barnes, rev. Oxford translation, 2 vols. [Princeton: Princeton University Press, 1984], 1:328).

an imperfect act of generation. Every female born was considered a "defec-
tive" or "mutilated" male (as Aristotle's terminology has variously been trans-
lated), a "monstrosity" of nature.[2]

For Greek theorists, the biology of males and females was the key to
their psychology. The female was softer and more docile, more apt to be
despondent, querulous, and deceitful. Being incomplete, moreover, she
craved sexual fulfillment in intercourse with a male. The male was intellec-
tual, active, and in control of his passions.

These psychological polarities derived from the theory that the uni-
verse consisted of four elements (earth, fire, air, and water), expressed in
human bodies as four "humors" (black bile, yellow bile, blood, and phlegm)
considered respectively dry, hot, damp, and cold, and corresponding to
mental states ("melancholic," "choleric," "sanguine," "phlegmatic"). In this
scheme the male, sharing the principles of earth and fire, was dry and hot;
the female, sharing the principles of air and water, was damp and cold.

Woman's psychology was further affected by her dominant organ, the
uterus (womb), *hystera* in Greek. The passions generated by the womb made
women lustful, deceitful, talkative, irrational, indeed—when these affects
were in excess—"hysterical."

Aristotle's biology also had social and political consequences. If the
male principle was superior and the female inferior, then in the household,
as in the state, men should govern and women must be subordinate. That
hierarchy did not rule out the companionship of husband and wife, whose
cooperation was necessary for the welfare of children and the preservation
of property. Such mutuality supported male preeminence.

Aristotle's teacher Plato suggested a different possibility: that men and
women might possess the same virtues. The setting for this proposal is the
imaginary and ideal Republic that Plato sketches in his dialogue of that
name. Here, for a privileged elite capable of leading wisely, all distinctions
of class and wealth dissolve, as consequently do those of gender. Without
households or property, as Plato constructs his ideal society, there is no
need for the subordination of women. Women may therefore be educated
to the same level as men to assume leadership. Plato's Republic remained
imaginary, however. In real societies, the subordination of women remained
the norm and the prescription.

The views of women inherited from the Greek philosophical tradition
became the basis for medieval thought. In the thirteenth century the su-
preme Scholastic philosopher Thomas Aquinas, among others, still echoed

2. Aristotle, *Generation of Animals* 2.3 737a27–28 (Barnes, 1:1144).

Aristotle's views of human reproduction, of male and female personalities, and of the preeminent role of the male in the social hierarchy.

ROMAN LAW AND THE FEMALE CONDITION. Roman law, like Greek philosophy, underlay medieval thought and shaped medieval society. The ancient belief that adult, property-owning men should administer households and make decisions affecting the community at large is the very fulcrum of Roman law.

About 450 B.C.E., during Rome's republican era, the community's customary law was recorded (legendarily) on twelve tables erected in the city's central forum. It was later elaborated by professional jurists whose activity increased in the imperial era, when much new legislation was passed, especially on issues affecting family and inheritance. This growing, changing body of laws was eventually codified in the *Corpus of Civil Law* under the direction of the emperor Justinian, generations after the empire ceased to be ruled from Rome. That *Corpus*, read and commented on by medieval scholars from the eleventh century on, inspired the legal systems of most of the cities and kingdoms of Europe.

Laws regarding dowries, divorce, and inheritance mostly pertain to women. Since those laws aimed to maintain and preserve property, the women concerned were those from the property-owning minority. Their subordination to male family members points to the even greater subordination of lower-class and slave women, about whom the laws speak little.

In the early republic the *paterfamilias*, "father of the family," possessed *patria potestas*, "paternal power." The term *pater*, "father," in both these cases does not necessarily mean biological father but denotes a householder. The father was the person who owned the household's property and, indeed, its human members. The *paterfamilias* had absolute power—including the power, rarely exercised, of life or death—over his wife, his children, and his slaves as much as his cattle.

Male children could be "emancipated," an act that granted them legal autonomy and the right to own property. Those over fourteen could be emancipated by a special grant from the father, or automatically by the father's death. But females could never be emancipated; instead, they passed from the authority of the father to that of a husband or, if widowed or orphaned while still unmarried, a guardian or tutor.

Marriage in its traditional form placed the woman under her husband's authority, or *manus*. He could divorce her on grounds of adultery, drinking wine, or stealing from the household, but she could not divorce him. She could possess no property in her own right, nor could she bequeath any to her children upon her death. When her husband died the household property passed not to her but to his male heirs. And when her father died she had no claim to any family inheritance, which was directed to her brothers or more remote male relatives. The effect of these laws was to exclude women from civil society, itself based on property ownership.

In the later republican and imperial periods these rules were significantly modified, and women rarely married according to the traditional form. The practice of "free" marriage allowed a woman to remain under her father's authority, to possess property given to her by her father (most frequently the "dowry," recoverable from the husband's household on his death), and to inherit from her father. She could also bequeath property to her own children and divorce her husband, just as he could divorce her.

Despite this greater freedom, women still suffered enormous disability under Roman law. Heirs could belong only to the father's side, never the mother's. Moreover, although she could bequeath her property to her children, she could not establish a line of succession in doing so. A woman was "the beginning and end of her own family," said the jurist Ulpian. Moreover, women could play no public role. They could not hold public office, represent anyone in a legal case, or even witness a will. Women had only a private existence and no public personality.

The dowry system, the guardian, women's limited ability to transmit wealth, and their total political disability are all features of Roman law adopted by the medieval communities of western Europe, although modified according to local customary laws.

CHRISTIAN DOCTRINE AND WOMEN'S PLACE. The Hebrew Bible and the Christian New Testament authorized later writers to limit women to the realm of the family and to burden them with the guilt of original sin. The passages most fruitful for this purpose were the creation narratives in Genesis and sentences from the Epistles defining women's role within the Christian family and community.

Each of the first two chapters of Genesis contains a creation narrative. In the first "God created man in his own image, in the image of God he created him; male and female he created them" (Gen. 1:27). In the second, God created Eve from Adam's rib (2:21–23). Christian theologians relied principally on Genesis 2 for their understanding of the relationship between man and woman, interpreting the creation of Eve from Adam as proof of her subordination to him.

The creation story in Genesis 2 leads to that of the temptations in Genesis 3: of Eve by the wily serpent and of Adam by Eve. As read by Christian theologians from Tertullian to Thomas Aquinas, the narrative made Eve responsible for the Fall and its consequences. She instigated the act; she deceived her husband; she suffered the greater punishment. Her disobedience made it necessary for Jesus to be incarnated and to die on the cross. From the pulpit, moralists and preachers for centuries conveyed to women the guilt they bore for original sin.

The Epistles offered advice to early Christians on building communities of the faithful. Among the matters to be regulated was the place of women. Paul offered views favorable to women in Gal. 3:28: "There is neither Jew nor Greek, there is neither slave nor free, there is neither male nor female; for you are all one in Christ Jesus." Paul also referred to women as his coworkers and placed them on a par with himself and his male coworkers (Phil. 4:2–3; Rom. 16:1–3; 1 Cor. 16:19). Elsewhere Paul limited women's possibilities: "But I want you to understand that the head of every man is Christ, the head of a woman is her husband, and the head of Christ is God" (1 Cor. 11:3).

Biblical passages by later writers (though attributed to Paul) enjoined women to forgo jewels, expensive clothes, and elaborate coiffures; and they forbade women to "teach or have authority over men," telling them to "learn in silence with all submissiveness" as is proper for one responsible for sin, consoling them however with the thought that they will be saved through childbearing (1 Tim. 2:9–15). Other texts among the later Epistles defined women as the weaker sex and emphasized their subordination to their husbands (1 Peter 3:7; Col. 3:18; Eph. 5:22–23).

These passages from the New Testament became the arsenal employed by theologians of the early church to transmit negative attitudes toward women to medieval Christian culture—above all, Tertullian ("On the Apparel of Women"), Jerome (*Against Jovinian*), and Augustine (*The Literal Meaning of Genesis*).

THE IMAGE OF WOMEN IN MEDIEVAL LITERATURE. The philosophical, legal, and religious traditions born in antiquity formed the basis of the medieval intellectual synthesis wrought by trained thinkers, mostly clerics, writing in Latin and based largely in universities. The vernacular literary tradition that developed alongside the learned tradition also spoke about female nature and women's roles. Medieval stories, poems, and epics also portrayed women negatively—as lustful and deceitful—while praising good housekeepers and loyal wives as replicas of the Virgin Mary or the female saints and martyrs.

There is an exception in the movement of "courtly love" that evolved in southern France from the twelfth century. Courtly love was erotic love between a nobleman and noblewoman, the latter usually superior in social rank. It was always adulterous. From the conventions of courtly love derive modern Western notions of romantic love. The tradition has had an impact disproportionate to its size, for it affected only a tiny elite, and very few women. The exaltation of the female lover probably does not reflect a higher evaluation of women, or a step toward their sexual liberation. More likely it gives expression to the social and sexual tensions besetting the knightly class at a specific historical juncture.

The literary fashion of courtly love was on the wane by the thirteenth century, when the widely read *Romance of the Rose* was composed in French by two authors of significantly different dispositions. Guillaume de Lorris composed the initial four thousand verses about 1235, and Jean de Meun added about seventeen thousand verses—more than four times the original—about 1265.

The fragment composed by Guillaume de Lorris stands squarely in the tradition of courtly love. Here the poet, in a dream, is admitted into a walled garden where he finds a magic fountain in which a rosebush is reflected. He longs to pick one rose, but the thorns prevent it, even as he is wounded by arrows from the god of love, whose commands he agrees to obey. The rest of this part of the poem recounts the poet's unsuccessful efforts to pluck the rose.

The longer part of the *Romance* by Jean de Meun also describes a dream. But here allegorical characters give long didactic speeches, providing a social satire on a variety of themes, some pertaining to women. Love is an anxious and tormented state, the poem explains; women are greedy and manipulative, marriage is miserable, beautiful women are lustful, ugly ones cease to please, and a chaste woman is as rare as a black swan.

Shortly after Jean de Meun completed *The Romance of the Rose*, Mathéolus penned his *Lamentations*, a long Latin diatribe against marriage translated into French about a century later. The *Lamentations* summed up medieval attitudes toward women and provoked the important response by Christine de Pizan in her *Book of the City of Ladies*.

In 1355 Giovanni Boccaccio wrote *Il corbaccio*, another antifeminist manifesto, though ironically by an author whose other works pioneered new directions in Renaissance thought. The former husband of his lover appears to Boccaccio, condemning his unmoderated lust and detailing the defects of women. Boccaccio concedes at the end "how much men naturally surpass women in nobility"[3] and is cured of his desires.

3. Giovanni Boccaccio, *The Corbaccio, or The Labyrinth of Love*, trans. and ed. Anthony K. Cassell, 2d rev. ed. (Binghamton, N.Y.: Medieval and Renaissance Texts and Studies, 1993), 71.

WOMEN'S ROLES: THE FAMILY. The negative perception of women expressed in the intellectual tradition is also implicit in the actual roles women played in European society. Assigned to subordinate positions in the household and the church, they were barred from significant participation in public life.

Medieval European households, like those in antiquity and in non-Western civilizations, were headed by males. It was the male serf, peasant, feudal lord, town merchant, or citizen who was polled or taxed or succeeded to an inheritance or had any acknowledged public role, although his wife or widow could stand as a temporary surrogate for him. From about 1100, the position of property-holding males was further enhanced. Inheritance was confined to the male, or agnate, line—with depressing consequences for women.

A wife never fully belonged to her husband's family nor a daughter to her father's. She left her father's house young to marry whomever her parents chose. Her dowry was managed by her husband, and at her death it normally passed to her children by him.

A married woman's life was occupied nearly constantly with cycles of pregnancy, childbearing, and lactation. Women bore children through all the years of their fertility, and many died in childbirth. They also were responsible for raising young children up to six or seven. In the propertied classes that responsibility was shared, since it was common for a wet nurse to take over breast-feeding, and servants performed other chores.

Women trained their daughters in the household duties appropriate to their status, nearly always tasks associated with textiles: spinning, weaving, sewing, embroidering. Their sons were sent out of the house as apprentices or students, or their fathers assumed their training in later childhood and adolescence. On the death of her husband, a woman's children became the responsibility of his family. She generally did not take "his" children with her to a new marriage or back to her father's house, except sometimes in artisan classes.

Women also worked. Peasants performed farm chores, merchant wives often practiced their husbands' trades, the unmarried daughters of the urban poor worked as servants or prostitutes. All wives produced or embellished textiles and did the housekeeping, and wealthy ones managed servants. These labors were unpaid or poorly paid but often contributed substantially to family wealth.

WOMEN'S ROLES: THE CHURCH. Membership in a household, whether a father's or a husband's, meant for women a lifelong subordination to others. In western Europe the Roman Catholic Church offered an alternative to the career of wife and mother. A woman could enter a convent parallel in function to the monasteries for men that evolved in the early Christian centuries.

In the convent, a woman pledged herself to a celibate life, lived according to strict community rules, and worshiped daily. Often the convent offered training in Latin, allowing some women to become considerable scholars and authors as well as scribes, artists, and musicians. For women who chose the conventual life the benefits could be enormous, but for numerous others placed in convents by paternal choice, the life could be restrictive and burdensome.

The conventual life declined as an alternative for women as the modern age approached. Reformed monastic institutions resisted responsibility for related female orders. The church increasingly restricted female institutional life by insisting on closer male supervision.

Women often sought other options. Some joined the communities of laywomen that sprang up spontaneously in the thirteenth century in the urban zones of western Europe, especially in Flanders and Italy. Some joined the heretical movements that flourished in late medieval Christendom, whose anticlerical and often antifamily positions particularly appealed to women. In these communities some women were acclaimed as "holy women" or "saints," whereas others often were condemned as frauds or heretics.

Though the options offered to women by the church were sometimes less than satisfactory, they were sometimes richly rewarding. After 1520 the convent remained an option only in Roman Catholic territories. Protestantism engendered an ideal of marriage as a heroic endeavor and appeared to place husband and wife on a more equal footing. Sermons and treatises, however, still called for female subordination and obedience.

THE OTHER VOICE, 1300–1700

When the modern era opened, European culture was so firmly structured by a framework of negative attitudes toward women that to dismantle it was a monumental labor. The process began as part of a larger cultural movement that entailed the critical reexamination of ideas inherited from the ancient and medieval past. The humanists launched that critical reexamination.

THE HUMANIST FOUNDATION. Originating in Italy in the fourteenth century, humanism quickly became the dominant intellectual movement in Europe. Spreading in the sixteenth century from Italy to the rest of Europe, it fueled the literary, scientific, and philosophical movements of the era and laid the basis for the eighteenth-century Enlightenment.

Humanists regarded the Scholastic philosophy of medieval universities as out of touch with the realities of urban life. They found in the rhetorical discourse of classical Rome a language adapted to civic life and public speech. They learned to read, speak, and write classical Latin, and eventually classical Greek. They founded schools to teach others to do so, establishing the pattern for elementary and secondary education for the next three hundred years.

In the service of complex government bureaucracies, humanists employed their skills to write eloquent letters, deliver public orations, and formulate public policy. They developed new scripts for copying manuscripts and used the new printing press to disseminate texts, for which they created methods of critical editing.

Humanism was a movement led by males who accepted the evaluation of women in ancient texts and generally shared the misogynist perceptions of their culture. (Female humanists, as we will see, did not.) Yet humanism also opened the door to a reevaluation of the nature and capacity of women. By calling authors, texts, and ideas into question, it made possible the fundamental rereading of the whole intellectual tradition that was required in order to free women from cultural prejudice and social subordination.

A DIFFERENT CITY. The other voice first appeared when, after so many centuries, the accumulation of misogynist concepts evoked a response from a capable female defender: Christine de Pizan (1365–1431). Introducing her *Book of the City of Ladies* (1405), she described how she was affected by reading Mathéolus's *Lamentations:* "Just the sight of this book . . . made me wonder how it happened that so many different men . . . are so inclined to express both in speaking and in their treatises and writings so many wicked insults about women and their behavior."[4] These statements impelled her to detest herself "and the entire feminine sex, as though we were monstrosities in nature."[5]

The rest of *The Book of the City of Ladies* presents a justification of the female sex and a vision of an ideal community of women. A pioneer, she has received the message of female inferiority and rejected it. From the

---

4. Christine de Pizan, *The Book of the City of Ladies*, trans. Earl Jeffrey Richards, foreword Marina Warner (New York: Persea, 1982), 1.1.1, pp. 3–4.

5. Ibid., 1.1.1–2, p. 5.

fourteenth to the seventeenth century, a huge body of literature accumu-
lated that responded to the dominant tradition.

The result was a literary explosion consisting of works by both men
and women, in Latin and in the vernaculars: works enumerating the achieve-
ments of notable women; works rebutting the main accusations made
against women; works arguing for the equal education of men and women;
works defining and redefining women's proper role in the family, at court,
and in public; works describing women's lives and experiences. Recent
monographs and articles have begun to hint at the great range of this move-
ment, involving probably several thousand titles. The protofeminism of
these "other voices" constitutes a significant fraction of the literary product
of the early modern era.

THE CATALOGS. About 1365, the same Boccaccio whose *Corbaccio* re-
hearses the usual charges against female nature wrote another work, *Concern-
ing Famous Women*. A humanist treatise drawing on classical texts, it praised
106 notable women from pagan Greek and Roman antiquity, from the Bible
(Eve), and from the medieval religious and cultural tradition; his book
helped make all readers aware of a sex normally condemned or forgotten.
Boccaccio's outlook nevertheless was unfriendly to women, for it singled
out for praise those women who possessed the traditional virtues of chastity,
silence, and obedience. Women who were active in the public realm—for
example, rulers and warriors—were depicted as usually being lascivious and
as suffering terrible punishments for entering the masculine sphere. Women
were his subject, but Boccaccio's standard remained male.

Christine de Pizan's *Book of the City of Ladies* contains a second catalog,
one responding specifically to Boccaccio's. Where Boccaccio portrays fe-
male virtue as exceptional, she depicts it as universal. Many women in his-
tory were leaders, or remained chaste despite the lascivious approaches of
men, or were visionaries and brave martyrs.

The work of Boccaccio inspired a series of catalogs of illustrious women
of the biblical, classical, Christian, and local pasts, among them Filippo da
Bergamo's *Of Illustrious Women*, Pierre de Brantôme's *Lives of Illustrious Women*,
Pierre Le Moyne's *Gallerie of Heroic Women*, and Pietro Paolo de Ribera's *Immor-
tal Triumphs and Heroic Enterprises of 845 Women*. Whatever their embedded
prejudices, these works drove home to the public the possibility of female
excellence.

THE DEBATE. Yet many questions remained: Could a woman be virtu-
ous? Could she perform noteworthy deeds? Was she even, strictly speaking,
of the same human species as men? These questions were debated over four

centuries, in French, German, Italian, Spanish, and English, by authors male and female, among Catholics, Protestants, and Jews, in ponderous volumes and breezy pamphlets. The whole literary genre has been called the *querelle des femmes,* the "woman question."

The opening volley of this battle occurred in the first years of the fifteenth century, in a literary debate sparked by Christine de Pizan. She exchanged letters critical of Jean de Meun's contribution to *The Romance of the Rose* with two French royal secretaries, Jean de Montreuil and Gontier Col. When the matter became public, Jean Gerson, one of Europe's leading theologians, supported her arguments against Jean de Meun, for the moment silencing the opposition.

The debate surfaced repeatedly over the next two hundred years. *The Triumph of Women* (1438) by Juan Rodríguez de la Camara (or Juan Rodríguez del Padron) struck a new note by presenting arguments for the superiority of women to men. *The Champion of Women* (1440–42) by Martin Le Franc addresses once again the negative views of women presented in *The Romance of the Rose* and offers counterevidence of female virtue and achievement.

A cameo of the debate on women is included in *The Courtier,* one of the most widely read books of the era, published by the Italian Baldassare Castiglione in 1528 and immediately translated into other European languages. *The Courtier* depicts a series of evenings at the court of the duke of Urbino in which many men and some women of the highest social stratum amuse themselves by discussing a range of literary and social issues. The "woman question" is a pervasive theme throughout, and the third of its four books is devoted entirely to that issue.

In a verbal duel, Gasparo Pallavicino and Giuliano de' Medici present the main claims of the two traditions. Gasparo argues the innate inferiority of women and their inclination to vice. Only in bearing children do they profit the world. Giuliano counters that women share the same spiritual and mental capacities as men and may excel in wisdom and action. Men and women are of the same essence: just as no stone can be more perfectly a stone than another, so no human being can be more perfectly human than others, whether male or female. It was an astonishing assertion, boldly made to an audience as large as all Europe.

THE TREATISES. Humanism provided the materials for a positive counterconcept to the misogyny embedded in Scholastic philosophy and law and inherited from the Greek, Roman, and Christian pasts. A series of humanist treatises on marriage and family, education and deportment, and the nature of women helped construct these new perspectives.

The works by Francesco Barbaro and Leon Battista Alberti, respectively

On Marriage (1415) and *On the Family* (1434–37), far from defending female equality, reasserted women's responsibility for rearing children and managing the housekeeping while being obedient, chaste, and silent. Nevertheless, they served the cause of reexamining the issue of women's nature by placing domestic issues at the center of scholarly concern and reopening the pertinent classical texts. In addition, Barbaro emphasized the companionate nature of marriage and the importance of a wife's spiritual and mental qualities for the well-being of the family.

These themes reappear in later humanist works on marriage and the education of women by Juan Luis Vives and Erasmus. Both were moderately sympathetic to the condition of women without reaching beyond the usual masculine prescriptions for female behavior.

An outlook more favorable to women characterizes the nearly unknown work *In Praise of Women* (ca. 1487) by the Italian humanist Bartolommeo Goggio. In addition to providing a catalog of illustrious women, Goggio argued that male and female are the same in essence, but that women (reworking the Adam and Eve narrative from quite a new angle) are actually superior. In the same vein, the Italian humanist Maria Equicola asserted the spiritual equality of men and women in *On Women* (1501). In 1525 Galeazzo Flavio Capra (or Capella) published his work *On the Excellence and Dignity of Women*. This humanist tradition of treatises defending the worthiness of women culminates in the work of Henricus Cornelius Agrippa *On the Nobility and Preeminence of the Female Sex*. No work by a male humanist more succinctly or explicitly presents the case for female dignity.

THE WITCH BOOKS. While humanists grappled with the issues pertaining to women and family, other learned men turned their attention to what they perceived as a very great problem: witches. Witch-hunting manuals, explorations of the witch phenomenon, and even defenses of witches are not at first glance pertinent to the tradition of the other voice. But they do relate in this way: most accused witches were women. The hostility aroused by supposed witch activity is comparable to the hostility aroused by women. The evil deeds the victims of the hunt were charged with were exaggerations of the vices to which, many believed, all women were prone.

The connection between the witch accusation and the hatred of women is explicit in the notorious witch-hunting manual *The Hammer of Witches* (1486), by two Dominican inquisitors, Heinrich Krämer and Jacob Sprenger. Here the inconstancy, deceitfulness, and lust traditionally associated with women are depicted in exaggerated form as the core features of witch behavior. These inclined women to make a bargain with the devil— sealed by sexual intercourse—by which they acquired unholy powers. Such bizarre claims, far from being rejected by rational men, were broadcast by intellectuals. The German Ulrich Molitur, the Frenchman Nicolas Rémy, and the Italian Stefano Guazzo coolly informed the public of sinister orgies and midnight pacts with the devil. The celebrated French jurist, historian, and political philosopher Jean Bodin argued that because women were especially prone to diabolism, regular legal procedures could properly be suspended in order to try those accused of this "exceptional crime."

A few experts, such as the physician Johann Weyer, a student of Agrippa's, raised their voices in protest. In 1563 Weyer explained the witch phenomenon thus, without discarding belief in diabolism: the devil deluded foolish old women afflicted by melancholia, causing them to believe they had magical powers. His rational skepticism, which had good credibility in the community of the learned, worked to revise the conventional views of women and witchcraft.

WOMEN'S WORKS. To the many categories of works produced on the question of women's worth must be added nearly all works written by women. A woman writing was in herself a statement of women's claim to dignity.

Only a few women wrote anything before the dawn of the modern era, for three reasons. First, they rarely received the education that would enable them to write. Second, they were not admitted to the public roles— as administrator, bureaucrat, lawyer or notary, university professor—in which they might gain knowledge of the kinds of things the literate public thought worth writing about. Third, the culture imposed silence on women, considering speaking out a form of unchastity. Given these conditions, it is remarkable that any women wrote. Those who did so before the fourteenth century were almost always nuns or religious women whose isolation made their pronouncements more acceptable.

From the fourteenth century on, the volume of women's writings rose. Women continued to write devotional literature, although not always as cloistered nuns. They also wrote diaries, often intended as keepsakes for their children; books of advice to their sons and daughters; letters to family members and friends; and family memoirs, in a few cases elaborate enough to be considered histories.

A few women wrote works directly concerning the "woman question," and some of these, such as the humanists Isotta Nogarola, Cassandra Fedele, Laura Cereta, and Olympia Morata, were highly trained. A few were professional writers, living by the income of their pens: the very first among them was Christine de Pizan, noteworthy in this context as in so many others. In addition to *The Book of the City of Ladies* and her critiques of *The Romance of the Rose,* she wrote *The Treasure of the City of Ladies* (a guide to social decorum for women), an advice book for her son, much courtly verse, and a full-scale history of the reign of King Charles V of France.

WOMEN PATRONS. Women who did not themselves write but encouraged others to do so boosted the development of an alternative tradition. Highly placed women patrons supported authors, artists, musicians, poets, and learned men. Such patrons, drawn mostly from the Italian elites and the courts of northern Europe, figure disproportionately as the dedicatees of the important works of early feminism.

For a start, it might be noted that the catalogs of Boccaccio and Alvaro de Luna were dedicated to the Florentine noblewoman Andrea Acciaiuoli and to Doña María, first wife of King Juan II of Castile, while the French translation of Boccaccio's work was commissioned by Anne of Brittany, wife of King Charles VIII of France. The humanist treatises of Goggio, Equicola, Vives, and Agrippa were dedicated, respectively, to Eleanora of Aragon, wife of Ercole I d'Este, duke of Ferrara; to Margherita Cantelma of Mantua; to Catherine of Aragon, wife of King Henry VIII of England; and to Margaret, duchess of Austria and regent of the Netherlands. As late as 1696, Mary Astell's *Serious Proposal to the Ladies, for the Advancement of Their True and Greatest Interest* was dedicated to Princess Ann of Denmark.

These authors presumed that their efforts would be welcome to female patrons, or they may have written at the bidding of those patrons. Silent themselves, perhaps even unresponsive, these loftily placed women helped shape the tradition of the other voice.

THE ISSUES. The literary forms and patterns in which the tradition of the other voice presented itself have now been sketched. It remains to highlight the major issues around which this tradition crystallizes. In brief, there are four problems to which our authors return again and again, in plays and catalogs, in verse and letters, in treatises and dialogues, in every language: the problem of chastity, the problem of power, the problem of speech, and the problem of knowledge. Of these the greatest, preconditioning the others, is the problem of chastity.

THE PROBLEM OF CHASTITY. In traditional European culture, as in the cultures of antiquity and others around the globe, chastity was perceived as woman's quintessential virtue—in contrast to courage, or generosity, or leadership, or rationality, seen as virtues characteristic of men. Opponents of women charged them with insatiable lust. Women themselves and their defenders—without disputing the validity of the standard—responded that women were capable of chastity.

The requirement of chastity kept women at home, silenced them, iso-

lated them, left them in ignorance. It was the source of all other impedi-
ments. Why was it so important to the society of men, of whom chastity
was not required, and who more often than not considered it their right
to violate the chastity of any woman they encountered?

Female chastity ensured the continuity of the male-headed household.
If a man's wife was not chaste, he could not be sure of the legitimacy of
his offspring. If children who were not his acquired his property, it was
not his household, but some other man's, that had endured. If his daughter
was not chaste, she could not be transferred to another man's household
as his wife, and he was dishonored.

The whole system of the integrity of the household and the transmis-
sion of property was bound up in female chastity. Such a requirement per-
tained only to property-owning classes, of course. Poor women could not
expect to maintain their chastity, least of all if they were in contact with
high-status men to whom all women but those of their own household were
prey.

In Catholic Europe, the requirement of chastity was buttressed by
moral and religious imperatives. Original sin was inextricably linked with
the sexual act. Virginity was seen as heroic virtue, far more impressive than,
say, the avoidance of idleness or greed. Monasticism, the cultural institution
that dominated medieval Europe for centuries, was grounded in the renunci-
ation of the flesh. The Catholic reform of the eleventh century imposed a
similar standard on all the clergy and a heightened awareness of sexual
requirements on all the laity. Although men were asked to be chaste, female
unchastity was much worse: it led to the devil, as Eve had led mankind to
sin.

To such requirements, women and their defenders protested their inno-
cence. Following the example of holy women who had escaped the require-
ments of family and sought the religious life, some women began to con-
ceive of female communities as alternatives both to family and to the
cloister. Christine de Pizan's city of ladies was such a community. Moderata
Fonte and Mary Astell envisioned others. The luxurious salons of the French
précieuses of the seventeenth century, or the comfortable English drawing
rooms of the next, may have been born of the same impulse. Here women
not only might escape, if briefly, the subordinate position that life in the
family entailed but might make claims to power, exercise their capacity for
speech, and display their knowledge.

THE PROBLEM OF POWER. Women were excluded from power: the
whole cultural tradition insisted on it. Only men were citizens, only men
bore arms, only men could be chiefs or lords or kings. There were excep-

tions that did not disprove the rule, when wives or widows or mothers took the place of men, awaiting their return or the maturation of a male heir. A woman who attempted to rule in her own right was perceived as an anomaly, a monster, at once a deformed woman and an inadequate male, sexually confused and consequently unsafe.

The association of such images with women who held or sought power explains some otherwise odd features of early modern culture. Queen Elizabeth I of England, one of the few women to hold full regal authority in European history, played with such male/female images—positive ones, of course—in representing herself to her subjects. She was a prince, and manly, even though she was female. She was also (she claimed) virginal, a condition absolutely essential if she was to avoid the attacks of her opponents. Catherine de' Medici, who ruled France as widow and as regent for her sons, also adopted such imagery in defining her position. She chose as one symbol the figure of Artemisia, an androgynous ancient warrior-heroine who combined a female persona with masculine powers.

Power in a woman, without such sexual imagery, seems to have been indigestible by the culture. A rare note was struck by the Englishman Sir Thomas Elyot in his *Defence of Good Women* (1540), justifying both women's participation in civic life and their prowess in arms. The old tune was sung by the Scots reformer John Knox in his *First Blast of the Trumpet against the Monstrous Regiment of Women* (1558); for him rule by women, defects in nature, was a hideous contradiction in terms.

The confused sexuality of the imagery of female potency was not reserved for rulers. Any woman who excelled was likely to be called an Amazon, recalling the self-mutilated warrior women of antiquity who repudiated all men, gave up their sons, and raised only their daughters. She was often said to have "exceeded her sex" or to have possessed "masculine virtue," since the very fact of conspicuous excellence conferred masculinity even on the female subject. The catalogs of notable women often showed those female heroes dressed in armor and armed to the teeth, like men. Amazonian heroines romp through the epics of the age—Ariosto's *Orlando Furioso* (1532), Spenser's *Faerie Queene* (1590–1609). Excellence in a woman was perceived as a claim for power, and power was reserved for the masculine realm. A woman who possessed either was masculinized and lost title to her own female identity.

THE PROBLEM OF SPEECH. Just as power had a sexual dimension when it was claimed by women, so did speech. A good woman spoke little. Excessive speech was an indication of unchastity. By speech, women seduced men. Eve had lured Adam into sin by her speech. Accused witches were commonly accused of having spoken abusively, or irrationally, or simply too much. As enlightened a figure as Francesco Barbaro insisted on silence in a woman, which he linked to her perfect unanimity with her husband's will and her unblemished virtue (her chastity). Another Italian humanist, Leonardo Bruni, in advising a noblewoman on her studies, barred her not from speech, but from public speaking. That was reserved for men.

Related to the problem of speech was that of costume, another, if silent, form of self-expression. Assigned the task of pleasing men as their primary occupation, elite women often tended toward elaborate costume, hairdressing, and the use of cosmetics. Clergy and secular moralists alike condemned these practices. The appropriate function of costume and adornment was to announce the status of a woman's husband or father. Any further indulgence in adornment was akin to unchastity.

THE PROBLEM OF KNOWLEDGE. When the Italian noblewoman Isotta Nogarola had begun to attain a reputation as a humanist, she was accused of incest—a telling instance of the association of learning in women with unchastity. That chilling association inclined any woman who was educated to deny that she was, or to make exaggerated claims of heroic chastity.

If educated women were pursued with suspicions of sexual misconduct, women seeking an education faced an even more daunting obstacle: the assumption that women were by nature incapable of learning, that reasoning was a particularly masculine ability. Just as they proclaimed their chastity, women and their defenders insisted on their capacity for learning. The major work by a male writer on female education—*The Education of a Christian Woman: A Sixteenth-Century Manual*, by Juan Luis Vives—granted female capacity for intellection but argued still that a woman's whole education was to be shaped around the requirement of chastity and a future within the household. Female writers of the following generations—Marie de Gournay in France, Anna Maria van Schurman in Holland, Mary Astell in England—began to envision other possibilities.

The pioneers of female education were the Italian women humanists who managed to attain a literacy in Latin and a knowledge of classical and Christian literature equivalent to that of prominent men. Their works implicitly and explicitly raise questions about women's social roles, defining problems that beset women attempting to break out of the cultural limits that had bound them. Like Christine de Pizan, who achieved an advanced education through her father's tutoring and her own devices, their bold questioning makes clear the importance of training. Only when women were educated to the same standard as male leaders would they be able to raise that other voice and insist on their dignity as human beings morally, intellectually, and legally equal to men.

THE OTHER VOICE. The other voice, a voice of protest, was mostly female, but also male. It spoke in the vernaculars and in Latin, in treatises and dialogues, plays and poetry, letters and diaries and pamphlets. It battered at the wall of prejudice that encircled women and raised a banner announcing its claims. The female was equal (or even superior) to the male in essential nature—moral, spiritual, intellectual. Women were capable of higher education, of holding positions of power and influence in the public realm, and of speaking and writing persuasively. The last bastion of masculine supremacy, centered on the notions of a woman's primary domestic responsibility and the requirement of female chastity, had not as yet been assaulted—although visions of productive female communities as alternatives to the family indicated an awareness of the problem.

During the period 1300–1700, the other voice remained only a voice, and one dimly heard. It did not result—yet—in an alteration of social patterns. Indeed, to this day they have not been completely altered. Yet the call for justice issued as long as six centuries ago by those writing in the tradition of the other voice must be recognized as the source and origin of the mature feminist tradition and of the realignment of social institutions accomplished in the modern age.

We thank the volume editors in this series, who responded with many suggestions to an earlier draft of this introduction, making it a collaborative enterprise. Many of their recommendations and criticisms have resulted in revisions, though we remain responsible for the final product.

PROJECTED TITLES IN THE SERIES

Giuseppa Eleonora Barbapiccola and Diamante Medaglia Faini, *The Education of Women*, edited and translated by Paula Findlen and Rebecca Messbarger

Marie Dentière, *Prefaces, Epistles, and History of the Deliverance of Geneva by the Protestants*, edited and translated by Mary B. McKinley

Isabella d'Este, *Selected Letters*, edited and translated by Deanna Shemek

Maria de Gournay, *The Equality of Men and Women and Other Writings*, edited and translated by Richard Hillman and Colette Quesnel

Anibale Guasco, *Discussion with D. Lavinia, His Daughter, concerning the Manner of Conducting Oneself at Court*, edited and translated by Peggy Osborn

Olympia Morata, *Complete Writings*, edited and translated by Holt N. Parker

Isotta Nogarola, *Selected Writings*, edited by Margaret L. King and Albert Rabil Jr. and translated by Diana Robin, with an introduction by Margaret L. King.

Christine de Pizan, *Debate over the "Romance of the Rose,"* edited and translated by Tom Conley

François Poulain de la Barre, *The Equality of the Sexes* and *The Education of Women*, edited and translated by Albert Rabil Jr.

Olivia Sabuco, *The New Philosophy: True Medicine*, edited and translated by Gianna Pomata

Maria de San Jose, *Book of Recreations*, edited and translated by Alison Weber and Amanda Powell

Madeleine de Scudéry, *Orations and Rhetorical Dialogues*, edited and translated by Lillian Doherty and Jane Donawerth

Sara Copio Sullam, *Apologia and Other Writings*, edited and translated by Laura Stortoni

Arcangela Tarabotti, *Paternal Tyranny*, edited and translated by Letizia Panizza

GENDER AND RELIGION
IN FIFTEENTH-CENTURY FLORENCE

F lorence's main library, the Biblioteca Nazionale Centrale, preserves a
beautifully decorated manuscript containing a collection of poems by
a writer whom F. W. Kent has suggested was the first prominent Medici
woman in Florence: Lucrezia Tornabuoni de' Medici.[1] Possibly copied while
she was still alive, and to this day never published in its entirety, the volume
contains a single *laude*, or poem written in praise of a divine figure, and five
storie sacre, innovative verse retellings of biblical narratives. While the mere
fact that the poetry by a well-known fifteenth-century woman survives at
all is worthy of note, what makes its existence particularly compelling are
the stories Tornabuoni chose to put into verse. For this Florentine manu-
script, which may have been copied for her granddaughters, focuses primar-
ily on biblical women: the tales of two very unconventional Old Testament
heroines who risk their lives for the good of their people, the trials and
triumph of a slandered wife, an account of Florence's patron saint and a
vivid portrait of the queen who undid him, and an inventive retelling of
the travels of one of the Bible's first merchants and the extraordinary faith

---

1. Kent, "Sainted Mother, Magnificent Son," 5. Kent's lively and informed article is one of
the best treatments of Tornabuoni to date; he makes a convincing case both for Tornabuoni's
centrality in fifteenth-century Florence and, though he is not a literary historian, for the impor-
tance of her poetry. Pezzarossa's introduction to the *Poemetti sacri* and Martelli's several essays
on Tornabuoni focus more on the poetry, and both critics succeed in rescuing Tornabuoni's
poems from the disparaging comments and general neglect they had suffered for several centu-
ries. Other major accounts of Tornabuoni's life and work are Levantini-Pieroni's excellent
chapters on her biography; Yvonne Maguire's chapter in *Women of the Medici*; the brief remarks
of Natalie Tomas in "*A Positive Novelty*"; and Patrizia Salvadori's excellent introduction to the
edition of the *Lettere*. Mary Bosanquet's *Mother of the Magnificent: A Life of Lucrezia Tornabuoni* is a
fanciful, freely improvised account of Tornabuoni's life drawn largely from early twentieth-
century accounts, in English, of the Medici family.

of his wife. In these spirited lives of Judith, Esther, Susanna, John the Baptist, and Tobias, Tornabuoni gives her readers portraits of public and thus problematic women whose stories may have enabled her to reflect on aspects of her own situation in patriarchal Florence.

Today Tornabuoni is largely known for her family ties to Medici men. She was the wife of Cosimo Vecchio's son Piero, mother of the Magnificent Lorenzo de' Medici, and grandmother of two popes (Leo X and Clement VII). Yet she was also an influential woman in her own right. She supported numerous public projects in Tuscany and engaged in charitable works in Florence; she also patronized important writers and artists. Less appreciated in the historical annals is that she helped to run Florence in the years between her husband Piero's early death and the maturity of her son, Lorenzo.[2] Such accomplishments are attested in her forty-nine surviving letters, some written in her own hand, as well as the almost five hundred extant letters that were addressed to Tornabuoni by abbesses, priests, dignitaries from Tuscan hill towns, the queen of Bosnia, and leading writers and humanists of the day.[3]

The recent publication of a number of these letters in Italy has begun to alert the scholarly community to this industrious woman who influenced Florence in an era when the city was beginning to assume international prominence. Yet that much of her influence was necessarily indirect may be apparent from her treatment of biblical women who excel at "meddling." As Judith boldly says to the priests when she is about to leave the besieged city of Bethulia to seduce Holofernes, "[God] has put it into my heart / to meddle in things so that your vows will be heard." Tornabuoni, too, clearly "meddled" in her sons' education, in Florentine social and cultural affairs, in the Tuscan literary tradition of Dante and Petrarch, in a tradition of religious verse dominated by men who were members of religious orders, and finally, in the biblical stories themselves. Her bold and elegant poetry draws as much from popular culture as it does from the elite circle of writers and artists with whom she was intimate, so that Tornabuoni emerges as an "other voice" who dared to challenge, with cunning indirection, conservative Florentine assumptions about women's limitations in the fields of poli-

2. Although the following verdict of Tornabuoni's control over Florence may be overstated ("From the death of old Cos[i]mo until the coming of age of her son Lorenzo, hers were the strong hands which retained power"), it is equally clear from her letters and from Lorenzo's deference to her that Tornabuoni possessed authority unprecedented for a woman in fifteenth-century Florence; see Robert de la Sizeranne, *Celebrities of the Italian Renaissance in Florence and in the Louvre*, 73.

3. For a complete edition of Tornabuoni's own letters and 120 of the letters written to her, see Patrizia Salvadori's collection, *Lettere*.

tics and poetry alike. Her verse thus not only gives us a glimpse into Florence at the very height of its Renaissance but also offers us a reflection on the constraints, for women, *of* that Renaissance while justifying women's occasionally necessary interventions in the public domain. That Tornabuoni herself consistently meddled with the distinctions between private and public, social and political, feminine and masculine spaces so valued by Florentines such as Leon Battista Alberti and Niccolò Machiavelli is another reason her poetry is of such vital interest today.

CONTEXTS

One of the most elegant fresco cycles in Florence is in the Tornabuoni Chapel in the Dominican church of Santa Maria Novella. Commissioned by Giovanni Tornabuoni in 1485, three years after the death of his sister Lucrezia, the frescoes, painted by Domenico Ghirlandaio, portray in seven scenes from the life of John the Baptist some of fifteenth-century Florence's most eminent citizens, perhaps including Lucrezia herself in the painting of the Baptist's birth. Head veiled and hands clasped, she stands with other patrician women, contemplating the newborn in a nurse's arms and his imperious mother Elizabeth in her bed.[4]

Lucrezia Tornabuoni had a more intimate attachment to this scene than most Renaissance scholars might realize. Even though they were conserved only in manuscript, her poetic writings, which include the life of John the Baptist featured in Ghirlandaio's cycle, enjoyed far wider currency in her own day than in ours. In the late 1470s the noted humanist Angelo Poliziano writes to Tornabuoni that he is returning her lauds, sonnets, and "ternari"—most likely her *storie sacre* written in terzinas.[5] Luigi Pulci, whose

4. See the suggestion of Gaetano Pieraccini, "L'effige di Lucrezia Tornabuoni," 179. In this article he also calls attention to a portrait painting of Ghirlandaio's at the National Gallery in Washington, D.C., of a woman resembling the woman in the fresco; on the back of the Washington portrait is written LU[ ]TIA TORNABUONI MEDICI. Shelley Zuraw also suggests that a bust of a fifteenth-century woman currently in the Palazzo dell'Opera della Primaziale, Pisa, may represent Tornabuoni; her argument that the bust is a pendant to a known existing bust of Piero is convincing. She observes that this bust, which can plausibly be dated to 1453 if it is indeed the companion piece to Piero's, would be the earliest female portrait bust in Florence. Zuraw also notes that it could be related to portraits of emperors and their wives that had a distinctively dynastic component. See "The Medici Portraits of Mino da Fiesole," particularly 324–25; a photograph of the busts is on 318.

5. Poliziano formed a close enough friendship with Tornabuoni to lament her absence when he traveled to the family house at Cafaggiolo in December 1478 and found himself overcome by boredom: "I sit by the fire in slippers and a greatcoat, and if you could see me, you would think I was melancholy personified. . . . I do not find my Madonna Lucrezia, so that I may unburden myself to her" (trans. Maguire, *Women of the Medici*, 215n, in Salvadori, *Lettere*, 153–

idiosyncratic epic *Morgante* was commissioned by Tornabuoni herself, imagines the Virgin Mary reading his patroness's poems in heaven.[6] The burlesque poet Bernardo Bellincioni, with whom Tornabuoni exchanged at least one jocular sonnet, comments on having received her book: "Like all your other works, it has brought great pleasure to whomever has desired to see it."[7] A contemporary Florentine play on Judith and Holofernes that was published in 1518 seems to echo passages and an entire stanza from Tornabuoni's own *Storia di Iuditta*.[8] The sixteenth-century historian Niccolò

---

54 [letter 105]). In a letter written two months later, we learn specifically about Tornabuoni's poetry. On February 8, 1479, the former tutor of Lorenzo claims that he is "returning with [the messenger] Tommaso your lauds and sonnets and *ternarii* that you gave me when I was there [at Cafaggiolo?]. These gave us enormous pleasure, and Madonna Lucrezia or, better, Lucrezia [Tornabuoni's granddaughter] has learned by heart all of 'Lucrezia,' and many sonnets." If the "ternarii" refer to the three *storie sacre* that Tornabuoni had written in terzina—Susanna, Esther, and Tobias—then, as Paolo Orvieto has suggested, we have a precise terminus ad quem for these poems. Poliziano's letter is quoted in Martelli, 48.

6. Author of the *Morgante*, an epic poem spawned from the popular chivalric romances, Pulci wrote his great work at Tornabuoni's behest, beginning in 1461. In canto 28 of the *Morgante*, Pulci pays homage to his patroness—specifically the written works she left to the world before her premature death in 1482. ("Ma non pensai che innanzi al fin morisse!" [But I didn't think she would die before I reached the end!], he laments.) He imagines Lucrezia in heaven, seated alongside the Virgin Mary: "E canta o forse le sue sante laude. // Quivi si legge o della sua Maria / la vita, ove il suo libro è sempre aperto, / e di Esdram, di Iudit e di Tobia; / quivi si rende giusto premio e merto; / quivi s'intende or l'alta fantasia / a descriver Giovanni nel deserto; / quivi cantono or gli angeli i suoi versi, / dove il ver d'ogni cosa può vedersi" [And perhaps even now she sings her holy lauds. Here they are reading her life of Mary, to which the book always falls open, or the life of Esdras, Judith, and Tobias; here they are rendering her just merit and praise. And here they appreciate her powers of imagination as she depicts John the Baptist in the desert. Now the angels are singing her rhymes, here where they are able to glean the truth of all things].

Pulci's memory may not be exact; of the five extant *storie* we have, the only ones that overlap with the list from the *Morgante* are the *vite* of John the Baptist, Judith, and Tobias. The *Vita della Vergine* and *Esdram* may, it is true, one day appear, and the lives of Susanna and Esther go unmentioned.

7. Quoted in Tornabuoni, *Poemetti sacri*, 40n: "Reverendissima tamquam matre, io ho fatto a sicurtà del vostro libro: come di ogni altra simile vostra opera ell'è piaciuta assai a chi l'a desiderata vedere" (from August 22, 1479).

8. I have not seen the text of *La rappresentazione di Judith hebrea*, but Frank Capozzi quotes from it extensively in his 1975 dissertation for the University of Wisconsin–Madison, "The Evolution and Transformation of the Judith and Holofernes Theme in Italian Drama and Art before 1627." At least six lines are virtually identical to a stanza in Tornabuoni's *Judith*: lines 313–19 from the play, which contain the order to Holofernes to be merciless to the Hebrews: "Non usar' misericordia, / destruggi le lor terre e le persone; / chi volessio di lor pace o concordia, / non la pigliate per nessuna cagione! / Non voler' con loro altro che discordia, / mettigli in fuga e gran confusione, / e ardi e guasta e ruba il lor paese!"

These lines introduce only minor changes from stanza 35 of the poem, which begins, "Et punto non usar misericordia / distruggi le lor terre et le persone." The lines from the *rappresentazione* are cited by Capozzi (45), who speculates that the play was performed close

Valori noted that she "was extremely eloquent, as one can see from the sacred stories that she translated into our tongue and put into verse," and in 1711 Giovanni Crescimbeni suggested that with her vulgar poetry Tornabuoni "surpassed the majority of the poets—if not all of them—of her time."[9]

Even if this latter judgment must be deemed excessive, it is clear that Tornabuoni's poetry has suffered undeservedly from neglect.[10] One reason for this neglect is the versatile assembly of Florentine poets with whom Tornabuoni must inevitably be compared. Her contemporaries constituted a staggeringly innovative and influential group. Hers was, after all, the era of Poliziano's *Stanze per la giostra*, Pulci's *Morgante*, the impressive collection of pastoral poetry called the *Bucoliche elegantissime*, Marsilio Ficino's philosophical writings, and the poetry of Tornabuoni's own son, Lorenzo de' Medici. Even if stylistically she must appear inferior to these Florentine giants, we must be wary of belittling her achievement because it lacks linguistic innovation. Moreover, its devotional tones should not blind us to the way Tornabuoni intentionally deviates from the biblical accounts in both the Vulgate and the vernacular translations. And finally, despite their origins in the Bible, the *storie sacre* Tornabuoni composed are fundamentally linked to the civic and social life of Quattrocento Florence. The lives of the Old Testament heroines Susanna, Judith, and Esther are striking meditations on contemporary women's private and public lives. John the Baptist and Tobias, moreover, played highly symbolic roles within the city of Florence: the Baptist was the city's patron saint, and Tobias was a model of the charitable merchant. As poems attesting to a highly educated and creative woman, as well as to a lively sense of Florentine cultural and social life in the second half of the fifteenth century, the *storie sacre* and *laudi* alike deserve

---

to the time of its publication in 1518, "when the *sacre rappresentazioni* were not anymore in vogue" (32). The date of performance may in fact have been much earlier, but it is far more likely that the writer would have drawn from Tornabuoni's text, which was circulating in at least several manuscripts, than vice versa.

9. Cited in Levantini-Pieroni, *Lucrezia Tornabuoni*, 77–79.

10. As Levantini-Pieroni rightly suggests; see his comment on "poor Crescimbeni" (ibid., 78). But even so, twentieth-century assessments have erred in the other direction. In *Poesia religiosa del secolo XV*, Domenico Coppola accuses Tornabuoni of monotony and of using stereotypes in her several *laudi*, then excuses her when he acknowledges that "she had no real literary pretensions when she set out to compose her rhymes" (64). In his thorough biography of the young Lorenzo de' Medici, André Rochon observes disparagingly that even if Tornabuoni's letters reveal her talents in crafting a lively and revealing scene, her poetic work shows far less literary sensibility. Citing the "exclusively religious character" of her poetry, Rochon denies any redeeming value to either her *laudi* or her *storie sacre*, suggesting that at best they reveal to us the "fervent faith of a woman who was pious without being completely orthodox or overly prudish" (*Jeunesse de Laurent de Médicis*, 23).

our attention. In particular, they argue for the inextricable link between female religiosity and social and cultural practices of Renaissance Florence—a link that Tornabuoni, given her prominent and unique position in city life and her deep familiarity with "popular" and "official" culture alike, exemplifies perhaps better than any other Florentine figure.[11]

This is a link, moreover, that should force us to revise our understanding of the elite family Tornabuoni belonged to. The Platonic Academy that Marsilio Ficino was said to have established in the hills outside Florence during the 1460s, hence during Lorenzo's formative years, was a sign of a growing divorce between popular forms and "princely" culture—or perhaps more accurately, a culture distinguished by its attempt to gentrify the popular forms disseminated throughout Florence and stamp them with the mark of classical antiquity.[12] This poetry, moreover, is characterized by a pervasive secularism. By the 1480s, the fervent religiosity that had been such a crucial component of earlier Florentine cultural life had waned so much that it would take Girolamo Savonarola's reform of 1494 to bring it back—if only briefly. And yet that Lorenzo wrote almost exclusively in the *volgare*, the vernacular, is of great importance; so is the observation that some of his last poems are *laudi*, and his *sacra rappresentazione* of 1490 has much in common with his mother's *storie sacre*. Mario Martelli has even attributed Lorenzo's innovative use of Italian primarily to his mother, who, unlike her husband Piero de' Medici, came from one of the old, noble Florentine families. "Following in the footsteps of his mother, he showed that he loved the vulgar language and the kinds of poetry that Florence's oligarchs loved as well. Thus on the one side, that of the oligarchy, we have Italian and poetry; on the other, that of the Medici, we have Latin and philosophy."[13]

While one may not wish to credit Tornabuoni with a crucial if conservative role in this shift in Florentine cultural and religious sensibilities, her own engagement in vernacular literary forms is undeniable. She turned for her writing not only to the Bible, but also to oral forms that had long been heard in Florence's churches and piazzas. The *cantari* of strolling players who sang the tales of heroes of romances as well as saints' lives and biblical episodes are behind Tornabuoni's two *storie sacre* written in eight-line stanzas

11. For the now well known distinction between "popular" and "official" cultures, see Mikhail Bakhtin, particularly *Rabelais and His World*.

12. Thus, as Marco Santagata and Stefano Carrai note, members of Lorenzo's circle attempted to elevate and ennoble the literary genres they inherited from their predecessors (*Lirica di corte*, 108).

13. Martelli, *Letteratura fiorentina del Quattrocento*, 58.

(ottava rima) about Judith and John the Baptist. She was also familiar with the tradition of the *sacre rappresentazioni* or sacred plays performed by boys' companies and confraternities on feast days, many of them composed by the devout Feo Belcari and dedicated to the Medici.[14] The metrics and rhythms of Tornabuoni's nine extant short poems likewise reflect the popular forms practiced by her contemporaries Pulci, Bellincioni, and Matteo Franco. Written in all likelihood for an intimate group of friends, perhaps her grandchildren and immediate family, Tornabuoni's *storie* rather evoke the popular language of a Florence increasingly shunned by elite Florentine culture.[15] Her poetry thus represents another voice in two senses. Not only was she a woman writing in a culture dominated by men, but she wrote in a style and a genre that went against the grain of literary trends in late Quattrocento Florence—trends that were largely inhospitable to a woman writer, particularly one who was probably not skilled in classical Latin.[16]

Yet if we acknowledge, with Martelli, that Tornabuoni's vernacular and religious verse may well have aroused Lorenzo's interest not only in using Italian but in writing religious poetry,[17] then she reflects not so much a minor undercurrent as an unacknowledged cultural force in her own right. In fact it is difficult to justify the divorce that literary history has tended to make between the canonical and latinizing—if not always Latin—writings of the Florentine Renaissance and the supposedly inferior religious works of the same era.[18] The very fact that Tornabuoni sent her poetry to

---

14. For recent work on Belcari, see Martelli, *Letteratura fiorentina del Quattrocento;* Coppola also devotes a lengthy chapter to his *laudi* in *Poesia religiosa del secolo XV.*

.15. Critics of Luigi Pulci point out very much the same thing, calling attention to the "medieval" traces found in Pulci's and Tornabuoni's poems alike. Orvieto makes the argument most strongly in his recent study, titled, significantly, *Pulci medievale:* noting that Pulci's "true patron was not, or was only for a brief time, Lorenzo . . . but the oft-praised Lucrezia Tornabuoni, under whose protection the *Morgante* was born and written. . . . Once her protection collapses, along with the literary world which she authorized, Pulci will collapse as well" (282).

16. Pezzarossa makes a similar point when he observes that Tornabuoni's literary activity is representative of her gender, her class, and particularly her religious sentiments (Tornabuoni, *Poemetti sacri,* 43).

17. Maguire suggests that Lorenzo's letter in 1466 to the king of Naples defending the *volgare,* as well as his commentary on his *Simposio,* may owe a good deal to Tornabuoni's emphasis on writing in Italian (see *Women of the Medici,* 126).

18. The tendency to devalue religious overtones in Renaissance poetry goes back at least to Jacob Burckhardt, who was emphatic about seeing the fifteenth and sixteenth centuries as overwhelmingly secular; since Benedetto Croce's works, there has also been a great deal of resistance among Italian literary historians to a "religious Renaissance." Coppola makes some judicious points about the ongoing importance of religious poetry, particularly in Florence, in the first chapter of *Poesia religiosa del secolo XV.*

Poliziano, whose princely pupils included the young Lorenzo, suggests that the Florentines themselves may have perceived no such divorce. Indeed, Ghirlandaio's paintings in the Tornabuoni Chapel call attention to a very real urgency on the part of Florence's elite in the late fifteenth century to locate its works within the context of sacred history. By the time Ghirlandaio had finished the cycle in 1490, Ficino had long left Florence and Poliziano had departed for Mantova; Lorenzo, who like Poliziano, would die in 1492, would soon begin penning his *laudi* and *The Martyrdom of Saints John and Paul.*

By placing Tornabuoni's writings within the context of both her life and mid-fifteenth-century Florence, we can begin to understand why she cultivated a vernacular, religious discourse in order to situate her complex life within a sacred space and to conceive of her civic duties in a religious register. (Her efforts thus parallel those of her brother in the Tornabuoni Chapel through the sure hand of Ghirlandaio.) This seems to be the most compelling reason to compose *storie sacre* that were apparently never performed, unlike Lorenzo's *sacra rappresentazione* or those of Tornabuoni's near contemporary Antonia Pulci.[19] But it also seems clear that Tornabuoni wrote for an audience who would listen to her poetry as well as read it: "Whoever hears or reads this little work [odi et legge] / may they take compassion on the innocent," she notes at the end of *The Story of Devout Susanna,* and it is possible that her *storie* were used as devotional texts. Yet they are never merely devotional. Her choice and treatment of subject matter demonstrate an interest in, and deep familiarity with, not only biblical material but a wide range of Florentine social and cultural practices. A brief account of Tornabuoni's life will suggest how intimate this familiarity was.

LIFE

Lucrezia Tornabuoni de' Medici (1427–82) lived during one of the most glorious periods of Florence's eminent history. During these fifty-five years, Florence was host to painters such as Masaccio, Filippo Lippi, Fra Beato Angelico, Leonardo da Vinci, Angelo Pollaiuolo, and Sandro Botticelli. When Tornabuoni was a child, Filippo Brunelleschi was at work on the magnificent cupola of the Duomo; when she was a young woman, Leon

---

19. Martelli speculates that one of her *laudi,* "Ecco el Messia," might have served as part of a performance, perhaps even for nuns: it may have functioned as "the briefest of *sacre rappresentazioni,* the extreme brevity of which certainly does not negate the decisively dramatic nature of the composition" (*Letteratura fiorentina del Quattrocento,* 20). For Antonia Pulci's works, see the recent translation of her plays by James Cook and Barbara Cook in this series.

Battista Alberti designed the palace and the facade to Santa Maria Novella commissioned by Giovanni Rucellai. (One of Tornabuoni's daughters later celebrated her wedding with festivities in the small triangular piazza across from the Rucellai palace when she married Giovanni Rucellai's son.) Politically, the small but powerful city grew to international prominence in the course of the fifteenth century, as the long tradition of republicanism was supplemented by increasing Medici control, first under the sure hand of Cosimo de' Medici, then under those of Piero and Lorenzo. Chosen to host the Council of Florence in 1439, the city became a site for meetings and a necessary stop for dignitaries traveling the length of the peninsula. Hence the noted visits of Pope Pius II, Galeazzo Maria Sforza, and Eleonora of Aragon between 1459 and 1473. Florence also expanded its territorial surroundings in the period, although in doing so it antagonized the pope and the king of France.

Much of Florence's growing prominence was due to the wealth and strategies of the Medici family, into which Tornabuoni married in 1444. The marriage itself was a sign of Medician shrewdness. Tornabuoni was the descendant of a noble Florentine family that could trace its roots back to Giovanni Tornaquinci, who fought in the battle of Montaperti in 1260.[20] Tornabuoni's grandfather, Simone Tornaquinci, had changed the family name to Tornabuoni in 1393, abandoning noble status to cater to Florence's democratic leanings and to earn himself a seat in the magistracy. At the time of Lucrezia's birth, the Tornabuonis were prosperous bankers; Lucrezia's well-known brother, Giovanni, would eventually become head of the Medici bank in Rome. In the meantime Cosimo Vecchio had catapulted the Medici faction to prominence in the 1440s and 1450s, using the money gained from his banking and mercantile practices to transform an already prosperous city into an architectural jewel. His son Piero's marriage to a Tornabuoni afforded him the opportunity to link his ascendant family with the older Florentine oligarchy and with a family that had always been extremely loyal; the Tornabuonis had supported Cosimo when he went into exile in 1433.

The sickly Piero de' Medici (nicknamed "il gottoso" [the gouty one]) lacked Cosimo's energy and political vision. But he continued his father's legacy of artistic patronage, commissioning the famous frescoes by Benozzo Gozzoli for the chapel in the Medici palace, Pollaiuolo's three canvases of the labors of Hercules, and Michelozzo's rebuilding of Santissima Annunzi-

---

20. For background on the Tornabuoni family see Levantini-Pieroni, *Lucrezia Tornabuoni,* and Pampaloni, "Tornaquinci poi Tornabuoni," 351–63.

ata. He was active in patronizing Florentine churches and convents, and not merely those, like San Marco and San Lorenzo, that were in the Medici quarter but also San Miniato al Monte across the Arno.[21] Perhaps most important, thanks to Piero's competent and apparently mild rule, the Medici retained their considerable influence during some difficult years after Cosimo's death in 1464. The most threatening event during Piero's brief rulership (1464–69) was a plot to murder Piero hatched in 1466 by the ambitious Pitti family. But the intended assassination was foiled, largely by Lorenzo's quick thinking, and in the long run it galvanized popular support for the Medici. (The famous Pazzi Conspiracy of 1478, which caused the death of Tornabuoni's younger son, Giuliano, was treated rather differently; a quick and very public death to the traitors, memorialized in the macabre drawings of Andrea Castagno, provoked a more spectacular response than Piero's, for in this instance a Medici son had been killed.)[22] When the twenty-year-old Lorenzo took over the city after his father's death in December 1469, he seems to have deliberately adopted policies that clarified his position as primus inter pares—first among equals. When visiting dignitaries came to Florence, they were hosted not by Lorenzo but by the city, and the ruling Cento, or Council of One Hundred, continued to control Florence's military and political agendas.

Tornabuoni's own place in this maelstrom of activity is seldom acknowledged. The death of Piero in 1469 forced Lucrezia to take a larger part in Florence's civic affairs, although she had done a great deal even before his early demise. Piero's illness had confined him to his room for weeks at a time, and he entrusted to his wife several delicate diplomatic missions, including a trip to Rome in 1467 to inform the pope of Venice's designs against Florence.[23] Tornabuoni also influenced Piero to permit the

---

21. On Piero's patronage, see Diane Finiello Zervas, "'Quos volent et eo modo quo volent': Piero de' Medici and the *Operai* of SS. Annunziata, 1445–55." Also noteworthy is the recent talk by Linda Koch on Piero's relationship to a chapel in San Miniato al Monte, given at the meeting of the Renaissance Society of America. On Tornabuoni's and her husband's joint patronage of projects, see Katherine J. P. Lowe, "A Matter of Piety or of Family Tradition and Custom? The Religious Patronage of Piero de' Medici and Lucrezia Tornabuoni." More generally, see Andres, Hunisak, and Turner, *Art of Florence*, 504–7, 547.

22. The danger posed by Florentine exiles is alluded to in a letter from Piero to his wife of October 1, 1467, even if he dismisses the exiles' threats as "mere dreams" (in *Lettere*, ed. Salvadori, 96 (letter 50). Tornabuoni herself was at times in danger from the infighting that constantly threatened to break out among Florence's leading families and those embittered by exile; thus she was urged to leave the baths where she was recovering from illness in 1467 when it appeared that some exiles intended to seize her and her son as hostages.

23. Rochon, *Jeunesse de Laurent de Médicis*, 23.

Strozzi family to return from a lengthy exile; Giuseppe Levantini-Pieroni speaks of her as "the most direct instrument" of their return in 1465.[24] At the same time, during her marriage to Piero she was engaged primarily in family care, having borne seven children, five of whom survived birth: Bianca (1445), Lucrezia, also called Nannina (1447), Lorenzo (1449), Giuliano (1453), and Maria.[25] Tornabuoni influenced her sons' education, helping choose their tutors, such as Lorenzo's first and perhaps most important teacher, the well-known scholar and future bishop of Arezzo Gentile Becchi.[26] In the years to come her children's tutors would include Cristoforo Landino, Pulci, and Poliziano. Tornabuoni was also closely involved in marriage negotiations for her children; for example, she traveled to Rome in 1467 to meet Lorenzo's prospective bride, Clarice Orsini. In an often quoted passage from her long letter to Piero, she describes the young woman's looks (not as beautiful as women from Florence, but acceptable), her dress (much against the fashion of Florentines), and perhaps most important, her apparent corrigibility ("she is very modest and will soon learn our customs").[27] The marriage was without question a shrewd move on the part of the Medici. The same political sagacity that had led Cosimo Vecchio to arrange a marriage between his son Piero and the aristocratic Tornabuoni compelled Piero to seek out a bride from a respectable, noble Roman family, extending the Medici's sway into papal affairs. Celebrated in June 1469, only months before Piero's death, the marriage ceremonies went on for several days. As Machiavelli would describe them in his *Istorie fiorentine*, they were carried out "with much pomp and fanfare, and all the magnificence that a man [such as Piero] required: each day the guests consumed themselves with new types of dancing, with feasting, and with spectacles drawn from antiquity."[28]

Tornabuoni's daughters in turn were married to young men from prominent local families. Nannina married Bernardo Rucellai in 1466. (The wedding festivities were recorded in scrupulous detail by his father, Giovanni, from whom we learn that seventy bushels of bread and fifty barrels of trebbiano wine were ordered for the six banquets held in the Piazza Rucellai.)[29]

---

24. Levantini-Pieroni, *Lucrezia Tornabuoni*, 37.

25. No birthdate is known for Maria, apparently the oldest of the five; it has been suggested that she was Piero's illegitimate daughter but raised within the Medici household.

26. Salvadori prints one lengthy letter from Becchi to Tornabuoni (see letter 74).

27. Translated in Maguire, *Women of the Medici*, 129. The letter is printed in *Lettere*, ed. Salvadori, 62–63 (letter 12).

28. Machiavelli, *Istorie fiorentine*, bk. 8; quoted in Levantini-Pieroni, *Lucrezia Tornabuoni*, 55–56.

29. Cited in Maguire, *Women of the Medici*, 74.

Maria's husband, Lionetto de' Rossi, was director of the Medici bank in Lyons.[30] Bianca married Guglielmo de' Pazzi over a decade before the conspiracy that took the life of Tornabuoni's younger son, Giuliano. When Giuliano was murdered in the Duomo in April 1478, in an attack that wounded Lorenzo, Tornabuoni stepped in to provide for the illegitimate child her son had fathered; Tornabuoni sought out the boy who would become Pope Clement VII and had him educated with Lorenzo's children.[31] Her solicitude with regard to her children is apparent from her letters, the earliest of which are detailed chronicles of the young Giuliano's delicate health. One can only assume that Lorenzo's sentiments, recorded after her death in 1482, were genuine: he writes to the duchess of Ferrara that he has lost "not only my mother, but my only refuge from my troubles and my relief in many labors."[32]

A different kind of eulogy spoken upon Tornabuoni's death gives us more detail regarding the kind of "relief" she may have provided her son in the years after Piero died, when she became especially involved in Florence's affairs. Francesco da Castiglione, one of the canons from the Cappella dei Chierici in San Lorenzo, which Tornabuoni had founded, addresses himself with some lack of discretion to Lorenzo:

> What part of the state did the wisdom of Lucrezia not see, take care of, or confirm! . . . Sometimes [your mother's] actions, from the political point of view, were more prudent than yours, for you attended only to great things and forgot the less. . . . She advised the most important persons as well as the magistrates, and she also admitted the humblest to her presence and all she sent away happy and contented. . . . She knew how to manage the most important affairs with wise counsel, and to succor the citizens in time of calamity.[33]

30. For additional details, see Rochon, *Jeunesse de Laurent de Médicis*, 29–30.

31. See Maguire for further details (*Women of the Medici*, 109–10). Levantini-Pieroni sees the incident as exemplary of Tornabuoni's authority in the household: "And that in the Medici household she exercised a level of authority that generally Florentine men did not permit their women to have, is also shown by the fact that it was she who took in the son of her Giuliano" (*Lucrezia Tornabuoni*, 61). Jacopo Nardi, whom Levantini-Pieroni cites, refers explicitly to Tornabuoni's agency in seeking out the young Giulio: "Se non fosse stata la intercessione e l'autorità dell'avola madonna Lucrezia de' Tornabuoni . . . forse non sarebbe stato questo fanciullo ricevuto, né allevato come figliuolo di Giuliano" [Were it not for the intervention and authority of Madonna Lucrezia de' Tornabuoni . . . perhaps this child would never have been acknowledged, let alone raised, as Giuliano's son] (Levantini-Pieroni, *Lucrezia Tornabuoni*, 62n).

32. Cited in Maguire, *Women of the Medici*, 220n; the Italian text is from Levantini-Pieroni, *Lucrezia Tornabuoni*, 69.

33. Quoted in Maguire, *Women of the Medici*, 220n, with minor revisions.

Although one might suspect some hyperbole in such immediate eulogies, Castiglione's words reveal that Tornabuoni was far more than a supportive mother and spouse engaged primarily in household affairs. Her day-to-day role in the young Lorenzo's life during years of instability—in addition to the Pazzi Conspiracy that took Giuliano's life, there were other instances of internal unrest, as well as threats from powers surrounding Florence— is especially evident in the many letters she wrote to her son and received from those soliciting her influence and favor after 1469.

Indeed, numerous letters attest to the not always subtle pressures that Tornabuoni placed on her son after Piero's death. She beseeches Lorenzo for such "favors" as the choice of a new rector for a parish church (letter 18); she petitions him for the poor messenger who carries her letter, noting that his five children are dying of hunger (letter 30); she insists that a man has been removed from local office on trumped-up charges (and she has apparently done a great deal of work to verify this; letter 33). Florentine citizens were quick to recognize a mother's potential power over her son. Several letters ask Tornabuoni to try to change Lorenzo's mind on a given matter, to "work on him" [operiate][34] to effect a pardon, to proffer charity, to secure a position. But Tornabuoni could influence affairs more directly as well, and she was not always beholden to her son or husband.[35] In a letter interesting for its allusion to Tornabuoni's learnedness (it opens with, "You have read so much, your study is full of books, you have understood the epistles of Saint Paul, you have, throughout your entire life, frequented the company of valorous men"), Gentile Becchi, former tutor of Lorenzo, recommends to Tornabuoni the brother of a friend who wishes to obtain a post at the University of Pisa.[36] She is also asked to influence the choice of a new chancellor for the University of Pisa,[37] and many letters from informants traveling outside Florence enlighten her on the development of the war against the Turks and the fragile balance of power among Italian city-states.[38]

34. For the term, see letter 54, from Francesco Dovizi: "Vi prego operiate con Lorenzo che ne scrivi una letter di buono inchiosto al vicario" [I beseech you to work on Lorenzo so that he will write a well-meaning letter to the vicar]; Salvadori, *Lettere*, 100.

35. Patrizia Salavadori observes: "Numerous comments from her interlocutors enable us to infer that Tornabuoni had a certain margin of autonomy in her activities" (*Lettere*, 33).

36. "Voi havete sempre tanto lecto, sì pieno lo scriptoio di libri, udito pìstole di sam Paolo, praticho tutto il tempo di vostra vita con valenti huomini" (Salvadori, *Lettere*, 122 [letter 74]).

37. See Maguire, *Women of the Medici*, 98, who cites a letter from Ser Niccolò da Volterra asking that she recommend him for the chancellorship; the letter, not published by Salvadori, is in the Archivio Mediceo avanti Principato, Av. fol. lxxx.38.

38. See Levantini-Pieroni, *Lucrezia Tornabuoni*, particularly 65, for a discussion of the many figures who wrote to her about international affairs.

At the same time, one should not exaggerate Tornabuoni's influence on civic and social affairs—or, for that matter, that of her husband and son. As a growing body of scholarship is insisting, Lorenzo was hardly in sole control of Florence's many domestic and international affairs. Far from being a youthful tyrant, as he tended to be portrayed by earlier historians, Lorenzo was subject to a number of forces within a Florence that maintained not simply the vestiges but the reality of a republic.[39] In a city where civic and military power continued to lie in the hands of so many citizens— needless to say, all of them men—it is not surprising that women as a rule had little direct say in the ongoing events of Florentine life. Moreover, unlike the duchesses of northern Italian courts, such as Bona Sforza, who visited Florence in March 1471 and expressed surprise that women had not come out to meet her as she approached the city, Tornabuoni and other leading Florentine women conducted their affairs out of the public eye. The duchess was officially welcomed only once she was within the Palazzo Medici, "where there were many women gathered to greet her."[40]

Certainly Tornabuoni was counted on to entertain visiting dignitaries and to represent the women of the city to them, and she was no doubt influential in orchestrating the visits of famous members of royalty to Florence while Piero and Lorenzo were Florence's first citizens. In addition to the Sforza, members of the d'Este court and Eleonora of Aragon were solemnly received in Florence during the 1470s. But Lorenzo needed to pay more than lip service to the city's republican origins; Florence was not one of the despotic northern courts in which duchesses might have as free and powerful a presence as dukes. Hence Bona Sforza's surprise when she approached the city. The resulting constraints on women's behavior formed a large part of a humanist tradition that emphasized women's limited participation in the public realm. In his *Libri della famiglia*, Leon Battista Alberti writes: "It would hardly win us respect if our wife busied herself among the men in the marketplace out in the public eye. It also seems somewhat demeaning for me to remain shut up in the house among women when

---

39. Hence Nicolai Rubinstein argues for the ongoing validity of groups like the Council of the One Hundred, or the Cento, and after 1471, the existence of the Balìa, which consisted of a first group of forty citizens elected by the Signoria and the Accoppiatori, who in turn elected another two hundred members of the commission. See "Lorenzo de' Medici: The Formation of His Statecraft," 49. Even though Rubinstein argues for the skillful diplomacy that marked Lorenzo's years guiding Florence, he notes the "considerable restraints" to which many of Lorenzo's actions were subject (46 and passim).

40. "Dove era de molte done per accogliere Madona" (quoted in Riccardo Fubini, "Margine," 171–72). Citing Fubini, Salvadori makes the point that "women's presence in public . . . was unheard of in the city's tradition" (Tornabuoni, *Lettere*, 6).

I have manly things to do among men, fellow citizens and worthy and distinguished foreigners."[41] As will become clear, the lives of the biblical women Tornabuoni chose to depict in her *storie* have a curious resonance with her own, in large part because of their compromised positions regarding their political influence and visibility. It is noteworthy that all of them work consistently for the good of their *families* and their *people*, and it is possible that Tornabuoni saw her allegiances in terms of her family rather than of Florence. At the same time, almost all the women she focused on ran risks similar to those she may have taken as she wielded influence in the city and surrounding provinces. Women were not expected to act in these ways and were on occasion criticized for doing so.[42]

Some of these undertakings were specifically economic. One of Tornabuoni's projects during the last years of her life was the renovation of Bagno a Morba, a hot spring ten miles south of Volterra that she leased from the Monte di Firenze in 1477. F. W. Kent has only half facetiously called her work with Bagno a Morba Italy's first experiment in *agriturismo*.[43] Certainly for her own benefit as much as anyone else's (she suffered from painful arthritis and had been going to the baths long before she sought to have a hand in restoring them), she supervised the construction not only of a thermohydraulic plant but of lodgings for her family and a hotel for paying guests. Her dealings with her manager and the workers who sought to improve the grounds reveal a sage businesswoman wanting to keep abreast of the details of a major economic and civic project. Tornabuoni also collected rents from numerous shops and buildings, especially in Pisa (at times revealing impatience with her renters).[44] But strictly speaking her most time-

41. Alberti, *Family in Renaissance Florence*, 207. There is a wide literature on the humanist texts destined for women readers, even if there is considerable disagreement as to how to interpret them. See, for some important contributions, Isidoro del Lungo, *La donna fiorentina del buon tempo antico*, 190–220; R. A. Sydie, "Humanism, Patronage and the Question of Women's Artistic Genius in the Italian Renaissance"; F. W. Kent, *Household and Lineage*; Constance Jordan, *Renaissance Feminism*; Pamela Joseph Benson, *The Invention of the Renaissance Woman*; and Natalie Tomas, *"Positive Novelty."*

42. Kent notes the condemnation of Tornabuoni when she traveled to Rome in 1467 and visited the Roman Curia, in part to influence the papal curate regarding Venice's designs on Florence. The exile Iacopo Acciaiuoli (no friend of the Medici) complained that she "reduced Florence to the lowest level of repute"; quoted in Kent, "Proposal by Savonarola for the Self-Reform of Florentine Women," 339. See Natalie Tomas's insightful interpretation of this event: "Acciaiuoli was effectively condemning Lucrezia for her 'public' display of Medici *de facto* power, and, I suggest, expressing his disapproval at the idea that a *woman* could be sent to the Roman Curia" (*"Positive Novelty,"* 62).

43. "Kent, Sainted Mother, Magnificent Son," 10.

44. See Salvadori's wry comment: "In her handling of rents, Lucrezia does not seem as though she can be easily moved by the economic difficulties of her clients." She cites a letter from

consuming public "work" was neither economic nor political, but her day-to-day charitable enterprises, and it is in the letters requesting her assistance that Tornabuoni's public presence most fully emerges. She is begged to help release a man from prison or to intervene in the case of a priest who wants to move to a new parish. Young girls petition her for dowries, friars request positions, and prioresses, who address her as "madonna pietosa de' poveri e maxime delle religiose" [pitying lady of the poor, especially of religious women], ask for "panno grosso," or coarse cloth to make habits (letter 85). She also practiced a more conspicuous piety: hence her funding of special feast days at convents such as San Domenico in Pisa, her support of a canonicate in the chapter of Fiesole, and her instituting an annual anniversary mass for Piero's soul in San Lorenzo.[45]

Such activities attest to a sense of public life very different from that expected by the visiting duchess from Milan, one made possible primarily through a conception of charity that insists women take on a visible role in the daily life of urban society in order to help the needy, feed and clothe the poor, tend the sick, and assist the dying. This was a model of charitable works that had been promulgated most famously by Catherine of Siena, who died a century before Tornabuoni, and by Francesca Romana, who was her contemporary.[46] Catherine, however, was only the most vociferous of the *mantellate* or Dominican tertiaries who lived in communities scattered throughout urban areas and dedicated themselves to an apostolic life of helping others.[47] Tornabuoni, of course, was no *mantellata*. Yet her many undertakings in Florence and throughout Tuscany had much in common with the work the tertiaries performed, while the wealth of her own family and that of the Medici enabled her to attain a visibility in her civic and domestic projects that most tertiaries did not enjoy. Perhaps ironically, in the prologue to a book that appears to have been dedicated to her, the *Opere a ben vivere*, Antoninus Pierozzi, archbishop of Florence (later Saint Antoninus), argues that women like Tornabuoni should *not* spend so much time in the various social exchanges that made their charitable work possible. In his concern with public morality and female chastity, Antoninus

---

the wife of a barber, who turns to Lorenzo in the hope that he will be more generous than his mother (Tornabuoni, *Lettere*, 25n).

45. For these details and others, see Lowe, "Matter of Piety or of Family Tradition and Custom?" 63.

46. See the work of Karen Scott and my essay on Saint Catherine, "Caterina da Siena and the Legacy of Humanism."

47. On the work of the *mantellate* and women's vernacular writings, see Katherine J. Gill, "Women and the Production of Religious Literature in the Vernacular."

prefers that women go to mass only on the holiest feast days. Otherwise they should remain at home, reading their offices and avoiding the many public occasions that would induce them to sin.[48]

On the other hand, Antoninus grudgingly observes that at times women in Tornabuoni's position must attend public events—marriage ceremonies, religious vigils, feast days, public festivals, and dances—all of them occasions that might easily draw them into sin.[49] Yet even if Antoninus may have been overly strict in his cautions and restrictions, it is easy to imagine a conflicted Lucrezia confronting the ambiguous question of just what the city and the Medici family did expect of her, and to what extent she must wander into what Antoninus considered the domains of vice.[50] Her considerable work with the spring at Bagno a Morba; her obvious familiarity with lavish parties, as indicated by her lengthy descriptions of feasting; and her knowledge of the dynamics of power and intrigue at court, made clear in *Esther* and *John the Baptist*, all suggest that she was not, and could not be, either the enclosed housewife of Alberti's imaginings or the pious and long-suffering widow of Antoninus's treatises. This is not to say that Tornabuoni's reflections on her role in the public space, where women are placed in almost all of her *storie sacre*, do not display some wariness about the potential of such a space for compromising female virtue. Her at times contradictory remarks on the way her biblical heroines intervened in political matters reveal her own uncertainty about the roles women could and should play in civic affairs.

But Antoninus's anxieties, as well as the many extant letters both to and from Tornabuoni, nonetheless demonstrate a consistent and solid network of connections in Florentine life—whose very informality opened up a place for women to interact and wield unusual influence. F. W. Kent has been crucial in assessing how informal these networks were, given that Florence's civic and social spaces frequently overlapped. Largely because of this overlap, Kent envisions a woman in Tornabuoni's position as having

48. Enzo Maurri, in *Un fiorentino tra Medioevo e Rinascimento*, 138–40, argues with particular effectiveness that Tornabuoni was the dedicatee of a second copy of *Opere a ben vivere*; he believes that the first copy had been dedicated to Tornabuoni's sister, Dianora Tornabuoni, wife of Tommaso Soderini. The one I consulted, in the Biblioteca Riccardiana, is the later copy of the manuscript, done in Antoninus's own hand.

49. "You ought not to attend [these events], unless you believe that not to go will create some kind of scandal, or dishonor your husband, in which case I leave it up to your discretion, and the weight of your conscience" (Antoninus, *Opere a ben vivere*, fol. 56r).

50. Martelli notes that Tornabuoni was not as loyal to Antoninus as her contemporary Feo Belcari; see "Lucrezia Tornabuoni," 64–65.

access to important people.[51] Despite Florence's austere republican tradition, Tornabuoni did seem capable of working within the interstices of society to effect change. But we must bear in mind the fine distinction Constance Jordan has made between power and authority in women's lives in the early modern era.[52] Authority, for Jordan, signifies holding a position that is recognized per se as legitimate, whereas the exercise of power involves the very "informalities" Kent has called attention to—putting to use eloquence, persuasion, and petition. That Tornabuoni wielded power—if not authority—during her lifetime, and that such power and influence did not seem to fade even in her last few years of declining health, is apparent not only in her letters but in the homage paid her when she was buried in 1482 in the Medici church of San Lorenzo. Poems written upon her death attest to her centrality in Florence as both a symbol—most frequently of the Madonna—and an energetic agent who worked on behalf of its citizens.[53] As we turn to the poems, we will observe resonances between Tornabuoni's life and the lives of the biblical women she celebrated.

WRITINGS

Exactly when Tornabuoni composed her poetry is unknown, although Poliziano's letter of 1478 indicates that she wrote at least some of her *laudi* and no doubt several of her *storie sacre* before then. Scholars surmise that most of her writings date from after Piero's death.[54] Of the three literary genres in which Tornabuoni wrote, two are included in this volume: her surviving *laudi* and the five extant *storie sacre*. (There is only one extant sonnet by Tornabuoni, although according to Poliziano's letter of 1478 she must have written many more.)

---

51. Kent, "Sainted Mother, Magnificent Son," as well as Kent's work more generally.

52. In her review of the series in which this translation appears, Jordan observes that "women [in the early modern period] *were* powerful; they were eloquent, persuasive, and influential. What they were not was authoritative; they lacked the means to make their desires more than the motive force behind a request, petition, or plea; for the most part, they were excluded from those institutions that would have given their positions legitimacy" ("Listening to 'the Other Voice' in Early Modern Europe," 186). Tornabuoni, even in this scenario, emerges as something of an exception; her positions were recognized as legitimate by a great many in Renaissance Florence, even if she was more constrained than men.

53. Kent calls attention to eulogies written upon her death and discusses the persistent symbolism linking Tornabuoni to the Madonna ("Sainted Mother," 10–11, 26–29).

54. See the comment of Pezzarossa, who argues for Pulci's extensive influence on Tornabuoni and suggests that this influence can be traced to the late 1460s (Tornabuoni, *Poemetti sacri*, 41).

The vast body of poetry loosely called *laudi* is best defined by Francesco Cionacci, the seventeenth-century editor of a volume of religious lyric poetry written by members of the Medici family, including Tornabuoni: *"Laude* are nothing other than spiritual canticles or *canzoni,* which correspond to the hymns of the Greeks and the Romans. One of the distinguishing features of this poetic genre is that it must be accompanied by a song that one alludes to by providing instructions that it should be sung to the tune of this or that *canzone.* This was done to call people away from their profane music [*cantilene*], as pious folk composed their lauds according to these popular tunes."[55] For four of her own *laudi,* Tornabuoni avails herself of one of the period's most "popular tunes," Angelo Poliziano's famous *ballata* "Ben venga maggio" [Welcome to May]. The Florentines Feo Belcari, Poliziano, and Lorenzo de' Medici all composed *laudi* that employ a variety of metrical forms (not just the *canzone,* pace Cionacci). Literally hundreds of *laudi* can be found in manuscripts compiled in the fifteenth and sixteenth centuries (called *laudari*); most of the poems—such as Tornabuoni's—are without attribution.

Tornabuoni's eight *laudi* and one religious *canzone* translated here are of varying poetic quality. They use standard, quasi-dramatic settings—the birth of Christ, his death on the cross, his descent into hell, the Last Judgment—in order to engage the reader directly with the agony and ecstasy of Christ's life. Nativity scenes, the subject of three *laudi,* are virtually orchestrated by a stage director who calls to the scene of Christ's birth the patriarchs, angels, shepherds, and wise men.[56] One of the more moving of Tornabuoni's *laudi* involves direct dialogue between the dying Christ and a spectator, who is asked to contemplate his wounds; another, more enigmatic *laude* is sung by a recent convert who is addressing the demonic forces that attempt to lure her back into sin. The longest of the poems retells the fall of Adam and Eve and prophesies Christ's redemption, as Tornabuoni dwells on "our first parents'" befuddlement when first exiled from paradise. Although the account in Genesis and passages from the New Testament are central, we may detect other influences in a few passages—Dante's *Inferno* informs the rousing "Ecco il Re forte," and another *laude* is derived from a liturgical hymn.[57] That Tornabuoni's poems circulated in many *laudari*

55. Cionacci, "Rime sacre di Mona Lucrezia de' Medici," a chapter in *Rime sacre del magnifico Lorenzo de' Medici il Vecchjo, di Maddona Lucrezia sua madre e d'altri della stessa famiglia;* Cionacci's comments on the origins of the *laudi* are on 28–29.

56. Martelli in fact speculates that this poem may have been composed for a convent performance (*Letteratura fiorentina del Quattrocento,* 20).

57. Tornabuoni, *Laudi di Lucrezia de' Medici,* ed. Volpi, 18.

suggests that her writings may have influenced others; Coppola even speculates that Savonarola may have derived one of his poems from the "lyric tonalities" of her "Venitene pastori."[58] In turn, for many years, a *laude* of Savonarola's was attributed to Tornabuoni, largely because of its "joyous and expansive spiritual happiness"—a quality said by Coppola to mark Tornabuoni's poetry, and evident in Savonarola's best work as well.[59]

Although the *laudi* were occasional pieces, Tornabuoni's Italian adaptations of biblical stories probably were not. Nor can they be said to be as derivative as the *laudi* undoubtedly are. There were, of course, many writings that took Old and New Testament stories as their focus and expanded on them in either Latin or the vernacular; the *Meditations on the Life of Christ*, said by some to have been written by Saint Bernard, are perhaps the best-known example of an extended translation of biblical materials. That Tornabuoni composed her *storie sacre* in two different metrical forms—the ottava rima, or eight-line stanza, and the terzina, or three-line stanza—suggests that she had more than one model in mind when she sat down to "turn [the stories of Judith and others] into rhyme, and in a manner that would please."

The lives of Judith and John the Baptist are in octaves, and these two *vite* seem to have enjoyed wider circulation than the poems about Esther, Susanna, and Tobias, which are in terzinas. The poems in octaves look to two important contemporary forms, the *cantari* and the *sacre rappresentazioni*, or sacred plays. The former are poetic narratives that emerged from oral traditions going back at least to the thirteenth century, composed in eight-line stanzas with a regular rhyme scheme of ABABABCC. Perhaps the best known of the *cantari* focus on chivalric episodes and legends (*cantari cavallereschi*): examples include *Lancelot, The Queen of the Orient*, and *The Story of Patrocolo and Insidoria*.[60] Tornabuoni and other Florentines could have heard these *cantari* in the Florentine piazzetta of San Martino and the Piazza of San Felice.[61] The Medici's interest in linking their family to the city's *rifondatore*,

---

58. Coppola, *Poesia religiosa*, 65n, where he speculates: "Is it outrageous to think that the gentle poet may have left some germ of inspiration in the severe soul of the friar?"

59. Coppola, *Poesia religiosa*, 64.

60. Gaetano Mariani has a convenient list of recently published *cantari* in *Morgante e i cantari trecenteschi*, 3–4n.

61. Dale Kent's paper for the 2000 Renaissance Society of America conference, titled "Civic Culture as Popular Entertainment: Political and Patriotic Texts in Public Performances and Private Literary Compilations in Early Medicean Florence," explored in fascinating detail the role of the piazza of San Martino in the city's popular culture. In her abstract she suggests that "San Martino was particularly the place where politics became entertainment."

Charlemagne, encouraged the cycles of chivalric songs to become intensely popular in mid-fifteenth-century Florence, as did their attempts to link Florence to the northern Italian courts with their rich legacies of Gothic art and knightly tournaments and their connections to the lavish world of French nobility.[62] The poems written to celebrate the *giostre* [jousts] of Lorenzo and Giuliano, respectively, by Pulci (1469) and Poliziano (1475) owe a great deal to this tradition. But perhaps the best-known poem with clear ties to these Carolingian cycles is the one Tornabuoni herself commissioned in 1461, Pulci's *Morgante*. Gaetano Mariani has elucidated the stylistic features shared by the popular *cantari* and Pulci's far more ambitious poem. Both engage in frequent moralizing, stereotypes of female beauty, and lavish descriptions of the countryside and the battles that take place there, and the poems are marked by a tendency toward parataxis and hyperbole. As Mariani notes, the most significant difference between these poems and the *Morgante* is the presence of "uno spirito geniale" [a genial spirit] who presides over the whole of Pulci's epic. Yet it is abundantly clear that the author of the *Morgante* relies on the world of the songs for his own whimsical forays into the life of his giant.[63]

These are stylistic features that mark Tornabuoni's *storie sacre* as well, though her poems naturally draw more on the *cantari* that took religious themes as their topic.[64] Whether the religious poems were sung as frequently as the chivalric poems is not clear; in his edition of fourteenth-century *cantari* from Siena, Giorgio Varanini argues that such texts were probably destined not for piazzas and crossroads but for reading alone or in small groups. The religious *cantari* of Neri Pagliaresi, Niccolò Cicerchia, and Fra Felice Tancredi exemplify certain striking traits: invocations for grace and help from God that include a confession of the writer's inferiority; the tendency to parataxis also notable in the courtly *cantari*; an inclination to focus on the homely or domestic detail; and direct references to the

---

62. For a discussion of the "profound link" between the Medici and Charlemagne that *cantari* focusing on the Carolingian cycle exploited, see *Tems revient*, ed. Ventrone, 55–56.

63. Mariani, *Morgante e i cantari trecenteschi*, 1–28.

64. That contemporary compilers of these materials did not bother to distinguish between the content of the *cantari* seems clear from at least one important manuscript in the Biblioteca Riccardiana, 2816, titled "Rappresentazioni, storie, e rime diverse." Copied in what seems to be a mid- to late sixteenth-century hand, the manuscript contains nineteen selections, including several *sacre rappresentazioni*, such as the "Representation of the Sacrifice of Abraham" of Feo Belcari and Giovanni de' Medici, several arguably religious *cantari* such as the "Esempio di S. Panuzio," a *cantare* drawn from chivalric materials titled "La Sala di Malagigi in ottava rima," and two of Tornabuoni's *sacre storie*, without attribution (*Judith* and *John the Baptist*, both in ottava rima).

project at hand. In the third stanza of the *Legend of Saint Giosafa,* Pagliaresi
asks his Lord to "give me the grace to do this, to tell such a devout tale"
[di dir questa istoria sí devota]; Cicerchia, at the beginning of *The Passion,*
asks that his heart might be inspired so that he can put the story of Christ's
death into verses ("a ciò ch'i' possa dir ne' versi in rima"), and at the begin-
ning of the second part of *The Resurrection* he calls on Christ so that he might
faithfully follow "la santa storia" [the holy story].[65] These are all conventions
that Tornabuoni's *sacre storie* share as well, as she asks Mary to "give [her]
the skill / to draw [the life of John the Baptist] all together, and put it
into rhyme, / so that it may be worthy of honor and esteem" and as she
acknowledges at the beginning of *The Story of Queen Esther* her "feeble
talents / as I compose in rhyme this entire story." And just as, at the end
of *Susanna,* Tornabuoni addresses "whoever hears or reads this little work,"
so does Cicerchia, at the end of *The Resurrection,* call on those who "hear or
read" his poem to correct any defects they may find.[66]

Such common patterns in the works' invocations and epilogues place
Tornabuoni's long poems squarely within a tradition of popularized reli-
gious stories that borrow freely from the Bible as well as other sources:
apocryphal tales, such as the Gospel of James, that circulated widely in the
Middle Ages; hagiographies such as the *Legenda aurea;* and commentaries
designed to instruct readers, particularly female readers, such as *Meditations
on the Life of Christ.* While at least one of Tornabuoni's stories was the subject
of other religious *cantari* as well—hence the existence of *La storia di Susanna
e Daniello,* of which Tornabuoni was apparently unaware[67]—she was also
indebted to the chivalric poems for more than one stylistic nuance. Her
descriptions of feminine beauty or of the sumptuous banquet at the begin-
ning of *The Story of Queen Esther* or the garden that is at the center of *Susanna*
surely owe some of their details to the chivalric poems. And her stylistic
choices place her squarely in the ambiance of the *cantari,* religious and chi-
valric alike. Her style is admittedly simple, and at times disarmingly paratac-
tic. Tornabuoni connects most of her clauses with *et* [and], seldom making
use of overt patterns of subordination even when the biblical context calls
for them. In this she resembles the writers of the *cantari,* and to a lesser

---

65. Citations are all from Giorgio Varanini's edition of *Cantari religiosi senesi del Trecento;* he
provides a brief but excellent account of the religious *cantari* tradition on 451–54. Citations
are from 7, 309, and 405.

66. *Cantari religiosi senesi del Trecento,* 447.

67. See Parducci's comments on this particular *cantare* and his conclusion that there is virtually
no common ground between it and Tornabuoni's *Story of Devout Susanna* ("Ystoria della devota
Susanna," 180–82).

extent Pulci, who often sacrificed subordinate clauses for a more evenly flowing verse form.

Yet another popular Florentine genre based on these traditions and often composed in ottava rima is the *sacra rappresentazione*, which was popular in Florence during the 1460s and 1470s. Unlike the *cantari*, which were sung throughout the year, the "sacred plays" tended to be tied to specific liturgical feast days or, importantly for Tornabuoni's place in Florentine society, diplomatic occasions. The visit of Duke Galeazzo Maria Sforza in 1471 occasioned a wide range of festive events including the performance of a number of *sacre rappresentazioni*. (One of them, the *Descent of the Holy Ghost*, was being performed when the church of Santo Spirito caught fire and almost entirely burned down.) Two years later, dinner entertainments were performed for Eleonora of Aragon by Florentine *festaiuoli* at the Roman palace of Pietro Riario: they included a *sacra rappresentazione* of Susanna, a play on the harrowing of hell, scenes from the Nativity, and *Giovanni Baptista*. Lorenzo de' Medici would compose his own sacred play on Saints John and Paul a decade after Tornabuoni's death. Tornabuoni's *storie sacre* were not destined for performance, but the topics she chose overlapped with those of contemporary plays, such as *San Giovanni nel deserto*. Moreover, her long *canzone* on Adam and Eve features brief dialogues similar to those of the anonymous *Notabile rappresentazione chiamata la creazione del mondo*, probably first performed in 1451.[68]

Even though the three *storie sacre* composed in terza rima are likewise indebted to the *cantari*, one must also consider the possible influence of literary epic on Tornabuoni—namely, of course, Dante's *Commedia*, which like *Susanna*, *Tobias*, and *Esther*, was written in terzinas. Not surprisingly, Dantesque allusions and echoes abound; Tornabuoni's most blatantly moralizing passages may betray Dante's legacy.[69] But if Dante's distinctive blend of intimacy and fidelity to the larger Christian narrative that unfolds within

68. The tradition of the *sacra rappresentazione* changed dramatically after Tornabuoni's lifetime; Newbigin suggests a crucial change in the roles of women in the *rappresentazioni* after the 1480s, as we see increasing reference to virgins, women terrorized by violence, saints from the *Legenda aurea*, and the Griselda tale: "Alongside the brides who survive to enjoy earthly rewards there are even more virgins who do not, and who pass directly to heavenly delights. How do we account for the resurgence of interest in the martyrdoms based on the *Vitae patrum* and the *Legenda Aurea*? . . . Did Savonarola's much touted *riforma delle donne* actually alter society's perception of women, or women's perception of themselves, so that they saw themselves depicted in these works?" ("Politics in the sacre rappresentazioni," 129).

69. Martelli, *Letteratura fiorentina del Quattrocento*, 15. He also notes that these moralizing passages are more suited to the metrics of the terzinas than those of the octaves; hence Tornabuoni's voice is more intrusive in the *storie* of Esther, Tobias, and Susanna.

his text can be said to be an important influence on Tornabuoni, there were other filiations as well. In addition to occasional Petrarchan echoes one can discern echoes of the contemporary poets Francesco d'Altobianco degli Alberti and Feo Belcari. Poliziano, whose description of the palace of Venus has been cited as an important model for Tornabuoni's elaboration of Aha-suerus's feasting in the first chapter of *Esther*, is especially interesting in this light. With his own wide range of interests and his versatility in working with various poetic forms, he helps us see Tornabuoni herself as a bridge between popular and more elite forms, between the neo-Gothic descriptive-ness of the *cantari* tradition and the desire to make vernacular poetry worthy of an educated audience.

Of course the Bible was the chief source of Tornabuoni's *storie*, even if we are unsure whether she drew on the Latin Vulgate or on translations of the Bible into Italian. As Kenelm Foster comments, surprisingly little work has been done on Italian vernacular translations of the Bible in the fifteenth century, even though numerous manuscripts survive of both the Old and New Testaments in Italian. Dante quotes considerably, in Italian, from both Testaments, and by the time Lucrezia was purportedly writing there existed at least two complete translations of the Bible into the vernacular.[70] Florence in particular emerged in the mid-fifteenth century as a center for such trans-lations, and Tornabuoni may well have been familiar with them. One of Tornabuoni's ancestors, in fact, translated a letter of Jerome's that has been found in a manuscript of the vernacular New Testament.[71] In particular, for her *Vita di Sancto Giovanni Baptista*, Tornabuoni may have availed herself of the Tuscan *Diatessaron*, a popular compendium and concordance of the four Gospels. And she no doubt knew others' versified treatments of stories and prayers from the Old and particularly the New Testament, such as the selections in a manuscript titled "Fiore di Virtu: Rime Sacre," now in the Biblioteca Riccardiana in Florence. Copied in 1472, it contains entries such as "L'ave Maria in versi ternari facta per Antonio di Macteo di Chuzzado,

70. On Dante's translations from the Vulgate, see Felicina Groppi, *Dante traduttore*, 20–47.

71. Foster points out this detail, prefacing it with: "We are left then with various indications, in the manuscripts, which show or suggest one or other part of the medieval Italian scene— a group or region within which the vernacular bible, or some part of it, circulated. The region is usually Tuscany, and more precisely, Florence. The Florentine predominance is remarkable. In no other city do we find the vernacular bible, as Berger puts it, 'so intimately mixed into literary culture and family life.' The majority of our manuscripts are preserved in Florentine libraries, and it is remarkable that many of these were copied by members of that wealthy mercantile class which was in effect the city's aristocracy" (Foster, "Vernacular Scriptures in Italy," 458). The Tornaquinci letter and New Testament are in the Biblioteca Nazionale, Pala-tine V.

cittadino fiorentino" (1763); it is followed by "Il pater nostro in versi tern-
ari." Even if Tornabuoni scholars have noted obvious instances where she
translates liberally from the Latin—and even where a mistranslation from
the Latin appears—it is not improbable that she would have worked with
vernacular retellings.[72] There were no clerical objections to translations dur-
ing this period, and in his *Opere a ben vivere* Antoninus assumes that women
are reading not only their offices but biblical texts in Italian as well. Hence
the vernacularization of the Bible in early Renaissance Florence, work in
which Tornabuoni was seriously engaged, can be said to have constituted
one part of the ongoing efforts in the vernacular as attested by Poliziano,
Ficino, and others, albeit practiced by a very different segment of Florentine
society than the humanist elite.[73]

WOMEN AS BIBLICAL STORYTELLERS

Finally we turn to the most interesting questions of all: not why did Torna-
buoni choose to write *storie sacre*, but why did she choose the biblical books
she did? And what do her choices and her treatment of them reveal about
her distinctiveness as an author and, more generally, about mid-fifteenth-
century Florence? The latter question is perhaps easier to answer. Despite
their relative fidelity to the biblical texts, in their frequent deviations from
the Vulgate—and possibly vernacular Bibles—the poems of Tornabuoni
reflect a lively picture of patrician and social life. As I mentioned earlier,
we have glamorous depictions of the feast that opens the Book of Esther,
lengthened from several descriptive sentences in the Latin to over one hun-
dred lines in Tornabuoni's poem. We hear of the dress, the draperies, the
garden, the enameled artworks, the servants who wait behind the chair of
each visiting dignitary, the young men, "like angels," who roam the gardens
with trays of delicacies and wine. The wedding ceremony between Sarah
and Tobias in *The Life of Tobias* is sketched in some detail, as Sarah's father
asks (anachronistically) for the Bible so that he may record the *parentado*

72. Jerome's Vulgate was no longer available in late medieval Italy; Dante himself, as Groppi
observes, would have worked from Latin texts derived from Jerome's fourth-century version,
known as the "Italian text" from the twelfth century, and the "Parisian text," from the four-
teenth. Like Groppi, I will be citing from the *Biblica sacra: Iuxta latinam vulgatam versionem* for
Old Testament passages and the *Novum Testamentum Domini nostri Jesu Christi* for New Testament
passages.

73. Pezzarossa supplies a very useful list of Florentine manuscripts that contain biblical stories
in the vernacular (Tornabuoni, *Poemetti sacri*, 61–63n). As Foster notes, there is still a great
deal of work to be done with these texts, very few of which have been either published or
studied ("Vernacular Scriptures in Italy").

[marriage] in the book in the presence of witnesses. We learn of Tornabuoni's concern that poverty-stricken or working women have the dowries they need to wed when Judith gives her serving maid ample gifts so she may find herself a worthy husband. Tornabuoni is also anxious to redeem the fallen morality of the many virgins who have slept with King Ahasuerus in *Esther* when she ensures that they are given appropriate dowries so they can contract respectable marriages. We see mothers nursing their own children; Anna gives the infant John her breast, and the elderly Tobias appeals to his son's necessary respect for his mother when he counsels him to "bear her in your mind, and keep her in your heart, / recalling the labors and suffering she sustained for you / when she gave you her milk, that sweetest of drinks." The same speech finds Tornabuoni inserting a nonbiblical passage about the dangers of sodomy. Recalling to his son "the terrible judgment / that was sent to Sodom and Gomorrah," Tobias instructs him to avoid a similar sin, telling him that he "must remain content with the woman / whom God has prepared for you, and this is your duty, / and this is what God has commanded of you." Some of the most emotional passages in Tornabuoni's *storie* involve mothers' tender solicitude for their children. Tobias's mother complains that her husband has sent Tobias on dangerous and unknown paths to recover money, and Elizabeth is reluctant to permit the young John to go off into the desert to live alone.[74]

Most interestingly, we get glimpses into a close, and in some ways closed, society obsessed with hearsay, reputation, and family pride.[75] When, in *The Life of Tobias*, Tobias's father-in-law, Raguel, believes that his daughter's eighth husband will meet the same grim fate as the other seven, he instructs his servants to dig a grave and has his wife send a handmaiden to see if Tobias, like all the others, is dead the next morning. The request is found in the Bible, but Tornabuoni's elaboration is telling: "If she finds him dead, she should not spread the news, / but they should bury him quickly before it is day, / wrapping him in clean white linen." Once it is clear that Tobias has survived his ordeal, Tornabuoni has Raguel happily tell his servants: "'Now quickly, fill the grave back up / before anyone can hear about it! / And before it is day, fill it with earth/ so that no one can find anything out; / do not reveal the order that I gave.'" King Herod worries

74. The emphasis on motherhood is at the same time not necessarily in conflict with the larger narratives themselves. Anne Barriault (*Spalliera Paintings*, 132) has commented on the inseparability of familial and political themes in the *disegni* embellishing many of the paintings and furnishings of Italian homes.

75. Rinaldina Russell's comment that "in [Tornabuoni's] view of human events . . . most contacts between people are seen as power struggles" is very apt ("Lucrezia Tornabuoni," 437).

that the people will discover his plans to murder the popular Baptist, and a number of passages are taken up with the byzantine negotiations between Herod and his wife to seal John's fate in a manner that will not arouse suspicion. A close, almost incestuous society in which great care must be taken to conceal a secret emerges in *Susanna* when the young, chaste wife is accused of adultery by the two false elders: "The servants from the house heard these noises, / and they and all the others / wondered greatly about it in their hearts; / they were drawn instantly to the sound, / and heard the old men tell of Susanna's adultery. / . . . / The people murmured of this at great length." The verb *bisbigliare*—"to mutter," or "to mumble," with ancillary meanings of "to gossip" and "to prattle"—vividly suggests an environment where gossip is a primary means of passing along information. Gossip itself was traditionally associated with women, and as I noted earlier, the meddling that comes from "gossip" and "prattle" enables Judith to distinguish herself before the town elders who are desperately trying to save their city: "May each of you note my words!/ through his grace, God has put it into my heart / to meddle in things so your vows will be heard." *Frammettersi,* a colloquialism for "to mix oneself up in," "to meddle," has no analogue in Scripture; it is Tornabuoni's way of suggesting that Judith will avail herself of "women's ways" to save Bethulia from the wicked Holofernes.

The allusion to Judith may suggest one answer to the more difficult question of why Tornabuoni picked the stories she did. There are, of course, obvious reasons for several of her choices. John the Baptist was Florence's patron saint, and Judith was seen in republican Florence as an example of a city's strength against tyrants as well as of humility conquering pride. Such is the meaning of two inscriptions attached, during the 1450s and 1460s, to Donatello's famous statue of Judith.[76] Most of Tornabuoni's interpolations take up this rejection of pride and its many manifestations—sensuality, anger, the urge to dominate others—and her works

76. After the overthrow of the conspirators in 1466, Piero de' Medici apparently had this inscription placed on the base of Donatello's statue, glorifying Judith as an emblem of civic virtue: "Petrus Medices Cos. Fi. libertati simul et fortitudini hanc mulieris statuam quo cives invicto constantique animo ad rem. pub. redderent dedicavit" [Pietro de' Medici, son of Cosimo, dedicated the statue of this woman to the strength and liberty that the citizens, through their constant and invincible spirit, restored to the republic]. This invocation was added to an earlier one that stresses Judith as a figure of humility: "Regna cadunt luxu surgent virtutibus urbes caesa vides humili colla superba manu" [Kingdoms fall through excess; cities rise up through virtue; see the proud neck being severed by the humble hand]. See Janson, *Sculpture of Donatello,* 198–200, which speculates on the origins of the inscriptions and observes that at the time of the conspiracy the statue was in the garden of the Medici palace in Via Larga.

are linked by their demonstrations of *superbia*'s ultimate downfall. But the agent of such downfall tends, in most of Tornabuoni's *storie sacre*, to be a "meddling" woman, four of them—Judith, Esther, Susanna, and the wife of Tobias—living in environments hostile to the Hebrews.[77] And almost all the women Tornabuoni chose to write about are invested, or invest themselves, with at times subtle forms of power. Thanks to her connections to the Hebrew community, Esther is almost always in the privileged position of knowing about dangers threatening both her people and the king, as when she learns through her uncle of an assassination attempt on her husband. Judith uses her great beauty and self-discipline to foil the enemy Holofernes. Herod's wife is wily and clever enough to convince her husband to kill John the Baptist, and her daughter employs her dancing to cunning effect. Susanna's prayer to God after she is accused of adultery inspires Daniel to pronounce her innocent. Anna's harsh berating of her husband Tobias precipitates the prayer to God that will produce an angel, and Sarah's conviction that God will save her from excessively lustful husbands releases her from despondency and allows her to contrive with the young Tobias against demonic possession. To some degree, all of them manipulate powerful men into fulfilling their plans, whether they are motivated by selfish reasons (Herodias) or by the desire to save their people (Judith, Esther). They thus represent the kind of "meddling" that was not acceptable behavior for women in fifteenth-century Florence, and Tornabuoni's writings may in some way, as Martelli has suggested, seek to surpass the limits imposed on her and her female contemporaries.[78] Yet with the exception of Herodias, the women also display qualities that Tornabuoni and other Florentines can be said to have prized: fidelity to their spouses, chastity, and loyalty to their people.

This fierce attachment to one's people and a selflessness that compels one to go against the grain of local custom and tradition constitute a constant theme in the five *storie sacre*, and such qualities mitigate the radical transgressiveness of a Judith or Esther. They also transcend differences of gender. In her invocations Tornabuoni herself does not always identify with

---

77. Tornabuoni's four Old Testament poems all draw on the rich narrative traditions of Hellenistic Jews, many of whose works—such as the four texts that are the starting points for Tornabuoni's poems—have been consigned to the list of deuterocanonical or apocryphal works. I will say more about the Apocrypha in the introduction to *The Story of Devout Susanna*, but note that the Hebrews in the first and second centuries B.C.E. were writing in captivity, and their preoccupation with figures of deliverance is evident in the stories composed during that time, mainly in Greek and Aramaic.

78. Martelli, "Lucrezia Tornabuoni," 51–52.

her female characters. While she admires the powers that God gave to Judith, the *vedovetta* or little widow, she aligns herself with Tobias, for example, in the opening of his *storia*. Her poem begins with the request for God's grace,

> that I might turn the little story of Tobias
>   into verse and please my readers.
> Oh, send me Raphael as my guide and companion,
>   he whom you sent to accompany the only son of Tobias
>   on unknown paths.
> He knew how to guide him in such fashion that
>   he might go and return in safety;
>   and he gave him a wife of noble standing.
> He recovered his gold and his silver;
>   he received as many sheep as he did oxen and camels,
>   and all was restored and he was greatly contented. . . .
> This Tobias was so fired with the love
>   of holy charity that he had no care
>   for worldly praise . . . .

A charitable figure who assists impoverished members of his tribe, buries the dead when such piety is prohibited by evil rulers, instructs his son to clothe the naked, and laments with those who mourn, Tobias is also astute in his business dealings, sending his son to reclaim the money he lent a needy relative, Gabael. Tobias thus may have symbolized for Tornabuoni a man who performs charitable works not *despite* his shrewd business dealings, but *because* of them; his wealth places him in a position of responsibility that mandates he help the poor when others cannot. That Tobias is supposedly punished for his generosity with ensuing poverty and blindness—or so says his nagging wife, Anna—is only a temporary state of affairs. It is a test, sanctioned by God, of his mercy and obedience, that turns him into what Tornabuoni calls "a new Job."[79]

The lives Tornabuoni wrote about exemplify a sanctity that is directed toward a larger community—whether it is the sanctity of the elderly Tobias, of Judith, or of John the Baptist—and thus these lives do not simply partake of contemplative virtues but sustain a balance between action and contemplation. That men and women play equal roles within this constella-

---

79. Daniel, the young prophet who reveals Susanna's innocence to a deceived community, is likewise endowed with extraordinary gifts that he uses for the ultimate good of his people—gifts Tornabuoni herself seeks to emulate, as I indicate in my introduction to *Susanna*.

tion of texts, four of them linked by their status as so-called apocryphal narratives written in the late second and first centuries B.C.E., is a corrective to the ideology of a republican humanism that insisted on the comparative inequality of the sexes. Considering, moreover, the many charitable and political ventures Tornabuoni engaged in—given the wide range of her "power," to once again use the word in Constance Jordan's sense—it also seems that the *reality* of Tornabuoni's life militated, if only in subtle ways, against the ideology of an Alberti or Antoninus. What largely enabled this opposition was, of course, her family standing, but the force of the religious environment within which she lived and worked cannot be denied. One might even say that the demands to perform charitable acts in Florence, which had far fewer *mantellate* than other Tuscan towns such as Siena, afforded a tempting if uneasy bridge between the exciting promulgations of a civic humanism pledged to the greater good of the city and the exacting claims of a tradition of female piety that had experienced its heyday in the fourteenth century with figures like Saint Catherine. Whether Tornabuoni could have articulated this bridge in such terms is unclear. But it is beyond question that her poems are dominated by the fierce civic-minded piety of her heroes and heroines. And while one must not turn the *storie sacre* into veiled autobiographies, Tornabuoni's obvious interest in women and men who defied social norms in order to perform charitable works suggests that she herself may have wrestled with justifying her works to the world. Her *storie sacre* thus may have been a means of placing these works within a context as broad and spiritually charged as Ghirlandaio's frescoes in Santa Maria Novella.[80]

Tornabuoni's self-consciousness about her complicated position in Florence extended to her role as writer. On the one hand, like the religious writers of *cantari*, she professes ignorance, humility, and poverty of imagination, expressing only the modest desire to turn stories into verse. In most of her lengthy departures from biblical texts, she articulates trepidation: shortly before she embarks on a long elaboration of Salome's dance before King Herod, she writes, "I know that I have entered onto shadowy paths, /

---

80. At the same time, one must not ignore the possibility that in so doing she may also have been knowingly, if only tacitly, justifying a Medicean ideology that sought to cast its political designs in the framework of Christian charity as well. See the perhaps overly cynical comments of Paolo Orvieto in his edition of *Susanna*, when he notes that "all of Tornabuoni's initiatives, whether public or private, seem to have conjoined . . . Christian charity with the far-sighted political design of a vaster project of political pacification." He cites Piero's predilection for courting the more powerful families in Florence as well as Tornabuoni's intercessions on behalf of Florentine exiles such as the Strozzi (Tornabuoni, *Istoria della casta Susanna*, 15).

and I hope to navigate safely to the end, / through the grace of God who was there in the beginning, / as I pray that he alleviate my ignorance." The "shadowy paths," to be sure, are real; what follows are over twenty stanzas that improvise on a single verse from the Gospel of Mark: "And Herodias' own daughter having come in and danced, she pleased Herod and his guests. And the king said to the girl, 'Ask of me what thou willest, and I will give it to thee'" (Mark 6:22).

But is Tornabuoni's anxiety real or merely rhetorical? Obviously, in works professing the value of humility the narrator must approach the biblical text in humble fashion, as Tornabuoni does specifically in her proems. At the same time, her modesty and simplicity of style may be more a strategic *choice*, geared for her audience, than a symptom of stylistic impoverishment. As Rinaldina Russell notes, her lengthy descriptions of feasts and domestic interiors are often offered with an air of "ironic appraisal; they do not display that naive astonishment of the outsider, which is redolent of the wandering story-teller."[81] At times she expresses high hopes for her poems: she believes that her *Life of Saint John the Baptist* will increase others' devotion to the saint, and her *canzone* on Adam and Eve is instructed to "go forth, with fervor, / Comforting them / Though they are rebels / So they may turn to seek God's mercy / And beseech his pardon." In the second chapter of *Esther* she has God himself complimenting her: "Do not fear, / take up your singing again in my name, / and you will have from it honor and great pleasure; / proceed with your verses and talk about . . . / the lords and citizens whom I recounted / in the first canto with such sweet style." At times, too, in the authority of Tornabuoni's poetic voice one senses a narrator who is in far more command than a halting preface might allow. "Non mi curo più di te" [I concern myself with you no more], the most haunting of Tornabuoni's *laudi*, is a stark dramatization of the essential solitude of the new convert, and the sure-handed verses of the *Life of Saint John the Baptist*, probably the most mature of Tornabuoni's works, give us compelling and original portraits of a John torn between his call to go into the desert and his love for his family.

More allusively, the verses of this last *vita* present us with a young daughter of Herodias who is at once drawn to John's sacred word and forced by respect to do her mother's will. In what must surely be an original stroke on Tornabuoni's part, the unnamed girl who dances with such consummate

81. Russell elaborates: "There is something distinctly personal in the use that Lucrezia makes of these *topoi*. . . . Value judgments are implied in her swift characterization and in the decisions that her characters take" ("Lucrezia Tornabuoni," 436–37).

skill is at least initially presented as an innocent on the order of the chaste Susanna, victimized by the power plays of others, compelled by her very beauty to take on a role in a play she herself has not written. Even as Tornabuoni gives us moving depictions of strong and extraordinary women—Judith, Esther, the evil Herodias—she is also sensitive to younger and more vulnerable figures who are caught between varying demands and compromised by their own female attributes. The characters who populate her biblical worlds thus can be said to represent a wide spectrum of male and particularly female personalities. The poems ultimately represent a fascinating intermingling of Florentine customs with Tornabuoni's respect for and devotion to the scriptural texts—texts she reads, and pointedly rewrites, with a confidence that even the most extreme tropes of humility cannot mask.

EDITIONS AND TRANSLATION

The present edition is drawn from both printed and manuscript sources. For the *storie sacre*, I have relied primarily on the manuscript in the Biblioteca Nazionale, Magliabechiano VII, 338, which contains all five of the *storie* translated here (*La vita di Sancto Giovanni Baptista, La ystoria di Judith vedova hebrea, La storia di Hester regina, La ystoria della devota Susanna,* and *La vita de Tubia*). I have chosen to rearrange the order slightly, beginning with the short *Ystoria della devota Susanna,* continuing with the *storie* from three contiguous Old Testament books (Tobias, Judith, Esther), and ending with the *Vita di Sancto Giovanni Baptista* based on the New Testament. The transcriptions of *Tobias* and *Esther* are my own, made exclusively from that manuscript. In 1978 Fulvio Pezzarossa published the lives of both Judith and John (the two *storie* in ottava rima) in *I poemetti sacri di Lucrezia Tornabuoni,* which offers a judicious transcription and edition, and I have also referred to Paolo Orvieto's useful edition of *Susanna.* Parducci's transcription of "La ystoria della devota Susanna di Lucrezia Tornabuoni" is marred by errors.

The *laudi* of Tornabuoni are scattered throughout numerous manuscripts in Florence and can be found in several versions. I worked from several manuscripts in the Biblioteca Nazionale (Magl. VII, 1083, Magl. XXXV, 119, and Magl. VII, 338, which contains Tornabuoni's *canzone* along with her *storie sacre*) and one in the Biblioteca Riccardiana (Ricc. 3112). Volpi's edition of the *laudi* from 1900 is unreliable, given the liberties he takes with punctuation and occasional errors in transcription. I have also consulted Francesco Cionacci's 1680 edition of *Rime sacre del magnifico Lorenzo de' Medici il Vecchio, di Maddona Lucrezia sua madre e d'altri della stessa famiglia.*

In translating the poems, I have attempted to respect Tornabuoni's paratacticism and her repetitive word choice. I have preserved the three-line stanzas for the three poems in terzinas and the eight-line stanzas for the poems in ottavas, attempting to obey the metrical pattern wherever possible and, particularly in the ottavas, retaining line breaks so that striking features of Tornabuoni's verse can emerge—such as her refusal, in *John*, to rhyme any word with "Cristo" other than itself. With the *laudi*, I take the most care to respect metrical patterns and, in situations where it does not seem entirely forced, the versification as well. Given that the *laudi*, unlike the *storie sacre*, would have been sung, it seemed important to convey as far as possible in English their gently lilting and in some cases lyrical quality. Most of the *laudi* do not alternate line lengths; these were the easiest ones to translate. For those that do—"Non mi curo più di te," which ends stanzas of tetrameters (four feet) with a seven-syllable line, and more complexly, "Contempla le mie pene" and the *canzone*, which alternate lines of seven syllables with, respectively, twelve-syllable and eleven-syllable lines—I have tried, with varying degrees of success, to be faithful to the changing metrical patterns. In transcribing an occasional line or passage in Italian from Tornabuoni's manuscripts, I have tried to edit conservatively, adding primarily diacritical marks and sometimes punctuation.

THE STORY OF
DEVOUT SUSANNA

INTRODUCTION

Tornabuoni's Old Testament translations are all drawn from the so-called apocryphal books of the Bible—works of questionable canonical authenticity that even today occupy an ambiguous status in regard to both Hebrew and Christian traditions.[1] Dating largely from after 200 B.C.E. and written by Jews, primarily in Greek and Aramaic and mainly in and around Palestine during a time of crisis for the Jewish community,[2] the apocryphal materials manifest stunning variety in terms of orthodoxy and literary quality. In particular, they draw on the literary genres dear to the vibrant Hellenistic traditions of the third and second centuries: the short story, autobiographical accounts, riddles, and interpolated folktales. Even if the authenticity of these books was questioned by the compilers of the Hebrew Bible, they were nonetheless translated into Greek in Alexandrian Egypt in the first and second centuries (the Septuagint). Jerome in turn suspected that they should not be considered strictly canonical, but he included them in his Latin Vulgate in the fourth century C.E. With some

1. Of the four stories treated by Tornabuoni, only Esther achieved canonical status in the Hebrew Bible.

2. For the historical background, see Pfeiffer, *History of New Testament Times with an Introduction to the Apocrypha* chaps. 1 and 2. With the conquest of Alexander the Great, Greek and Aramaic began to replace Hebrew as the primary language of the Jewish Diaspora, and many of the writings from the first and second centuries express concern with the loss of Jewish identity. Amy-Jill Levine's discussion of the books of Judith, Esther, and Tobias, as well as Daniel 13, is suggestive in its link between the fully developed female heroines in these books and the Hebrew community itself: "The shift in representation appears to be the means by which the Jews, suddenly finding themselves part of an alien empire, worked through their disorientation and the threat to cultural cohesion. . . . The women of the Apocrypha and Pseudepigrapha are the screen on which the fears of the (male) community—of impotence, assimilation, loss of structure—can be both displayed and, at least temporarily, allayed" ("Hemmed in on Every Side," 309–10).

he worked directly from the Hebrew. For others, such as Tobias and Judith, he apparently drew from Aramaic manuscripts, while for Esther and the chapters added to Daniel, one of which tells of the story of Susanna, he translated from Hebrew and Greek manuscripts that were not part of the Septuagint.[3]

That Tobias, Judith, and Esther are grouped together in the Vulgate, after the canonical historical texts of the Old Testament and before Job and the Psalms, suggests that Tornabuoni was turning to a portion of material in the Vulgate that she may have perceived as interrelated. Certainly they are related in terms of historical background. The stories take place either during periods of Jewish captivity in Persia or Babylon or while Israel is under threat from Babylonia or Assyria. Oriental potentates, whether of Persian, Assyrian, or Babylonian cast, appear in three of the apocryphal texts on which Tornabuoni based her *storie*. Their presence is only inferred in the briefest of those texts, *The Story of Devout Susanna*, where the manipulative elders themselves take on some of the characteristics of sinful foreign leaders; hence Daniel at one point accuses one of the would-be adulterers of behaving "far more like the people of Canaan."

Found in an appendix to Daniel, the tale of Susanna is extremely short. A mere sixty-three verses, it tells the story of the first manifestation of young Daniel's prophetic talents and his elevation by God. Susanna is the chaste and upright wife of the wealthy Joachim. "Beautiful and God-fearing," she takes noonday walks in her husband's gardens when the crowds who often gather there to hear legal cases disperse for lunch. The two elders, who had been appointed judges for a year, notice Susanna on her walks and begin to lust after her; they linger in the garden one afternoon to surprise her while she is bathing alone, and they ask her to sleep with them. If she resists, they will accuse her of adultery with a young man. Susanna gives them no choice other than to accuse her, but after she has been condemned to death by the assembly, the youthful Daniel in turn is inspired by God to know the truth. In a second, spontaneous trial scene he accuses the elders of foul play, and he cleverly interrogates them separately about the details of Susanna's "crime." Once he reveals their falsity, the elders in turn are killed and Susanna is avenged: "From that day onward . . . Daniel was greatly esteemed by the people" (Dan. 13:63).

---

3. For detailed information on the sources of apocryphal texts used by Jerome for his Vulgate, see Pfeiffer, *History of New Testament Times*; W. O. E. Oesterley, *Introduction to the Books of the Apocrypha*; and *Cambridge History of the Bible*, vol. 2.

Possibly originating in folktales about a slandered woman, the story in its present form dates to roughly 100–50 B.C.E. The style of the chapter is straightforward and does not lavish detail on descriptions of character or place. Still, its suggestive plot made the story popular in the Middle Ages and the early modern period, not least among artists, who delighted in depicting Susanna in her bath—most famously, Tintoretto, Paolo Veronese, and Artemisia Gentileschi.[4] The manuscript in the Biblioteca Nazionale in which Tornabuoni's writings are preserved uses this scene for the decorative miniature that opens *La ystoria della devota Susanna.* A more fulsome contemporary treatment is that of Domenico di Michelino, who painted the so-called Strozzi Cassone, now in Avignon. All of these depictions dwell, as the biblical text does not, on the lush details of the garden itself, and its characterization reminds one of the *locus amoenus* from medieval latinity and Petrarchan lyric.[5] Indeed, in her terzinas Tornabuoni uses several Petrarchan and Dantesque flourishes as she depicts a beautiful young woman who "facea ghirlandette" and "cantando le ponea in sul biondo crino" [weaves garlands and entwines them in her golden hair as she sings]. Like Dante's Matelda, she is portrayed as an innocent woman who wanders freely in paradise and gives no thought to the possibility that she is being watched. Tornabuoni freely indulges in the code of courtly love when she has one of the elders say that Susanna's beauty has led him into her prison ("Susanna mi tien qui per suo prigione"); he speaks of a burning in his heart that demands that he always be close to her ("m[h]anno acceso nel chore un tal disio, / chi sempre il viso bel vorre' vedere").

Even without Tornabuoni's variants, *Susanna* can be seen as a biblical version of a story well known in Renaissance Florence, the rape of Lucretia, insofar as it allows for the emergence of a new order—that of Daniel—over the body of the defamed woman.[6] The ending, of course, differs completely in that, unlike Lucretia, Susanna lives. At the same time, both stories suggest the vulnerability of women to the moral and public forces that would control them, and Tornabuoni makes the most of the passage from the garden's inner, protected space to the neighborhood beyond: "The servants from the house heard the noise, / and they and all the others / won-

---

4. See Orsella Casazza, "Per una storia iconografica," in Paolo Orvieto's edition of Tornabuoni's *Istoria della casta Susanna* for a brief overview of paintings derived from the story.

5. Paolo Orvieto's introduction to *Istoria della casta Susanna* is helpful in suggesting the medieval antecedents for Tornabuoni's descriptions (24–26).

6. For a discussion of the importance of this myth to republican Florence, see Stephanie H. Jed's *Chaste Thinking.*

dered greatly about it in their hearts; / they were drawn instantly to the sound, / and heard the old men tell of Susanna's adultery. / All were speechless and stunned; / to think that Susanna could have sinned in such fashion / filled them with marvel." Tornabuoni then delicately suggests the ubiquity and power of gossip: "The people murmured of this at great length." Such ubiquity lends itself to the ease with which the elders' story is believed: "And they all thought she was guilty, / because the old men were the elders that year, / and [so the people believed] they had found Susanna committing a crime." Throughout, Tornabuoni is at pains to emphasize Susanna's innocence as well as her closeness to God. Hence in a prayer that is not biblical, Susanna says, "My every hope is in you, O my God, / liberate me, Lord, if you choose, / from such false and evil torments!" The latter phrase ("tormento rio") is a possible echo of Dante.[7] In explicitly making Susanna God's handmaiden ("ancilla"), Tornabuoni strengthens the link between this chaste woman and the *ancilla* who is Mary: "Instantly her petition was heard, / and she did not become a martyr, / for her devout prayer was pleasing to God, / and he exalted his humble handmaiden / and abundantly showed that she was just. / Just as a spark will fly / from wood when it seems already spent—/ a mere breath awakens it, and the spark bursts outward—/ so did he awaken Daniel, / at an age when he was still boyish and young." Daniel's "cry" suggesting that he is literally possessed by Susanna ("Gridando disse: / 'Ciascuno stie atento, innocente son io!'") [Everyone listen to me: / I am innocent!]) echoes Susanna's earlier cry, a cry that now functions as a sign that Daniel speaks a divine language.

Perhaps more important, there is an implicit link between what Daniel is able to accomplish—revealing Susanna's innocence—and the accomplishments of the narrator, who in a brief proem asks God to enable her to write what she "holds clasped in her mind": "This is what happens to those who have confidence / in you, who are hopeful and strong in faith: / they will be magnificently recompensed. / As we see clearly from countless examples, / you never abandon your servants, / but shower them with grace as their reward." Much as Daniel's "parlar divino" [divine speech] is greeted as words that come from God, so, implicitly, may Tornabuoni's be as well— not to mention those of Susanna, who speaks more lines in Tornabuoni's *storia* than she does in the Book of Daniel.

7. Paolo Orvieto's note to the line suggests a link to *Inferno* 9:111: "Piena di duolo e di tormento rio": the sound that strikes Dante's ear after he and Virgil are let into the city of Dis following the angel's intervention.

While this *storia* departs less from Scripture than Tornabuoni's longer poems, it may nonetheless serve, particularly in its incisiveness, as exemplary of Tornabuoni's treatment of the biblical narrative. A contrast between Tornabuoni's account of Susanna and that of a contemporary *sacra rappresentazione* is instructive. In a recent article, Cristelle L. Baskins comments on the way *La festa di Susanna* (circa 1465) starkly opposes the passive Susanna to the prophetic Daniel, whose intervention not only rescues the young wife but "preempts Susanna's narrative account, demonstrating judicial as well as vocal authority."[8] Yet Tornabuoni's strategic placing of her own voice, here and elsewhere in the text, prevents this male gendering of narrative account and "vocal authority."[9] Susanna is not omitted from this divine dispensation; with the interpolation of an elegant simile from Isaiah, Tornabuoni makes it clear that it is Susanna's *prayer* that breathes life into the tender "spark" that is the young Daniel. The prayer that opens Tornabuoni's *storia sacra* can ultimately be said to have the same function of elevating the young judge to manifest the reviled innocence of a prominent Hebrew woman.[10]

Thus even if she can hardly be called a "redeemer" of her people— that title must be reserved for Judith and Esther—Susanna nonetheless enables the emergence of a prophet whose gifts will bring hope to a people who live in captivity. Surely Tornabuoni's interest in the story consists primarily in this aspect of the text, as well as in the possibilities the scene of the garden and the elders affords for elaborating along the lines of the tradition of courtly love. But in what is surely one of her finest *storie sacre*, she is also intrigued by the suggestive connections between her role as narrator and the important parts played by prophet and faithful Hebrew woman alike.

8. Baskins, *"Festa di Susanna,"* 335. One might also add to this the observation of Newbigin, who notes in this *sacra rappresentazione* the presence of political satire that is extremely rare before Lorenzo's own play in 1490: "The satire on the corruption of the judiciary that precedes the Susannah play is a notable exception" ("Politics in the *sacra rappresentazione,"* 124).

9. Similarly, in *La storia di Iuditta,* Tornabuoni suggests that her heroic role as female narrator (indebted though that role is to "God's son") is in some ways equivalent to Judith's heroism. "I found her story written in prose, / and I was greatly impressed by her courage: / a fearful little widow, / she had your help, and she knew what to do and to say; / Lord, you made her bold and helped her plan succeed. / Would that you could grant such favor to me, / so that I may turn her tale into rhyme, / in a manner that would please."

10. One must also mention another *storia* of Susanna roughly contemporary with Tornabuoni's work. In *Romania* 62, Parducci calls attention to "La storia di Susanna e Daniello, poemetto popolare italiano antico," which similarly amplifies the simple tale told in Daniel 13. He concludes that Tornabuoni was not familiar with this "storiella"; see his "Ystoria della devota Susanna," 181.

HERE BEGINS THE STORY OF SUSANNA, DEVOTED
DAUGHTER OF ELCHIA AND WIFE OF THE HEBREW JOACHIM.
WRITTEN BY MADONNA LUCREZIA, FORMERLY WIFE OF
THE MAGNIFICENT PIERO DE' COSIMO DE' MEDICI[11]

O God of Abraham, merciful and strong,
O God of Isaac, you are just and true;
O God of Jacob, I need no other guide
than you, who have inspired me with this plan
to recount the tale of an innocent woman
accused of adultery by two faithless liars.
Give me grace, my Lord, be lenient with me;
in your kindness give me the courage
to write the story that I hold clasped in my mind:
to tell how you rescued her from madness
and made her innocence manifest to all,
punishing those who committed the crime.
This is what happens to those who have confidence
in you, who are hopeful and strong in faith:
they will be magnificently recompensed.
As we see clearly from countless examples,
you never abandon your servants,
but shower them with grace as their reward.
I pray that you help me now, you who know and can do all,
assist my verses in this new undertaking
so that they will seem to be yours alone.
First of all, reader, I want you to know
and understand why the Hebrews
were in Babylon, and why their city
was taken. It was because of their evil sins
that Jerusalem was captured by that great leader
Nebuchadnezzar, lord of the Chaldeans.[12]

11. The title in Italian reads, "Fatta dalla sopradecta madonna Lucretia, donna fu del Magnifico huomo Piero de Coximo de' Medici cittadino fiorentino." That the *passato remoto* or distant past is used to describe Tornabuoni's married status ("donna *fu*") suggests that she is no longer the wife of Piero and may not have been for some time; hence the manuscript was obviously written after Piero's death in 1469, as Salvadori also notes (*Lettere*, 114).

12. Nebuchadnezzar was king of Babylon from 605 to 561 B.C.E., during the Babylonian captivity. This Nebuchadnezzar cannot be the same king mentioned in Judith, since in the latter text the Jews have already returned from captivity and rebuilt the Temple, finished forty-five

He stole the valuable treasure,
> he destroyed the temple, and he led everyone away,
> from the greatest of princes to the very least.

As one reads in the ancient histories,
> he put their royal family into prison,
> while the common folk were dispersed throughout the
>> country.[13]

One can hardly speak of all the labors and weariness
> suffered by the Hebrews in Babylon
> as they dwelled among a hostile people.

After many years had passed, they began
> to accustom themselves to the ways of the country,
> suffering their hardships in silence.

Among the Hebrews was a man who took himself a wife;
> his name was Joachim,
> and he was noble, wealthy, and very gallant.[14]

I will also speak of his wife,
> a noble and well-mannered girl
> who seemed like a white rose, a fresh fruit:

she was Susanna, gracious, honest, and lovely,
> the daughter of Elchia, who had raised her
> to honor the law of Moses.

She feared God, and led her life
> well, and with much love and devotion,
> always asking him that he might be her guardian.

Joachim was a man of discretion, and
> as I have said, he possessed much wealth;
> he lived contentedly in great joy.

He had a garden of such beauty
> that its likeness was not known in the land,
> so orderly and well-maintained it was.[15]

---

years after the death of Nebuchadnezzar. See Pfeiffer, *History of New Testament Times*, 293–96, for the historical details.

13. The siege of Jerusalem by Nebuchadnezzar and its subsequent captivity are described in 2 Kings 25.

14. Daniel 13 begins here: "In Babylon there lived a man named Joakim, who married a very beautiful and God-fearing wife, Susanna, the daughter of Helcia." I cite translations from the Confraternity-Douay edition of the Old Testament, based on the Vulgate. The Vulgate edition I have used throughout is the *Biblia sacra: Iuxta latinam vulgatam versionem*.

15. This and the following verses elaborate on the simple "he had a garden near his house" [erat ei pomarium vicinum domui suae] (Dan. 13:4).

It often remained open, and was not locked
   to the gentlemen of the city that came there
   (I speak of the Hebrew men, lest one think otherwise).
There they would engage in civic discourse,
   doing things of great importance,
   passing the time as best as they were able.[16]
This was a place of great delight;
   here you could find fresh fountains, an abundance
   of fresh, clear, pure water;[17]
and the Hebrews regarded it with great love.
   During that year, they had elected
   two of the eldest and most fit to govern
and serve as judges and give the people good precepts,
   and for a year they served as their leaders,
   chosen to admonish everyone in words and in deeds,
to act justly in matters great and small,
   to administer the law with equity,
   to settle quarrels and to correct errors.[18]
But as you will see, they were also wicked,
   which the almighty God foresaw when he spoke thus:
   "Two elders in a Babylon as perverse as they
   will commit a dishonest act
   that will displease me greatly.
   And it is particularly distasteful to me
because, out of all of my people there,
   it had fallen to them to rule and govern the Hebrews
   who had believed them to be the wisest."
It so happened that these elders would linger
   in that beautiful garden where they heard lawsuits;
   to stay there was delightful, and it pleased them.
When, around midday, their clients would return to their homes,
   lovely Susanna used to enter the garden
   to refresh herself and take her pleasure;[19]

16. One might see here a description of the typical activities in which Florence's leading citizens might engage in the city's piazzas.

17. A possible echo of Petrarchan allusions in the *Canzoniere* 126:1 to "chiare, fresche, e dolci acque": "quivi eran fonti fresche et molto chiare."

18. Once again, Tornabuoni elaborates on a single biblical verse: "That year, two elders of the people were appointed judges" (Dan. 13:5).

19. Daniel is emphatic that this is Susanna's *husband's* garden: "When the people left at noon, Susanna used to enter her husband's garden for a walk" ("ingrediebatur Susanna, et deambulabat in pomario *viri sui*," Dan. 13:7).

she would gather flowers and jasmine
and often entwine them into little garlands,
singing as she wove them into her blond hair.[20]
From here to there, the young woman would go
gaily about, never entertaining the thought
that there was something deceitful about the elders.
The elders, having often gazed
at this lovely and delightful girl,
both became overpowered by lust.
The one glances at the other while he conceals within
himself
the burning flame, even as he imagines
the act that would be an abominable sin.
But heeding neither the sin nor the shame that comes with
it,
each one walks about in blindness,
persevering in dishonest love.
So desirous are they of seeing Susanna one morning,
they fail to notice it is time to dine;
the hour is past, and vespers approach,
and thus they too must leave to eat.
All the others have already eaten,
while the lovers themselves have yet to begin.
Instantly, as if they had dined,
they made their return to the scene of their desire,
and it seemed to them both they had lingered too long.
Each man scorned his companion
as he stared him full in the face and demanded to know
the reason for his swift return.[21]
The first responded: "I will tell you
my intention, since you wish to know it:
Susanna holds me here in her prison;

---

20. The atmosphere is distinctly Petrarchan, although one is also reminded of Matelda in *Purgatorio* 28: as he enters Eden, Dante sees "una donna soletta che si gia / e cantando e scegliendo fior da fiore / ond'era pinta tutta la sua via" [a lady all alone, who went about singing and culling flower from flower, with which all her way was painted] (40–42).

21. The next eighteen lines embellish the dry biblical phrase: "But both turned back, and when they met again, they asked each other the reason. They admitted their lust" (Dan. 13: 15–16).

her gracious and gentle manners
   have inflamed my heart with such desire
   that I long to see her beautiful face before me always."
Said the other: "Oh woe is me! I
   am even worse off than you, so captured and bound am
      I,
   I do not know what to do and my heart is destroyed.
Since it seems that our love burns with equal intensity,
   let us seize a time to find her here alone,
   so that we may reveal to her our wishes."
See now how quickly the wits of these two take flight,
   toward foolish thoughts harbored by young boys,
   more appropriate to those who are still in school.
Having been led to such love,
   they sought a moment when they would be able
   to find her alone, to fabricate pleasing phrases
so that they might manifest and make known to her
   the great trials they had suffered,
   such that each of them fears death.
One day, into that very place came
   the young woman accompanied by
   two maidservants, there to assist her
in removing her garments, since she wanted
   to bathe in the clear, fresh springs.
   (She believed herself to be alone and thus feared
      nothing;
for the gates of the garden had been locked.)
   Thus she entered the bath to refresh her lovely limbs,
   as nude as the day she was born.
As she bathed in those frigid waters,
   she sent her maidservents to fetch oils
   that were used in times of great heat. Whence it
      happened
that these two elders who were so fervently
   in love, and who up to now had kept themselves
      concealed,
   were not slow when they saw her alone,
and they hastened impulsively to Susanna,
   and they attacked her with shrewd words:
   "For a long time we have wanted to tell you

how close we are to death,
    led there solely by your dazzling beauty.
    Now is the time to tell you, for the gates are closed.
O beautiful woman, be moved to pity;
    now you have time and no one else is here,
    please yield to our will!
But if you don't go along with our wishes"—each one reasons—
    "we will say that we found you here, caught in adultery,
    with a young man between the hour of vespers and nones
and that to better conceal your ugly sin,
    you sent away both of your maidservants,
    pretending that you left your precious oils behind."
When she heard such false words, Susanna
    was terrified, and turned pale and red at once;
    she conceals both her pudenda and her breasts.
Seeing how they are ruled by foolishness,
    by their blindness and wild thoughts, she said,
    "Fortune, today you have struck me
with anguish, with trials and falsehoods!
    They have hemmed me in on every side;
    if I fulfill their wishes,
eternal death readies itself for me;
    if I deny them, I will be helpless to flee from
    your cruel hands, and I will be condemned.
But it is better to die without cause,
    O lying and deceitful men, than to sin,
    and to distance my heart from the Lord."
Thus she began to shriek loudly,
    and the elders began crying out too,
    uttering against Susanna the accusation.
One of them unlocked the gate
    to the beautiful garden and immediately ran outside
    and recounted to all the people the falsehood.
The servants from the house heard the noise,
    and they and all the others
    wondered greatly about it in their hearts;
they were drawn instantly to the sound,
    and heard the old men tell of Susanna's adultery.
    All were speechless and stunned;

to think that Susanna could have sinned in such fashion
    filled them with marvel, since never before
    had they heard anything spoken against her.
The people murmured of this at great length;
    they had never heard of any stain
    besmirching Susanna, or her family or house.[22]
They came and gathered there together
    while the evil elders, who feared no one,
    persistently accused the young woman,
and many of them went to Joachim,
    the husband of the accused,
    because they believed the tale of the false ones.
And they all thought that she was guilty,
    because the old men were the elders that year,
    and [so the people believed] they had found Susanna
        committing a crime.
Amid great anxiety, she was led into the midst of the people
    by her friends and family
    so she could be judged and given a penalty.
Her beautiful face, with its sparkling eyes,
    was now pallid, without color, and full of tears,
    as she awaited the onslaught on her innocence;
she had covered her shame-filled face;
    all the people were moved to weep, to think
    that an angel could be so full of vice.
Both the elders commanded,
    "Now, may her face be uncovered,
    so that she might know even greater shame!"
With clear words and loud voices
    the elders began to speak,
    each of them certain as to how she had sinned.
Their hands on her head, they made her great crime
    manifest to all, and all began to murmur to themselves
    that truly she was deserving of death.

---

22. The biblical account is limited to the servants in Susanna's household ("When the people in the house heard the cries from the garden, they rushed in by the side gate to see what had happened to her," Dan. 13:26); Tornabuoni extends the initial interest in Susanna to "tutta gente," suggesting that the news of Susanna's infidelity quickly goes out into the town.

Susanna fixed her eyes full of pious tears
    on heaven, looking toward God,
    and with innocent heart she placed herself in his hands:
"My every hope is in you, O my God,
    liberate me, Lord, if you choose,
    from such false and evil torments!"[23]
The elders' speech is very bold,
    they turn their biting words to the people
    to make them see the counterfeited deed.
"When we were in the garden, we observed
    Susanna entering with two maidservants,
    and she undressed herself without fear.
The gate was locked and instantly she sent her handmaidens
    to fetch her oils; as soon as they were gone,
    we heard the fronds moving among the young palm trees,
and we turned our gazes to the sound:
    we saw emerge a young man who had been hidden
    by the leaves, and that bold one committed carnal sin,
and she did not resist.[24]
    And we, who had been standing apart,
    we saw this crime that was so malicious;
we ran toward them, but the young man
    instantly took flight, and we could not seize him,
    because he was much stronger than us.
We returned to her and demanded that she reveal
    the name of the young man;
    but we could not drag it out of her."
The people heard all that had taken place;
    and they believed the words of the elders
    because each of them affirmed it and swore to it.
That Susanna had sinned, all believed:
    and for her crime of adultery, they condemned her
    to a cruel death without hope of mercy.
Susanna heard she had been sentenced,
    and she cried out loudly and said, "O my Lord,
    I trust in you, blessed Majesty,

23. This brief prayer is not found in the Bible.
24. The phrase ("senza alcuna lite") is a pointed addition to the Bible, which simply says, "A young man, who was hidden there, came and lay with her" (Dan. 13:37).

one can never conceal from you any desire
that hides within the heart; you know it
before it comes to be what it is, whether good or evil.
O my Lord, you know I did not sin,
and you know that unjustly I go to die;
I am innocent, and not once have I erred.
I place myself within your hands!"[25] She spoke no more.
Instantly her petition was heard,
and she did not become a martyr,
for her devout prayer was pleasing to God,
and he exalted his humble handmaiden
and abundantly showed that she was just.[26]
Just as a spark will fly
from wood when it seems already spent—
a mere breath awakens it, and the spark bursts outward—[27]
so did he awaken Daniel,
at an age when he was still boyish and young.
Loudly he cried: "Everyone listen to me:
I am innocent!" These were his words.[28]
With this sign, the people who heard him
became suddenly attentive to that divine speech.
Each one asked Daniel,
"Why do you say this?" and he replied,
"In faith, you are foolish
and senseless, not to see through such lies
nor to be able to discern such tricks.
You ran in haste to do this vicious work;

---

25. This prayer of Tornabuoni's is more emotional than the one found in the Bible; the addition of the final two lines makes it particularly charged.

26. With the phrase "et piacque a Dio la divota orazione, / et exaudì la suo humile ancilla"—an elaboration of Scripture ("Exaudivit autem Dominus vocem ejus," Dan. 13:44)—Tornabuoni may purposefully allude to the "ancilla" who is also Mary.

27. "Suscito Daniel come faville / Chescie di legno": Tornabuoni beautifully elaborates on the mere suggestion of a simile provided in Dan. 13:45: "God stirred up the holy spirit of a young boy named Daniel" ("suscitavit Dominus spiritum sanctum pueri junioris").

28. Dan. 13:46 has the young boy crying out against the elders as he refuses to condone the false judgment: "I will have no part in the death of this woman," or literally, "I am clean of that woman's blood" [Mundus ego sum a sanguine hujus]. Tornabuoni makes the scene of revelation far more dramatic, as she has Daniel echo Susanna's last words (her "sono innocente" becomes his "innocente son io"), intimating a closer association between Susanna and the young prophet than Scripture would permit.

unjustly did you condemn Susanna
and sentence her to a cruel death
when she is worthy of praise, as these evil ones know.[29]
Turn back now to the court where you judged her,
because those cursed old men have given
false judgment, and you followed it."
Upon hearing this, the townspeople, marveling,
returned to take their seats,
saying to themselves, "This boy is sent from God;
he shows great intelligence and seems to know
how these proceedings have come about;
with his help, let us return to do our duty."
All beseeched him with much passion,
"Please, find out the truth of this matter, you who can;
tell us who it is that merits punishment!"
Daniel replied: "Now I want you
to separate these cursed men from one another;
I speak of the elders; then I will clarify all."
He was instantly obeyed,
and one of the evil elders was brought to him.
Daniel said: "Listen a little to what I tell you:
O aged one sunk in evil, through your crime,
today may all your sins come to fruition,
you who maneuver to sate your cursed desire
while judging the innocent and just!
Now tell me where Susanna committed
this act of adultery and her wicked deeds,
and in what place"—he said it in exactly this way—
"you saw that young man with her."
The old man replied and did not hesitate:
"Under the juniper tree I saw them both."
Daniel answered, "Truly you lie
through your teeth, and you should not:
the angel of God is here; turn your mind to that:
the sentence of God will break you in two!"
and he immediately sent him away.

29. Whereas the biblical Daniel bases his judgment of the people on their ignorance of trial proceedings ("Are you such fools, O Israelites! To condemn a woman of Israel without examination and without clear evidence?" Dan. 13:48), Tornabuoni's Daniel accuses them of loving

He then called the other, and said to him shrewdly,
    "Now you, what will you say, O cursed elder?
    Also for you has penance been prepared.
How well you resemble the people of this nation!
    You do not act like one born of Judea;
    the truth will be found out, to your shame.
You are far more like the people of Canaan;
    you thought you had found a Canaanite woman,
    who would consent to your foul-tasting sin!
But you were wrong: she is a woman of Judea.
    Now tell me: in what place did you see her sin?
    Under what tree did such an evil act take place?"
He answered: "Under a pine tree the dishonest ones
    were together and I saw them sin."
    Daniel said: "You too answer falsely;
you also lie, without shame;
    because of this the angel of God is here,
    he will take the knife to execute you;
he will cut you in half, cursed old man,
    and both of you will be put to death,
    because the law wants to cast you into oblivion."
The people saw all, they were admiring and stunned,
    they heard Daniel give a straight and true judgment
    and the falsehoods of the elders were revealed.[30]
In loud voices they cried out: "God without beginning
    and without end, may you be blessed!
    You have shown us who merits ruin.
Lord, whoever puts his trust in you
    lives with true faith and dwells in hope
    that every torment may be turned to delight.
We have seen the foolishness and ignorance
    of the elders: they should have given good rules
    to whoever fell into similar crimes;
they should have avoided shortcomings and vicious sin
    so they could admonish others;
    but they are the evil ones full of sly deceits."

---

gossip and scandal ("Corresti a furia in opere si viziose") and of thoughtlessly sanctioning the elders' authority.

30. This stanza and the following four are all additions to the Bible.

The people were heard to cry out loudly
    that they wanted the men who wronged Susanna to die;
    they wronged her because she would not yield to their
        wishes:
"Gather stones and let each of them die.
    What is written in the law must be accomplished
    so that the innocent may find comfort!"
And the men were unceremoniously killed;
    the stones were hurled at them in great fury.
    Thus was their crime justly punished.
Thus were their false and malign hearts
    revealed by means of the prophet Daniel,
    thus did Susanna go from grief to great joy.
Elchia, her aging and wretched father,
    and her mother thanked God
    for their daughter escaped from such penance.[31]
When he saw his wife liberated
    from filthy abomination and deceit,
    her husband, humble and pious in manner,
thanks the almighty God who released her;
    in similar fashion, her relatives and the townspeople
    all believed that she had been vindicated,
she who had barely escaped the cruel torments
    planned for her by the elders with their false words,
    so fervently bent on defaming Susanna.
God saw to such things, as happens
    with all those who have hope and faith:
    he wants to honor and exalt them.
And whoever does not esteem and believe in God
    will be treated as were those inveterate elders:
    he will never find mercy for his crimes.
These two were so completely blinded
    that neither one, as I have said, possessed wisdom.
    God punished them for their foul sins,

---

31. The rest of the poem elaborates on Daniel's terse conclusion: "Helcia and his wife praised God for their daughter Susanna, as did Joakim her husband and all her relatives, because she was found innocent of any shameful deed. And from that day onward Daniel was greatly esteemed by the people" (Dan. 13:63-64).

and he sent Daniel, of much wisdom,
    to discover their deceitful tricks
    that did not partake of reason and even less of wisdom.
Whoever hears or reads this little work,
    may they take compassion on the innocent
    and solace in the way justice disposed of those two.
After that, Daniel was held in esteem
    by all people always, for he had revealed
    the truth of what happened to that distressed woman:
he gave a judgment that was just and true.

THE LIFE OF TOBIAS

INTRODUCTION

The story of Tobias is one of the most charming books of the Apocry-
pha, or even the Bible as a whole. It is an apparently late first-century
tale narrating how two families tormented by devils, blindness, and poverty
at last find joy and wealth with the aid of the angel Raphael. Tobias not
only contains obvious echoes of folktales but is told by a skillful narrator.
Even the Aramaic version that Jerome used for the Vulgate preserves traces
of this skill, though some of the more innovative touches of the apparently
original Greek are lost, such as occasional first-person narrative from the
perspective of the elderly Tobias.[1] Its ultimately comic close is a testimony
to God's justice, for he is seen rewarding the faithful who have persevered
against almost impossible odds. Its many homely elements include a tender
parting of parents and their only child, a family's concern for an unmarried
daughter, and even a little dog who follows his master wherever he may
wander. This story about Jews suffering the outrages of political fortune
(like the apocryphal books of Judith and Esther, the Book of Tobias is
written by and about a Hebrew community in exile) is thus a delight to
read. At the same time, like Judith and Esther, it frequently moralizes about
duties essential to Hebrew life: fasting, the pious burying of the dead, alms-
giving, and belief in God no matter how severe the persecutions one is
forced to suffer.

Such moralizing was no doubt at the heart of Tornabuoni's interest in
the story of Tobias. But she along with many others was presumably also

---

1. The Vulgate Liber Tobiae (Book of Tobias), based on an Aramaic manuscript of the story,
gives both father and son the name Tobias, and I have followed this reading throughout. In
Greek manuscripts the book is called The Book of the Words of Tobit and distinguishes
between the father, Tobit, and the son, Tobias. See Pfeiffer, *History of New Testament Times*,
258.

attracted by the domestic details of a biblical book that served as a hand-book for proper sexual relations between newly married couples.[2] Torna-buoni preserves the long lecture that the angel Raphael gives the young Tobias before he goes to bed with his bride, in which he insists that sex is purely for procreation. Other elements relevant to married and domestic life not only were incorporated in Tornabuoni's retelling of the apocryphal story but were expanded, occasionally at some length. These additions tend to valorize the women's roles in the story; hence when Sarah, the daughter of Raguel, marries her eighth (!) husband and Tobias does not die on their wedding night, Raguel's wife Anna utters a lengthy prayer of thanks that is not in the Vulgate. Yet another expansion is more detrimental to a female character. The elder Tobias's wife Anna receives a young kid as wages for her work, but when she brings it home Tobias tells her to return it. As the Vulgate has it, "'For it is not lawful for us either to eat or to touch anything that cometh by theft.' At these words, his wife being angry answered: 'It is evident thy hope is come to nothing, and thy alms now appear.' And with these and other such like words she upbraided him" (Tob. 2:21–23). Tornabuoni takes it upon herself to inform us exactly what those "other such like words" were, as she gives us an Anna who shamelessly challenges her blind husband to give up the "governo" of the household now that he can no longer work. Tornabuoni introduces her expanded version of this domestic squabble with a disclaimer: "What I will say now is no delirium or dream; / one finds it written in the ancient histories." But in fact she *has* chosen to say far more than what is "written" as Anna goes on at length about Tobias's many failings: "You worship your own folly! / It seems to me that you have lost your senses! / In vain you have waited with hope; / once you were rich, and now you are poor. / You have thrown away all of our substance; / we have nothing left to live on, we barely survive; / and all of this has happened through your neglect."

But this portrait of a shrewish Anna is tempered by two things: her berating of Tobias leads to his prayer that will result in the arrival of an angel, and in the depiction of her later in the poem. Tornabuoni beautifully delineates her maternal solicitousness as she awaits her son's return. Since her husband is blind, she must go out to watch for their son Tobias, who left long ago to reclaim the money his father had lent a relative, Gabael (or Gabelus). The biblical narrative simply has Anna "sitting beside the way daily, on the top of a hill"; then she "presently perceived it was her son coming." Tornabuoni's version gives us the following:

2. Foster, "Vernacular Scriptures in Italy," 468.

> The mother of Tobias, who every day had gone
>   to a high mountain to wait and watch for him, to see
>   if her son was on his way,
> places her right hand upon her forehead,
>   and when she also puts her left hand there,
>   above her eyes, she makes for herself a shield
> so that the rays of the sun would not injure her,
>   as she sought to know from what direction he would return:
>   her son, for whom she often wept.
> Watching intently, she suddenly sees him—
>   "Here you are!"—her sweet son is returning,
>   and she sees his little dog following him with love.

As notable as these additions to Tobias are, they in themselves do not solely account for Tornabuoni's interest in the text, an interest that extended to medieval and fifteenth-century Florence as a whole. The book was one of the earliest to be translated into the Tuscan dialect; at least one anonymous fourteenth-century version of Tobias follows the Vulgate extremely closely. Moreover, there were a large number of paintings of Tobias in the mid-fifteenth century. From the many surviving works devoted to the travels of Tobias and the angel, it appears that the topic had acquired unprecedented importance. The most famous painting is that of Angelo Pollaiuolo, executed in Florence between 1465 and 1470, and Vasari records a canvas of this same subject in Orsanmichele, which was transferred to the Sala dei Capitani.[3] Other portraits of Tobias hung in the Bigallo, an orphanage across from the Duomo, which had begun the charitable practice of taking in abandoned children in the thirteenth century. A large fresco that had once been in the loggia shows Tobias and his son burying the dead, and in a tondo that dates from about 1480 Tobias appears with the Dominican martyr Saint Peter of Verona, Jesus, Mary, and Florence's patron saint John the Baptist. Alessandro d'Ancona also refers to several plays from the second half of the fifteenth century that are derived from the apocryphal book.[4] Tornabuoni's translation and revisions of the biblical story thus form part of a larger general interest, specifically Florentine, in the trials and tribulations of the family of Tobias.

The question, of course, is what provoked that interest; and at least

3. Vasari, *Vite*, 3:291–92, n. 1.

4. Gertrude M. Achenbach notes the discussion of the Tobias plays in Ancona's *Sacre rappresentazioni*, 1:97–126 ("The Iconography of Tobias and the Angel in the Florentine Painting of the Renaissance," 74).

part of the answer may reside in the growth in Florence of lay confraternities dedicated to pious works. One of them was devoted to Raphael and took as a model his self-abnegation in guiding Tobias on his travels. Gertrude M. Achenbach suggests that paintings of Raphael were commissioned for private worship, but as she observes, merchant groups often commissioned paintings of both Raphael and Tobias on their travels. We might then speculate on how a story that itemizes the charitable work all good Hebrews should undertake had relevance for Florentine businessmen concerned with squaring their spiritual lives with their flourishing economic ones.[5] When the elderly Tobias instructs his son before his journey, he sternly counsels him "to content yourself with what you have: / give alms, and never turn your face away / from those who must labor hard to earn their bread. / One can do nothing that pleases the Lord more / than to support the poor; /whoever does this with a good heart / finds that such work chases away sin." Strikingly, however, it is after proffering what all believe to be deathbed advice that Tobias gives his son detailed instructions regarding the money he lent to his relative Gabael: he should go to the city of Rages with the receipt (*scrittura*) for the ten talents of silver and politely ask Gabael to repay him. The story hinges on both the need for charity in one's community and the importance of being shrewd about one's business affairs; and it ends, of course, by rewarding the sage Tobias, who has been charitable and shrewd alike. In its own way, the Book of Tobias counsels one to be a generous member of the community and to be wise in business affairs. Indeed, it is success in the latter that enables one to be industrious in pursuing the former.

To this extent there is no need to suggest, as Achenbach does, that the two groups of patrons for paintings of Raphael and Tobias were distinct. Nor need one necessarily agree with her that, strictly speaking, "the story appealed to popular rather than to humanistic taste."[6] As John Henderson and others have recently shown, humanists played a large part in confraternal groups, and as the writings of Lorenzo de' Medici himself suggest,

5. Anna Maria Bernacchioni suggests another reason for the interest in Raphael in her discussion of Filippino Lippi's painting of young Tobias and the angel: "The angel Raphael was in fact the protector of travelers . . . and was often called upon so that he would protect sons when they would travel far from their families in order to enter the world of commerce. In these instances, the person who commissioned the painting would have his son depicted as the young Tobias" (*Maestri e botteghe: Catalogo della mostra, Firenze* 1992–93, 76).

6. Achenbach bases her judgment on the fact that "none of the great masters seems to have painted such pictures," suggesting that even if a painting on the theme was attributed to Botticelli, Verrocchio, or Pollaiuolo, it seems to have been farmed out to assistants ("Iconography of Tobias and the Angel," 78).

"popular" and "humanistic" were by no means antithetical terms.[7] Torna-buoni herself aligns charity with economic sagacity, for reasons that may be considered both self-serving and religiously motivated. At the same time, there is much in her treatment of the story that is not limited to this strict connection. As in her other *storie*, we see an emphasis on extraordinary faith in God and the power of prayer that results from that faith, on the willing-ness to rebel against political authority and to incur the heavy costs of the rebellion, and on the belief that suffering will eventually culminate in grace. While the elderly Tobias is most frequently seen as the exemplary believer and sufferer in the story—his sudden blindness, impoverishment, and Job-like resistance to his wife's complaints are indeed saintly qualities—one cannot ignore the equally important role of Sarah, the young Tobias's wife. Cursed by the deaths of her first seven husbands on their wedding nights, she too is harassed—by an impudent servant—and her shameful story is told far and wide throughout the kingdom. Thus when Tobias is instructed by Raphael to ask for Sarah's hand in marriage, he reveals that he knows about her dismal history, even though he lives hundreds of miles away: "I hear that she has had seven husbands, / and death has claimed them all." Sarah's own belief that God is saving her for a man of her tribe—an intima-tion she recognizes long before her father, Raguel, who has far less hope that things will work out—is highlighted by Tornabuoni, who makes the young woman a clear parallel for Tobias. At the same time, the moralizing about marriage practices that the story permits (the Bible makes it clear that couples who indulge in sex purely out of lust will be punished, perhaps by demons) is important to Tornabuoni as well. Nonetheless, her interest in the biblical book seems based much more on the resolution of trials and tribulations through persistent faith, prayer, and most important, the social and charitable practices of men and women alike.

HERE BEGINS THE LIFE OF TOBIAS, WRITTEN IN
TERZA RIMA BY THE ABOVE-NAMED MADONNA
LUCREZIA DE' MEDICI

[Preamble]

O gloriously eternal and magnificent God,
O infinite goodness, true majesty:
assist me in my new undertaking.

7. Henderson, *Piety and Charity in Late Medieval Florence*, 413–14.

Lord, if ever you acted charitably
 toward someone who beseeched you with humility
 and turned to you with goodwill,
then I ask of you grace, clement Lord,
 that I might turn the little story of Tobias
 into verse and please my readers.
Oh, send me Raphael as my guide and companion,
 he whom you sent to accompany
 the only son of Tobias on unknown paths.
He knew how to protect him in such fashion that
 he might go and return in safety;
 and he gave him a wife of noble standing.
He recovered his gold and his silver;
 he received as many sheep as he did oxen and camels,
 and all was restored and he was greatly contented.
And so it is then with all who serve God
 until they have reached a ripe old age,
 they are remunerated by their good Lord.

Chapter 1

This Tobias[8] was so fired with the love
 of holy charity that he had no care
 for worldly praise; he regarded it with horror.
He came from a city called
 Naphtali, from a tribe descended
 from Galilee.[9] And here he lived
before he was seized
 by Shalmaneser, king of the Assyrians,
 as I will recount further on.
He served God with devout tears and sighs
 before he was led among the pagans
 with many other men.

---

8. As I suggested in note 1, the Vulgate makes no distinction between father's and son's names; nor does Tornabuoni herself. (The anonymous Italian translator of the biblical book calls the younger Tobias "Tobiuzzo"—an affectionate name meaning "little Tobias.") I will follow Tornabuoni's use of the name Tobias for both men, trusting that the context will clarify which character is being discussed.

9. Thus does Tobias begin: "Tobias of the tribe and city of Naphtali . . . when he was made captive in the days of Shalmaneser king of the Assyrians, even in his captivity, forsook not the way of truth" (Tob. 1:1–2).

And to all those who lived near him,
    and to those who hailed from his family and his tribe,
    he gave alms with generous hands.
And although he was young, he never turned his thoughts
    to childish things
    but always acted with great wisdom and discretion.
And throughout Israel there was no
    other man who worshiped God
    with a more sincere or humble heart.
He fled the company of others[10] and grieved
    for those Hebrews who chose to disobey
    the law of God and take refuge in madness.
For they wished to adore the golden calves
    made by Jeroboam, son of Naba,
    who led all of Israel into sin.
But Tobias, to bring about good works,
    adored his Lord and offered
    him tithes with happy brow.
When he reached the proper age, it was time for him
    to take from his tribe a woman of good standing
    as his wife, and Anna was her name.
She gave birth to a son who resembled
    his good father, and he gave him his own name,
    and he had from her no other children.
Tobias placed his every hope in him,
    teaching him from the time he was a baby
    to fear God before all other things.
When he was captured, he was led in great misery
    to Nineveh, a city of great stature,
    where he came to live with his wife and son.
All the other Hebrews were eager
    to eat the food of the Gentiles that was forbidden,
    and they were entangled in their own wickedness.
Tobias alone was scrupulous; he
    observed the laws and feared his God,
    he despised not God's precepts or considered them vile.

---

10. Thus sounding very much like John, who in *La vita di Sancto Giovanni Baptista,* is said to prefer solitude (see stanza 44).

He placed his every hope in God
    and desired only to serve him,
    and God showered much grace upon him.
And he was so welcome to the king
    that he was given the freedom to go and to stay
    in the kingdom at his pleasure.[11]
And all the things that he wants to do
    are conceded to him by that lord,
    because he found him just and unique.
Tobias was encouraged and he took heart;
    without arousing suspicion he went all about
    teaching the captives without knowing fear.
And he traveled throughout the country, seeking
    to teach in every city,
    beseeching his people to remember the Mosaic law.
Because of his virtue and great goodness,
    the king ordered that he be given
    gold and silver in great quantities.
One day, when he had arrived in Rages,
    a city in Media, he saw in the crowd
    a member of his tribe, fallen into poverty,
who had the name of Gabael, and he was so distraught
    that Tobias took compassion on his great need
    and divided his silver with him, giving him half.
Gabael was gracious and kind;[12]
    he valued the service of his dear relative,
    who drew him out of his sufferings and gave him
        repose.
In his own hand he recorded the amount
    on paper, and gave it to Tobias
    so that he might always remember the debt.
Gabael became rich and drew himself out of poverty
    thanks to the silver Tobias lent him,
    of which he had received a great deal.

11. The Bible says that *God* "gave [Tobias] favor in the sight of Shalmaneser the king" (Tob. 1:13); Tornabuoni makes this special treatment dependent on the king's intervention alone.

12. The next three stanzas are Tornabuoni's addition to the Bible, which says nothing about the results of Tobias's charity.

After a long time the aforesaid
　　Shalmaneser died, and he left in his place
　　Sennacherib, his chosen son.
This Sennacherib little esteemed
　　the children of Israel; he detested them
　　and tortured them for his pleasure and his game.
But Tobias cared little for the dangers
　　that surrounded his people; rather, he followed
　　his usual ways both openly and in secret.
He provided clothing to the naked,
　　he fed the hungry, and he took care to bury
　　those from his tribe who had been killed.
And the story tells how the king returned
　　from Judea, when the plague was renewed
　　for his blasphemy against the Hebrews.
He was enraged and esteemed not at all
　　the sons of Israel, and he killed many of them;
　　throughout the whole country he persecuted
　　　　them.
He commanded his servants everywhere
　　to kill the Hebrews and leave
　　their unburied bodies for the beasts.
Tobias was attentive to these things,
　　and he set out to bury his people,
　　not wishing to leave them thus abandoned.
Enraged by what he heard of the good Tobias,
　　the king went beyond the bounds of anger
　　and ordered that he be sent to a dark death;
and all of his things were taken away,
　　all of his property,
　　so that the king's mandate would be passed.
Tobias knew his life was in danger and did not delay,
　　but naked he fled with his wife and his son,
　　leaving everything of importance behind.
And because his kindness for others' misery
　　had extended itself to those of that country,
　　they hid him, and they gave him clothing.
Similarly, they gave him as many things
　　as were needed by his family,
　　such was the compassion that they took on him.

Now listen, reader, to a great marvel:
    for God turned against that fierce tyrant
    the same cruelty he had inflicted on others;[13]
one of his sons tricked him, and he was killed
    after not even forty-five days had passed;
    thus did his wicked reign end with much trouble.
The evil that he did returned to find him:
    he who is cruel discovers cruelty;
    God did not want him to dwell any longer on earth.
When he heard of this turn in events,
    Tobias returned to his home,
    and all of his goods that were taken away
were restored to him.

Chapter 2[14]

The king was dead, and as I have told you,
    everything was returned to the good Tobias,
    and he once again ruled his own household.
If (as I have mentioned) in the past
    he had always served God in all his works,
    now he burns even more to perform them.
Having witnessed the vengeance taken on his enemy,
    he renews his vigor
    and pursues these works with virile heart.
On the occasion of a festival of the Lord,
    it was Tobias's custom, as always on that day,
    to hold a banquet in his home with happy heart.
And as usual, he sent out his son
    to invite all those who were needy
    to his table, and he told him quickly to return.
He fulfilled his commission and did not delay;
    he did his duty, inviting all the people
    that his father had asked to come.

---

13. This intervention ("Hor udirai lettor gran maraviglia"), as well as others like it, is Torna-buoni's addition, following the moralizing tradition of the *cantari* as well as an occasional Dantesque flourish (such as *Inferno* 9:61: "O voi ch'avete li 'ntelletti sani, / mirate la dottrina che s'asconde / sotto 'l velame de li versi strani" [O you possessed of sturdy intellects, / observe the teaching that is hidden here / beneath the veil of verses so obscure].

14. Thus far Tornabuoni respects the chapter divisions in Tobias; she will continue to do so until chapter 4, which incorporates materials from Tobias 5.

On his return, he saw something that left him speechless:
   a Hebrew youth had been killed,
   and he was overcome by fear and sorrow.
When he arrived home, he told his father
   that in the piazza he saw one of their people dead,
   sprawled on the ground, bathed in much blood.
Tobias instantly rose, greatly concerned;
   he left the banquet and ran there, still hungry,
   compelled by the words his son had brought him.
He took that body, darkened and stained,
   and secretly carried it to his house
   so that he was witnessed by no one.
He concealed it instantly, then ate his bread
   in sorrow and fear, remembering
   the words that God himself had uttered
through his prophet Amos, who said,
   "The days of your feasting will turn
   to lamentation";[15] and he recalled this with sighs.
He was disturbed, reflecting on this verse
   with troubled heart; he considers these words
   that he bury this body that had been forsaken.
In the hour when the sun sets
   he buried the man, and he was overtaken
   by his friends, and each of them wants to know
the reason for his actions. "Surely you will soon be
   seized and condemned to death, your property
      dispersed;
   it does not seem that you have understood [the law]."
But Tobias takes no heed; constant and strong,
   he fears God more than a terrestrial king
   and the threats that issue from his court.
He dexterously carries off the dead bodies,
   hiding them by day, and by night
   and under cover he buries them.[16]

---

15. A reference to Amos 8:10: "I will turn your feasts into mourning and all your songs into lamentations."

16. There is a play here in the Italian between "modo dextro" and "sinistro," or right hand and left, the left hand also having the connotation of sinister or undercover.

He is so exhausted by his work
  that he returned one day so tired
  that he went to cast himself down upon the walls,[17]
and he slept so soundly it seemed he was made of stone,
  so tired was he that he could not wait for nightfall,
  and he could not go a single step more.
Tobias had lost all of his senses,
  exhausted by his grief and hard work;
  he gave himself up to sleep, lying on a goatskin.
Like food, sleep is a source of nourishment;
  and nature seeks to be refreshed
  so that it does not do violence to itself.[18]
Exhausted, Tobias sleeps without fear,
  relieved from care, and gives no thought
  to a nest that hangs above him, the home
of a swallow and her children. By chance
  there falls from the nest some dung;
  it strikes the eyes of Tobias
and takes away his vision;
  he loses the sight of his corporeal eyes
  and is no longer able to make use of them.
Tobias does not do what foolish men do
  when they are struck by fortune;[19]
  they become full of rage and let loose a string
of curses; some cry out against the sun or the moon,
  others strike out against their great master;
  they have little patience for such things, if any.
But Tobias remained constant, fearing his God,
  nor was he disturbed by his blindness,
  but readied himself to do the will of the Lord,

---

17. I am translating "di sopre" as "upon the walls," although the sense is vague; Tornabuoni is translating the biblical "jactasset se juxta parietem" [he cast himself down by the wall] (Tob. 2:10).

18. There may be traces of a proverbial saying here: "Il dormir come il cibo ci notricha, / Et la natura vuol recreatione / Non violenza fargli si nimicha."

19. These three stanzas elaborate on Tob. 2:13: "He repined not against God because the evil of blindness had befallen him, but continued immovable in the fear of God." In the interest of suspense, Tornabuoni omits reference to the line that precedes this one: "Now this trial the Lord therefore permitted to happen to him, that an example might be given to posterity of his patience, as also of holy Job." This explanation is cleverly moved to chap-

who willingly consented to what had happened
  so that Tobias might conquer this new temptation
  and give an example of his humility.
The same thing had once happened to Job;
  from reading the ancient and well-known stories
  we know the great trials and afflictions he suffered
when consumed by leprosy.[20] There he lay, covered with
    mud,
  and his friends, his relatives, and his wife
  came to him saying, "now hope has deserted you."[21]
Such words did not increase his suffering;
  despite all the outrage he knew morning and night,
  he aligned his desires with those of God.
Thus did this excellent soul
  do the same when his relatives and cousins
  scorned him and sought to increase his burdens,
saying often to him, "Is this where your fervent prayers
  have led you? All the alms that you gave
  have made you blind!" But he heard nothing.
He answered them unperturbed,
  turning to them in a manner sweet and patient,
  refusing to be scandalized by what had befallen him.[22]
"You should not speak so basely
  about the sons of saints
  who happily await another life.
This is the life that will be given to all those
  who observe his commandments;
  he has promised to reveal it to all who bear his image.
Let not him who can see such things lament
  in any way throughout this brief life,
  even though it may engulf us in torments.

---

ter 7, when Raphael reveals his angelic origins and God's heavenly plan for Tobias and his family.

20. The extended allusion to Job is Tornabuoni's; it is worth noting that in the Vulgate Job follows the books of Tobias, Judith, and Esther.

21. Perhaps an allusion to the initial words of Job's wife in Job 2:9: "Are you still holding to your innocence? Curse God and die."

22. The following sermon from Tobias is Tornabuoni's elaboration on a single biblical verse: "[Tobias said] 'Speak not so, for we are the children of saints, and look for that life which God will give to those that never change their faith from him'" (Tob. 2:17–18).

Who loves God wears his burden lightly;
> the taste of him is sweet,
> he gains a stole whiter than snow.[23]

He shows us to the door; he has given us the keys
> of the eternal kingdom that is denied no one
> who has gained entrance with these means."

Tobias languished in neither hardship nor pain
> from his infirmity;
> his heart is one with his Lord's.

[But] he had fallen into such poverty and need
> that his wife had to go out
> and work so that they could survive.

What I will say now is no delirium or dream;
> one finds it written in the ancient histories,
> and I long to tell you about it.[24]

These servants of God had fallen into
> great hardship, and his wife was forced to do then
> what poor women[25] must do in our day:

to work day and night, and never could she rest
> or cease her work
> until she had earned enough to fill their needs.

She went out one day as was her wont,
> and for payment she received a little goat
> and brought it home, and when she had closed the
> door

Tobias heard it bleat. He suspected
> something, and said to his wife and son,
> "Make sure that you are careful:

---

23. A possible allusion to the Ancient One that Daniel sees in one of his visions: "His clothing was bright as snow, and the hair on his head was white as wool; his throne was flames of fire, with wheels of burning fire" (Dan. 7:9). Also, when Mary Magdalene comes to Christ's tomb in Matthew 28, an angel greets her whose "countenance was like lightning, and his raiment like snow" [et vestimentum ejus sicut nix] (Matt. 28:4).

24. What follows is Tornabuoni's rendition of the spat between Tobias and his wife. Tob. 2:21–22 portrays the domestic quarrel as follows: "[Tobias] said: Take heed, lest perhaps [the kid] be stolen. Restore ye it to its owners, for it is not lawful for us either to eat or to touch anything that cometh by theft. At these words, his wife being angry answered: It is evident thy hope is come to nothing, and thy alms now appear. And with these and other such like words she upbraided him."

25. "Mendiche": female mendicants or beggars. Clearly Anna is no beggar, since she goes out daily to work.

I don't know where this goat has come from;
    be wary lest it was stolen
    and scandal fall upon our heads.
Return it to the man who raised it,
    for it is not right that we eat such things;
    even to touch them is forbidden."
His wife heard him and could not contain herself;
    with a heart that was poisonous and cruel
    she addressed him: "You worship your own folly!
It seems to me you have lost your senses!
    In vain you have waited with hope;
    once you were rich, and now you are poor.
You have thrown away all of our substance;
    we have nothing to live on, we barely survive;
    and all of this has happened through your neglect.
You gave alms in vain;
    God should be rendering you a hundred for one;
    but all that you have left is your blindness and madness.
Here you sit complaining and quibbling;
    and indeed, you keep on doing it;
    and whoever sees you may well understand:
the best that you can hope for now
    is to leave off governing [your family], O poor man.
    I speak the truth, and don't think I'm prattling."[26]
And she upbraided him in much anger.

Chapter 3

Despite these bitter and injurious words, Tobias
    refused to change his mind,
    nor did he answer his wife.
Kneeling on the ground, tears falling from his eyes,
    he lifted himself up with humble heart,
    piously addressing his prayer to God:
"You alone are just, O creator,
    and there is truth in all your judgments;
    your ways are straight, without error.
Relent from punishing us for our sins;

---

26. "Cianciare": to prattle.

relax your just torments,
    so that our enemies will not rejoice,
even though my father or my mother was
    too removed from your commandments,
    and did not obey any of your precepts.
It's no marvel that we know these torments,
    that we are imprisoned and given over to death,
    that we are shamed, reproached, and made a fable of
among all nations to which we are sent,
    as one would do to a beast of prey;
    although one knows and sees only too well
that despite all the hardships that we bear,
    we merit sufferings graver than those we know now,
    and we should be deprived altogether of your favor.
For we have been thoughtless keepers of your word,
    we have not served you with pure hearts,
    nor have we sustained the burdens you gave us.
We are obstinate even in our failures.
    For this, Lord, may you welcome
    the departure of my spirit from this world,
so that it may join yours in peace,
    for it seems to me best that I lodge with you;
    better to die than to live disobedient."
On the very same day that Tobias
    received these insults from his wife,
    [a similar instance of] shame and rudeness occurred,
        as I will recount:[27]
It happened in a province of that empire
    of Medes, in a city called Rages;
    and such a mystery took place with good reason.
The story concerns a young girl,
    the daughter of Raguel, his only daughter,
    who was reproached by her handmaiden.
She said openly to her that she
    had already been given to seven husbands
    and had sent all seven to their deaths.

---

27. Both the Bible and Tornabuoni at this point move to the second strand in this marvelous short story, as they use the prayers of desperate followers longing for death to link the hopeless situations of two related families.

(And this was true, because all had perished
   through the hands of a demon named Asmodeus,
   who killed the men as they were going in to her.)
This uncouth servant flung at her these words:
   "Murderess! seven husbands are dead!
   and this has happened because of your horrible sins!
May you never bear
   daughter or son, may no seed be born of you,
   nor may anything bring you comfort.
I know that you hope to kill me off as well,
   just as you murdered all your bridegrooms."
   Sarah heard these words and was filled with sorrow
      and fear.
She departed, her thoughts shaken
   by the words of that insolent woman
   and the hostile reproofs she made to her.
Quickly she went up above
   into her room, where she stayed for three days,
   eating and drinking nothing,
her mind desolate and sad from such scornful words.
   She prayed humbly to her Lord,
   asking that he would rescue her and not delay,
and she sustained throughout that time such power
   of prayer, as she asked her Lord to liberate her
   from opprobrium and shame.
And after the third day of her withdrawal,
   she [still] prayed to the Lord of her Israel,
   and her hopes were not yet vanquished:
"Blessed are you," was her prayer;
   "O God of our fathers, and blessed
   be your name everywhere;
although in truth we do not follow
   your laws and your commandments,
   always you relent, and you love us without condition.
You are merciful, and content
   to pardon whoever asks pardon of you
   when he confesses and is truly repentant.
I turn my face and my gaze to your mercy
   so that you will liberate me from shame,
   so that [my innocence] may be clear to those who believe
      otherwise:

Oh, truly you should release me
    from this earth, so all will know
    that I wanted to preserve my chastity.[28]
You know, Lord, the simple life
    I have led; it has never been my intent
    to marry and give up my chastity.
I know that I am not a lustful woman;
    nonetheless, I consented to take a husband only
    out of fear and reverence for you.[29]
And as of yet, none of them has succeeded [in making me his
        wife];
    perhaps I was not worthy to be given
    to anyone, or to inhabit their homes.
[Or] would it be possible, O my Lord,
    that they were unworthy of me,
    because they did not seek to do your will?[30]
You see all of our designs,
    how none of them is brought to fruition;
    how neither quibbling nor cleverness is of any use.
And many times we take thorns for roses;
    if you do not help us,
    we will be led to great and unknown ruin.
And how many times has it happened in the world
    that we ask for something, and when we receive it,
    shortly thereafter we repent of having it!
Perhaps what seems to be such a disgrace
    will be the root of great goods; perhaps
    I am being reserved for another man.
But who loves you, Lord, with affection
    clearly merits worthy approbation
    for the good life that she leads.

28. Tornabuoni's Sarah doesn't offer God the same option that the biblical Sarah does: "I beg, O Lord, that thou loose me from the bond of this reproach, or else take me away from the earth" (Tob. 3:15).

29. There is an echo here of *The Story of Queen Esther*, from chapter 6: "You know, Lord, that I attained my glory unwillingly; / I did not come into my position [as Ahasuerus's queen] with happy heart, / but only to obey my uncle."

30. After coming to this crucial recognition, Tornabuoni's Sarah elaborates on what it might mean if God is in fact preserving her for a "good man" whose "will is united with God's." Thus does Tornabuoni draw a far more psychologically realistic portrait of the young woman who has first begged for death and then in the course of her prayer comes to realize that she may have other alternatives.

And every favor will be granted her,
    for she will patiently withstand injury
    if her will is united with God's.
Certainly you do not delight in our wrongs,
    and our rush to perdition displeases you;
    thus we appear to be dead rather than alive.
But after the afflictions of a tempest,
    there are nothing but tranquil times and good
        weather;
    and you raise us from our lowly state to one of
        exaltation.[31]
And who bathes her face with tears
    finds her sorrow converted into happiness
    because she follows your footsteps, O Lord.
You alone are our virtue, you alone are our strength.
    God of Israel, let your name be blessed
    by them who sit lowest and them who sit highest."
At this time both Sarah and Tobias
    directed their just prayers to God,
    as they told their stories of impudence and injury.
All their just and humble words were carried
    before the presence of God, and he was moved,
    and he had his angel, holy Raphael,
look after them, and he sent him below
    to care for them
    and transform their griefs into delight
and lighten their heavy thoughts.

Chapter 4

Tobias, thinking that his prayer was heard
    and that he would instantly die,
    [wanted to] reveal his worthy intentions
and called to him without delay
    his son, whose name was [also] Tobias.
    "Listen well to me now," he said; "don't waste a
        moment.

---

31. With this stanza, Tornabuoni returns to Tob. 3:22 ("For thou art not delighted in our being lost, because after a storm thou makest a calm, and after tears and weeping thou pourest in joyfulness").

When my soul has parted from me,
  bury my corpse, and honor your mother,
  my dear wife.
And bear her in your mind, and keep her in your heart,
  recalling the labors and suffering she sustained for
      you
  when she gave you her milk, that sweetest of drinks.
When she dies, her years completed,
  you will bury her next to me,
  and let my will be fulfilled.
Son, take care you never
  neglect to follow your Lord with upright mind
  and adore him alone.
Be careful never to consent for any reason
  to the breaking of his commandment;
  you must always be sage and prudent.
I want you to content yourself with what you have:
  give alms, and never turn your face away
  from those who must labor hard to earn their bread.
One can do nothing that pleases the Lord more
  than to support the poor;
  whoever does this with a good heart
finds that such work chases away sin.[32]
    Hear this, my sweet son: abstain from every vice,
    especially those that move to anger.
You have heard many times of the terrible judgment
  that was sent to Sodom and Gomorrah;[33]
  such cruel torment did they suffer.
So that you do not fall into such excess,
  never seek to know a similar sin,
  nor let your mind neglect to think on it.
But you must remain content with the woman
  whom God has prepared for you, and this is your duty,
  and this is what God has commanded of you.

32. The biblical passage on almsgiving is more detailed, as Tobias instructs his son on how much to give and lists the heavenly gifts he will gain. Tornabuoni's two stanzas on alms are elegantly succinct and retain much of the original force of Tob. 4:7–12.
33. The story of Sodom and Gomorrah is told in Genesis 19; Tornabuoni freely elaborates here with several terzinas about the act of sodomy, which in the fifteenth century was considered a grave sin punishable by fines and even death.

And the more you heed my words, the less
  you will be tempted to let pride rule you
  or seek to have worldly power.[34]
For if you read carefully the ancient histories,
  you will find that pride is the cause of every evil;
  embrace humility and despise no one.
O my son, listen with affection:
  I want to tell you even more precepts
  so that you will live well, with discretion.
When someone does some work for you,
  instantly give him his reward,
  and do not withhold it from the mercenary.
And take care that you keep your word;
  do not do to others what you would not want done
    to you;
  because he who is above you sees all things.
Eat your bread with the poor as if it were their own;
  cover their nakedness, give clothes to your neighbors,
  and give as much as you can to those who live near
    you.
And weep with those who are sad, be sorrowful with them
  over the death of their relatives;
  cry when they cry, grieve when they grieve.[35]
By no means should this ever leave your mind:
  always ask the wise man his counsel,
  trust in God and direct your thoughts upward to him.
I say this to you as well: now open your eyes
  because this is a thing of great importance;
  give careful thought to my words.
In my youth, I served my dear relative,
  Gabael, with great fidelity;
  I have yet a memory of the money I gave him—
if well I remember, ten talents—
  when I passed through
  the country of Media, for it was urgent.

34. A single verse in Tobias—"Never suffer pride to regain in thy mind, or in thy words: for from it all perdition took its beginning" (Tob. 4:14)—affords Tornabuoni the occasion to digress on the theme of pride that is so central to her *storie sacre.*

35. A touching elaboration of the flat Tob. 3:18: "Lay out thy bread and thy wine upon the burial of a just man."

Now, son, if you heed what I say,
　　you will go directly to that part of that kingdom
　　and request the weight of the silver.
And carry to Gabael this note,
　　which he wrote when I lent him the money,
　　when he was sorely afflicted by poverty.
Go, son, and have no fear
　　of the long way; do not be bewildered by it,
　　you will be able to go with tranquility.
You see that we are scarcely able to feed ourselves;
　　but I have hope that if we fear God
　　he will help free us from our loathsome suffering.
And if we flee from sin,
　　departing from evil and doing good deeds,
　　we will live with him in eternal glory."[36]
Tobias answered his aged father,
　　"I will do exactly as you command,
　　if through such deeds I can alleviate your suffering.
But I do not know the country to which you send me,
　　nor do I know Gabael, or
　　what road to take, or in what lands I must travel.
What sign will I give him, so that he trusts me
　　with the money that you lent him? because I
　　have never seen his face.
Nor does he know me, my father;
　　in what way, with what token might he believe me
　　so that your plan can succeed?"
His father answered, "So that it is clear
　　that you are my heir, show him at once
　　this writing, which is his, when he asks for it,
and you will have the money when you reach him.
　　But go and find first a good companion
　　who will be faithful and who will not leave you.[37]

---

36. In Tobias the fifth chapter commences here, with "Then Tobias answered his father." Tornabuoni will proceed to compress the remaining ten chapters of the biblical book into four and a half chapters.

37. "E non ti faccia gunto": I have not been able to find the word *gunto* in any contemporary dictionary; it is possible that it is an abbreviation for *disgiunto*, in which case the sense would be "may he not become separated from you."

I want him to earn from you a good wage,
   and you must pay him for his troubles
   so that he will never need to complain about us."
Tobias heard all that his father said,
   and he went to obey him,
   going outside the house, and there he met
a youth who seemed lively, full of spirit,
   girded for travel, suited to go with him,
   and his countenance shows that he would obey him.
Tobias made it clear that he wanted to speak with him:
   first he greeted him, then he beseeched him
   to tell him from what country he came.
The angel did not withhold his answer;
   he said that he was one of the sons of Israel;
   this pleased Tobias, and he bows before him,
asking him with pious speech:
   "Do you know the way that leads into the country
   of Media, where I desire to go?"
Responded the angel: "I know well how to guide you
      there;
   I often travel throughout the entire country,
   and there is not a single place that I cannot show
      you.
Often of late I have journeyed
   to the house of Gabael, our brother,
   and I have stayed with him."
Tobias heard all of this with uplifted heart
   and said: "I pray you, wait here for me a little while;
   I will return quickly, and waste no time.
I want to tell this to my father,
   [but] I will return to this place. If it is his wish
   that I travel with you, then it is joyful to me too."
He went back to his father, who was lying down,
   and he told him all that had happened;
   his father marveled, and sat up quickly:
"Beseech him, son, to come here,"
   and Tobias went and quickly brought him
   to his father, and he greeted him.
He said to [the elder] Tobias: "May you always know
      joy";

and Tobias replied: "How can I be glad,
 when I do not see the light, or the splendor of
  heaven?"
The young man told him: "Until now, this has been
 taken from you, but more than you have ever had will
  be restored
 through God's grace"; and he falls quiet.
Then Tobias said to the graceful youth,
 "Can you lead my son
 to the dwelling place of Gabael?
I would never forget such a favor
 if you could lead him there, and introduce him to
  Gabael,
 so that he can render him the money that was mine.
When you return, dear brother,
 I will repay you so well
 that you will never complain of him or of me."
"Fear not," said the angel; "I will protect him
 from all evil, and I will lead him back to you safely,
 because this good work is very important."
Tobias said, "My wife and I have a request:
 even though it seems to us that you come from
  heaven,
 we wish to know what tribe you are from."
The angel answered sincerely:
 "You are right to ask about this mercenary;
 do not fear; your son will wander safely with me.
But so that you may not remain in doubt,
 know that my name is Azariah,
 son of Hananiah and of his great nation."
The elderly Tobias answered him:
 "Great is your family, and pardon my request
 if you thought my question unworthy.
Have compassion on us, since I cannot see,
 and I beg you not to be angry with me;
 you see the shadows that surround me."[38]

---

38. This and the preceding stanza suggest Tobias's remorse at having asked the angel about
his lineage; the Book of Tobias simply has him say, "But I pray thee be not angry that I desired
to know thy family" (Tob. 5:19).

The angel told him: "Silence your desperate sighs;
　　I will lead him there safely
　　and safely he will return, as I wish."
Tobias answered him, humbly and plainly:
　　"May you travel in safety, and may God be with you;
　　may his angel accompany you over hills and plains
so that the adversary does not trouble you."

Chapter 5

Once they finished talking,
　　they made preparations for their journey,
　　and the elect travelers departed.
Tobias took leave of his mother and father,
　　and together with the angel he began his journey,
　　leaving the elderly couple disconsolate.
His mother said: "Oh, now what shall I do,
　　unable to see the source of happiness
　　in the presence of my wise son.
The support of our old age
　　travels far from us; he wanders to distant places,
　　taking away from us our treasure.
You want to overcome all of your trials,
　　but I wish that the money for which you send him
　　had never existed; you do not even know where
　　　　it is.
To me it seems that our riches are lost
　　when I can no longer see my son,
　　who is my sustenance and consolation."
Tobias said: "Do not cry, do not fear;
　　he will return safely, and you will see
　　with your own eyes the young man who will make you
　　　　happy.
And you will have from him great consolation;
　　the angel of God will be in his presence,
　　and I believe that he will never leave him,
so that even the most difficult road
　　will seem to them the easiest of paths,
　　and he will make all things turn out well, as he desires.

I imagine that things will fall out well,
    but you must first find peace,
    no longer cry, no longer hang your head.
He will return to us, now be peaceful";
    and she trusted in what he said,
    and silenced her weeping and her bitter words.
Tobias, son and heir of Tobias, made his way
    guided by his celestial companion
    and by his dog, who had seen him departing.
On the first day they arrived
    alongside the shores of the Tigris River,
    and here they were fiercely attacked
by a great fish that sprang up from the water.
    Tobias, who was standing there to wash his feet,
    saw the enormous fish racing behind him.
He said: "O sir, look at this! come and see
    what comes to devour me in great anger."
    The angel answered: "Don't let him grab you;
Take him by the gills and pull him from the water";
    and he grabbed him and soon drew him out onto dry
        land,
    where the fish wriggled and lay at his feet.
Tobias turned to the angel and said: "Here he is!
    What should I do?" and the angel said, "Be careful;
    slice him open up to his mouth
and take out his heart, his gall, and his liver;
    such things are necessary
    to produce good medicines."
The rest of the fish they put on the fire;
    they roasted it and carried it with them,
    and it provided food for them as they traveled on
        their dubious path.
They came to Rages without delay,
    to the city of Media, whence Tobias said,
    "Tell me, brother, so that I do not seem so dull,
What are these things that we carry on our travels,
    for what use are they? Please tell me."
    Azariah answered his question:
"I am knowledgeable in these matters;

if you put a little of the heart on the coals,
      you will have your troubles changed into joy.
The smoke chases away the demons
      from woman or man, and they will be powerless
      to return, and they will flee from you as if from
         thunder."[39]
Tobias answered: "To what lodging
      do you think we should go inside the city;
      in what place should we take our rest?"
Raphael answered him with confidence:
      "I want to stay with a relative of yours
      from your tribe; he is a man of substance.
His name is Raguel, a devout man;
      he observes the laws of Moses,
      and he is a wealthy man, and wise and powerful.
As you will see, he has only one child, a daughter,
      he has no other daughter or son;
      I want you to ask for her to be your wife.
If I am right, all that he has will be yours
      once you ask her father for her hand;
      he will give to you all that he has."
Tobias said: "I want to do all that you desire,
      but I hear that she has had seven husbands,
      and death has claimed them all.
Who refuses her does not know this evil;
      I would not want what happened to the others
      to befall me as well.
If I take her as my wife and then die,
      my mother and father would be disconsolate,
      and I would be the cause of their going down to hell.[40]
For their grief over my death would kill them in turn;

---

39. Raphael's instructions here are vaguer than those found in Scripture; Tornabuoni also omits, surely for dramatic suspense, Tob. 6:9: "And the gall is good for anointing the eyes, in which there is a white speck, and they shall be cured."

40. "Chagion sarei challon ferno sengissi": one of the few references in the Old Testament to an afterlife. See Tob. 6:15: "I should bring down their old age with sorrow to hell" [deponam senectutem illorum cum tristitia ad inferos]—or in the late medieval vernacular translation of *Il libro di Tobia*, "io li manderei allo inferno così vecchi con grande tristizia" (*Scrittori di religione del Trecento*, 1:12).

they have no other son
who can bring them comfort."
"Understand, Tobias, I am not trying to trick you,"
said Raphael; "I have the power
to chase away demons, and well do they know this.
They are attracted by those who are concupiscent
and who defile matrimony by banishing God
from their presence and their thoughts.
And who practices uxoriousness in such a way
turns himself into a mule or horse and loses his senses;
he becomes the prey and game of the devil.
When you take her, hear what I say:
Into her chambers you will go, and for three nights,
before you touch her, you must respect her.
Pray to God continually,
both of you pray together,
and do not touch her or even think of such things.[41]
Address to God all your desires and hopes;
then put the insides of the fish upon the coals,
and the demons will flee from that place.
The legions will descend from heaven,
so that their enemies will plunge below,
and you will have the grace of God for your purpose.
Then on the third night, when you are alone,
receive with fear and trembling the young lady,
thinking to lie with her only to bear children.
Nor must you unite with her in carnal delight,
but in the hope that in Abraham's seed
you will have a blessing at once old and new.
Now let us find Raguel, and you will see
how much delight and consolation
will come to you: more than ever before."
They found them quickly, and
Raguel gazed at the handsome man,
and his heart was filled with great tenderness.

---

41. Tornabuoni is more emphatic about avoiding carnal sin in marriage than the Book of Tobias, which merely instructs that Tobias should be "moved rather for love of children than for lust, that in the seed of Abraham thou mayest obtain a blessing in children" (Tob. 6:22).

To his wife he said: "How closely this young man
    resembles my dear cousin;
    see how modest and humble are his looks."
And turning back to them, after he spoke to his wife,
    he said: "Whence do you come, royal youths?"
The angel answered him, with benign gaze:
"From your brothers and relatives
    of Naphtalim; like you we are descended from them,
    nor do we worship vain idols.
We were led into that great city of Nineveh
    and made prisoners; we have lived there
    for many years, and many more months."
Raguel replied, and asked of them,
    "Would you know by chance my brother
    who dwells in that land, whose name is Tobias?"
They spoke to him, answering him with news
    of Tobias; they told him
    that through his patience he had become a new Job.
The angel spoke with fluent voice, telling him,
    "That Tobias whom you just named
    is the father of this young man," and Raguel hastens
to him, and said: "Son, how good it was of you to think
    of coming here, blessed are you now that you
    have arrived"; and he enfolded him in his arms.
Speaking thus, he kissed his face,[42]
    and it seemed as though he would never be satisfied
    with doing things that would please the youth.
Do not think that his wife could restrain herself
    from covering the young man with caresses;
    nor could their daughter refrain from drawing close.
They spent much time weeping, full of tenderness,
    everyone talking at once,
    exchanging gracious words and pleasantries.
Raguel showed great willingness
    to do honor to these strangers,
    and he instructed his servants to ready themselves
to kill a sheep; likewise

---

42. Tornabuoni dwells on this tender scene at greater length than does the author of Tobias,
who simply portrays all three family members as weeping.

he ordered them to prepare a feast,
   and to do it quickly and willingly.
And all was done and carried out as he wished,
   and Raguel invited his guests to dine,
   whence Tobias said to him with earnest words:
"I wish neither to eat nor drink today
   until you grant my pious wish,
   and do me a singular favor:
I would like to ask for Sarah,
   your daughter, to be my wife, if it pleases you,
   because this is my desire."
Once Raguel heard this, he began to be troubled,
   knowing what had already happened;
   he became fearful and sad
and did not answer but remained silent.
   He marveled over Tobias's request,
   for such things as had happened were known by all.[43]
The angel said: "Do not fear to give him your daughter,
   do not be afraid of what will happen,
   believe what I counsel you:
It is her good fortune to be given to a man
   who fears God. Take comfort in this request;
   have no suspicions, but rest secure."
Raguel answered him, speaking sweetly:
   "The tears I have shed, and the prayers I have uttered
   have come into the presence of God.
Let our tribulations be at an end;
   this youth has come to us so that
   she might marry a man from her tribe.
This is what I desired, and I still demand
   that the law of Moses be observed;
   thus may he be welcome to me and to her.
I am happy that you have asked for her hand;
   I, for myself, would not have offered her to you.
   That you yourself choose her [shows] that you come
      from God,
and I pray to him with pure heart

---

43. An example of one of Tornabuoni's additions that attest to her own sense of the small community she lived in.

that our past disgraces be converted into grace;
thus do I promise God to make a worthy offering.
So I know that you are trustworthy, do not hesitate
to put forth your hand; take hers in your own,
and may you always know happiness.
Live long lives, each of you secure
in the God of Abraham, who rules Israel,
and may the God of Isaac be with you.
May the God of Jacob bless you," said Raguel,
and be always with you."
And Raphael heard all of this,
he who had been Tobias's guardian on the wild way.[44]

Chapter 6

And as soon as these words were spoken,
Raguel had the Scripture brought to him,
as was usually done to seal a marriage.
Although he was not filled with much hope,
Raguel blessed God and called his wife
and said: "Make everything ready without delay.
Take her into another chamber,
and let her husband do as he will in a different room,
not the one where they are usually put."
Raguel then went to his daughter
and, weeping, said to her: "Dear child,
have a strong heart, be neither poor nor dejected;
may God in heaven enlighten your eyes
and raise you up from great unpleasantness,
and may there be good vigil before the feast."[45]
And then they went outside her chamber
and merrily they gave themselves to dining,
and as was their custom, they paid them great honor.

44. "Ch'era i[l] suo guardia alla silvestra via": One wonders if there is the faintest allusion here to Dante and Virgil and to the journey Tobias and the angel had taken as similar to traveling through "savage" hell.

45. Tob. 7:20 has Anna, Raguel's wife, uttering this prayer; Tornabuoni gives it to Raguel himself. Perhaps she is respecting a Florentine custom of the father's giving the blessing to his daughter on her wedding night? See Klapisch-Zuber, *Women, Family, and Ritual in Renaissance Italy,* for a detailed account of marriage practices; I have not, however, found any reference to a paternal blessing before the wedding banquet.

After they had eaten, without delay
   the young man was led
   into that chamber that was furnished so richly,
and when they were alone he remembered
   what Raphael had taught him,
   and from his wallet he drew out
a part of the liver that remained
   from that great fish, and thus he placed it
   upon the fire and commended himself to God.
Then the angel Raphael took up
   that demon and tied him up in the desert,
   so that he might not cast a spell on their marriage.
With sweet and open words Tobias
   comforted the young girl so she would
   raise her heart to God and offer everything to him.
He prayed to God, which none of her seven
   libidinous husbands had done;
   they had desired only to commit carnal sin.
Sarah heard his gracious and sweet words;
   and to better obey her dear spouse,
   she rose up and put her clothes back on.
Tobias spoke to her in this manner:
   "My sweet bride, hear what I say;
   I will reveal to you every secret.
Today, tomorrow, and the next day,
   we will spend our time in prayer, soliciting God
   so he will save us from tribulations.
The third night, then, you and I
   will be conjoined in holy matrimony,
   in temperate manner, with pure hearts.
Let our prayers be heard in heaven;
   let us ask him for a long and holy life
   so I do not finish like your seven dead husbands."
Their wills united, Sarah and Tobias
   began to pray with great fervor,
   asking that God bestow his grace on them.[46]

---

46. The Bible follows with a lengthy prayer in which both Tobias and Sarah make it clear that they are not "joining together like heathens that know not God" (Tob. 8:4–10).

The next morning, at the hour when the cock usually
    crows,
    Raguel indulged in his customary fear,
    and with much grief commands his servants
to prepare the tomb
    so that they might bury the youth quickly
    if the same thing had happened as always.
Then he asked his wife with cautious words
    that she send someone who would
    report to them the truth, and not fables.
If she finds him dead, she should not spread the news,
    but they should bury him quickly before it is day,
    wrapping him in clean white linen.
Without delay, his wife sends
    her faithful handmaiden
    to see if he lives, and bade her return quickly.
She went immediately to the richly furnished chamber,
    where she found them both healthy, sleeping in peace,
    and she hurried back to tell the good news.
Raguel said: "O glorious Lord,
    we thank you for having so contented us;
    now I am happy, and I am content to die."
His wife also, with fervent words,
    and in great gladness said: "Lord,
    who serves you need fear nothing.
May you always be blessed, O creator,
    for you take pity on your faithful ones;
    you have taken away our shame and shown us your love.
You have removed from our eyes the harsh veil,
    you chased away the fierce demon who held us in his
        grip;
    he left us lamenting a life more bitter than evil.
You treat your servants with clemency,
    you have pitied and preserved from harm
    the only children of their fathers.
Our struggles and griefs are at an end;
    we live to praise you, and to bless
    the grace that you send us as you will."[47]

47. The prayer of Raguel's wife is Tornabuoni's addition to Tobias, which has a short joint
prayer spoken by Raguel and Anna together (Tob. 8:17–19).

Happily, Raguel, his anguish chased away,
   said to his servants: "Now quickly, fill the grave back
      up
   before anyone can hear about it!
And before it is day, fill it up with earth
   so that no one can find anything out;
   do not reveal the order that I gave."
To his wife he said: "Go, do not delay;[48]
   prepare some tasty dishes
   so that we can pay homage to the young man.
Make ready a banquet, magnificent and grand,
   invite everyone, neighbors, relatives, and friends;
   my heart is full and bursting with joy!
God has heard our prayers! Who has a tongue to call out
   would never know that once we were dead;
   for now we are brought back to life."
Anna does not delay or turn a deaf ear;
   she has the sleek calves killed and the goats
   for the feast, and performs her duties willingly.
Raguel turns to witness what she has done;
   he adjures his son-in-law to remain
   and take his delight with them for two weeks.
He promised to give him half of his substance,
   offering it as a gift
   to his daughter and to Tobias.
And he declares that whatever remained after his death
   would similarly go to them as well,
   and this was just.
Tobias called Raphael and said to him:
   "If I should contract to make myself your servant,
   I would still be a pilgrim traveling through the world.
Because [such work] is neither haughty nor proud,[49]
   again I must ask you to wear yourself out;
   you are my hope, and you are my protection.

---

48. Raguel's instructions are not in Tobias; thus the joyfulness he displays in these three stanzas is Tornabuoni's elaboration.

49. An attempted translation of "Se mi facessi a te per charta servo / o peregrino anchor pel mondo gisse / perche non è altero ne protervo," which in turn must be Tornabuoni's rendition of "If I should give myself to be thy servant, I should not make a worthy return for thy care" (Tob. 9:2). It is unclear why Tornabuoni should introduce the idea of haughtiness into the biblical passage.

As you see, it is fitting that I remain here still
    for some days, and I cannot retract [what I have said],
    nor can I refuse to follow Raguel's wishes.
If I went, I would not be able to do
    what Raguel has sworn me to do;
    yet I want to obey my father
and return home at the appointed time, for
    I know that he numbers and counts the days.
    Still, I am also obliged to Raguel.
Please, go yourself to Gabael and tell him
    all that has happened, and ask that he come
    to the happy wedding feast of his dear cousin."
With alacrity, Raguel prepared
    camels and servants to make this trip;
    Raphael took them all, and so they departed.
He does not mind taking this journey;
    he travels and comes into Rages
    and renders to Gabael the evidence of his debt,
the note that he wrote in his own hand
    when he was helped by Tobias and in such need,
    and Gabael gave to Raphael the money.
And the angel told him everything
    that had befallen Tobias; and Gabael
    delighted in going to the wedding of his son.
To the house of Raguel they made their way;
    they found Tobias sitting at his wedding feast;
    they embraced and kissed, and weeping,
Gabael said with joy: "O my son,
    you are born of the best mother and father,[50]
    always has he served God without fear.
May my blessing be upon
    the bride who sits beside you,
    and on your children of this marriage,
and of the third and the fourth generations after that;
    may your seed be blessed
    for a long time, for many seasons!"
And then they all gave themselves up to eating.

---

50. Tobias mentions only the father at this point: "Thou art the son of a very good and just man" (Tob. 9:9).

Chapter 7

Tobias and Raguel and Anna and Sarah
   and the holy angel and Gabael compete
   with one another to see who can praise God best.
They take great pleasure and delight in feasting
   and observe the celebrations in awe of God.
   But the father of Tobias lingered in sadness,
for the appointed time had passed and he was torn,
   wondering what could have delayed his son
   for so long, and he was fraught with dread;
and with words that are as pitiful as they are humble,
   he asks what has happened: Is he perhaps dead?[51]
   And it seemed as though his heart would break.
Where did he end up, "to what harbor and in what fashion
   will you bring the money?" Perhaps he was
   poorly guided in his travels.
In these griefs they linger, torn with many cares,
   he and his wife weep with unmeasured plaint,
   wondering when they would hear from him, if ever.
Each went about desolate, full of tribulations;
   but Tobias began to comfort his wife
   and he spoke to her in this way:
"Oh, no longer let us lament;
   let us offer ourselves to God, because I hope
   that he will send him to us without delay; do not
     doubt.
For it seems to me, and I hold it as truth,
   that the man who went with him is faithful,
   full of goodness, and possessed of a sincere heart."
But she is torn apart thinking of him,
   and she left the house and went about outside,
   studying the road to lighten her thoughts.[52]

---

51. Tobias has the father wondering if it is Gabael who has died ("Why thinkest thou doth my son tarry, or why is he detained there? Is Gabael dead, and no man will pay him the money?" [Tob. 10:1–2]). Tornabuoni makes these questions even more painful as she suggests instead that Tobias wonders if his son has died: "Con parole pietose assa[i] dimesse, / Diciea che fa, et tanto forse, è morto / Et parea ch'el suo chore si distruggesse."

52. A touching addition to the biblical "daily she looked round about, and went into all the ways by which there seemed any hope he might return, that she might if possible see him coming afar off" (Tob. 10:7).

She continued to do this every day,
>   to see if she can see him coming from afar,
>   gazing out toward where her son should most likely
>   return.
He wants Their son was impatient with his father-in-law,
>   who had asked him to stay with them even longer
>   and thereby fulfill his duty.
He wants to return so he might bring joy
>   to his mother and father, who suffer in anguish,
>   and it seems that their hearts are eaten out for him.
Tobias was not content to remain there longer,
>   and he does not consent to stay; although he is
>   beseeched
>   by all of them, their speech was wind.
He makes up his mind: he has decided
>   no matter what to return to his father,
>   for he already seems to have delayed too long.
Raguel sees that Tobias will for no reason
>   heed his wishes, that he has made up his mind
>   and makes ready to go.
Half of what he owns, he gives to him:
>   camels, sheep, oxen, handmaidens, and servants,
>   and blessed all of them with good cheer.
He said to him: "God protect you;
>   may the good angel go as your companion,
>   neither may you have any cause for grief.
May the true God who sits in his high throne
>   give you his grace, so that you may find
>   prosperity even greater than what you have now."[53]
He kissed his daughter many times; her mother
>   also kissed her and hugged her,
>   and there was much tenderness and much compassion.
And she said, "My daughter, make sure that you honor
>   your mother-in-law and your father-in-law,
>   and may you never displease your husband.

---

53. This scene of parting is elaborated by Tornabuoni at some length; Tobias 10 has no direct conversation between daughter and parents, and there is no mention of singing, music, or giving presents to Raguel's servants.

Govern your house with love,
    in such manner that you may never be accused
    of negligence or any error."
Sarah said, "I have heard your words;
    and I pray to God that he give me such grace
    that I will always be ready to obey their wishes."
They took their leave, amid singing and music;
    Raphael and the bridegroom gave to the servants
    of Raguel magnificent gifts.
They were not slow in their travels
    but hurried so that on the eleventh day
    they arrived at Charan, healthy and well contented,
and that was midway in their journey.
    Here they rested to refresh themselves,
    and here they remained out of care for the women.[54]
The angel said to Tobias, "It seems to me best
    that we go a little ahead,
    and we will be able to gain several days on them,
so that we can put things in order
    and let your father know about your spouse,
    so that she will not arrive unprovided for.
This way, your wife and her handmaidens can travel
    with less hurry, and the horses and their guardians
    will find the rugged way less bothersome."
And they put into effect their sound plans
    and made their way toward the house,
    and Tobias carried the gall of the fish in his hands,
that part of the great fish that he had saved;
    he carried it because the angel told him to,
    and he never departed from his orders one jot.
The mother of Tobias, who every day had gone
    to a high mountain to wait and watch for him, to see
    if her son was on his way,
places her right hand upon her forehead,
    and when she also puts her left hand there,
    above her eyes, she makes for herself a shield

---

54. "Per amor delle donne fer soggiorno": Tornabuoni's addition, perhaps an allusion to occasions when the people she was traveling with would stop so she and other women could rest.

so that the rays of the sun would not injure her,
    as she sought to know from what direction he would
        return:
    her son, for whom she often wept.
Watching intently, she suddenly sees him—
    "Here you are!"—her sweet son is returning,
    and she sees his little dog following him with love.
She recognized him at once, and she rushes instantly
    to tell her husband with great happiness
    that their son had returned at last from his long travels.
With fitting and modest words, Raphael
    instructed Tobias: "As soon as you are home,
    praise God, and make yourself known to them;
embrace your father, and then prepare yourself
    to take that gall which you carry with you,
    and anoint each of his eyes.
For this is fitting: you will see presently
    that the eyes of your father will be opened,
    and the long shadows shall be removed.
He will see the light of heaven,[55] and his griefs
    will be converted into happiness,
    his eyes opened wide and uncovered."
Thus talking, they traveled at a fierce pace
    toward the house; but the dog of Tobias
    showed even less patience: he ran ahead
and lay down at the feet of the
    elderly father, and old Tobias heard him,
    and he put his hand out to the little dog.
Upright he stands, and he walks quickly,
    taking the hand of the young boy who guides him
    straight to his son who had been gone for so long.
There he is, and you have never heard or seen
    such tender greetings as they make to one another,
    those servants faithful to God.

---

55. The Italian here is "vedra ellume del ciglio" [he will see the light (with) his eyes], but
the Vulgate speaks of the light of heaven ("et videbit pater tuus lumen caeli" [Tob. 11:8]);
the scribe apparently misread "ciglio" for "cielo." See also the medieval translation of Tobias:
"E vederà il padre tuo il lume del cielo" (*Scrittori di religione del Trecento*, 1:17).

All of them kneel on the ground,
    worshiping God with humble heart,
    and then they sit down to refresh their spirits.
Fearlessly, Tobias comes
    and places the gall on the eyes of his father;
    the angel comforts him and gives him courage;
for half an hour, Tobias holds the gall,
    and there began to fall from the eyes of his father
    a white skin, then more skin emerges;
what came forth was like the albumen
    of an egg; the good Tobias quickly takes it away,
    and his father can see the light again.
The old man could know no greater comfort
    than to see himself surrounded by light,
    he can see his whole family, and the heavens above.
He said, "O Lord, you have castigated me,
    and all this has been done for my salvation,
    and as penitence for every sin.
Now you send me this consolation;
    I am able to see my son Tobias
    return healthy and rich to his home.
I know more joy now than I ever knew grief."

Chapter 8

One could not describe the feast
    that the mother and father gave for their dear son,
    and they did the same for his faithful companion.
Tobias tells them all of the great danger
    that happened to him by the banks of the river
    when he had his struggle with the fish and captured
        him.
And similarly he also spoke of
    the wise counsel of his faithful guide:
    "He showed me the way, and gave me light;
he enlightened me, and made me wise;
    he gave me courage, he made me take the wife
    who was singled out for me and given to me by
        fortune."

And he tells of Gabael and all his traveling,
  and he spends so much time talking,
  and he describes so many things that one cannot
    possibly write it all down.
Seven days after his return, he was joined by his bride
  and all of her family, and they brought with them
  money and an infinite number of goods.
She was modest and happy, she resembled an angel;
  Tobias's mother embraced her, and his father
  held her, and she knows great love from them all.
For seven days they held a great banquet,
  to which came Achior and Nabath,
  the cousins of Tobias, if I understand well.
When the seven days were over, on the eighth
  the elder Tobias said to his son,
  "What can we give this worthy baron?
He has protected you so well; in faith,
  I would like him to use what we have,
  sustenance and servants for his provisions."
"Oh, father, I have concluded the same myself,
  although we can never render him payment;
  whatever we had, it would be insufficient.
This is a man possessed of every virtue:
  he led me in safety and in health; he stayed with
    me,
  he made me know exactly what I had to do.
Thanks to his virtue, he liberated me
  from the fish who wished to devour me
  and taught me what I needed to know.
He made me take a wife whom no one wanted;
  he traveled to Rages and recovered the money
  that Gabael had had for so long.
He made Raguel and his wife happy,
  chasing away the fierce enemy Asmodeus,
  the one who had kept their daughter in distress.
And more than this, he restored to you the light;
  through him we have received great good,
  and I don't know how we can repay him.
You could not give anything to him that could equal

the many good things we have had thanks to him."
Then they called him, and the angel came to them,
and they took him aside, to a secret place,
    and they said to him: "Never will we be able
    to give you what you deserve.
Although it is only a small amount, we want to
    give you half the treasure that you brought
    from other places; this would satisfy us."
The angel answered that such worthy offerings
    are reserved for the Lord of heaven;
    all that he sought was their goodwill, and that was
        enough.
And he led them to an even more secret place[56]
    and said to them: "Blessed be the Lord,
    who is before all creatures.
Confess to him with all your heart
    that he has shown you his compassion,
    and to him alone should you give honor.
Who has peace from him knows gladness
    and celebrates his good works
    and never falls into discord with him.
Prayer and fasting are honorable indeed,
    but almsgiving is best, the best way
    to gather treasures that have been lost;
it liberates man from eternal horrors,
    and it is that alone that purges sin.
    Thus one finds life, and never again can he die.
But he who finds himself tempted
    to commit iniquity loses his soul;
    he is deceived about his end.
Truth stays always fresh and young;[57]
    I have no desire to hide from you my meaning,
    nor do I wish to go on deceiving you.
When you wept, when you prayed to God,
    when with holy zeal you buried the dead
    and converted your feasting into fasting,

---

56. An elaboration on the biblical "Tunc dixit eis occulte" [Then he said to them in secret] (Tob. 12:6).

57. "La verita è quella che sta verde": truth is always young.

keeping your mind upright and your eyes ready,
    hiding in your house the bodies of the dead
    and then going out by night to bury them,
I offered up your prayers and you never knew
    that it pleased God that you were tempted
    so he could see how you sustained such trials.
Once my Lord had proved
    how humble and patient you were,
    he sent me so that I could liberate
you and accompany your innocent son
    along the lengthy road
    and save Sarah from the fraudulent enemy,
from the insults that she bore
    when it was not her fault and she withstood her evil
        fortune,
    even as she suffered greatly.
Now I want you to know your great fortune,
    one that has never been seen or heard before:
    I am Raphael who has been sent for your care,
one of the seven visible spirits
    that stand above in the presence of God to
        contemplate
    the eternal, incomprehensible to you humans."
This angelic speech was received
    in great amazement, and they were all afraid,
    each one trembling when they heard his story.
With sweet and humane words, and kind,
    the angel said: "Peace be with you; you should have
        no doubts,
    you should act familiarly with me.
Blessed be the Lord, and sing to him;
    I only looked as though I ate and drank with you,
    but you saw me neither eat nor drink.
My secret food," he then said,
    "is unlike yours; and what I drink
    has never been seen in this world.
Now,"[58] he said to them with happy face,

---

58. Raphael's parting words and the simile of lightning ("Da loro occhi sparì come baleno")
are not in Tobias, which ends—albeit dramatically—with "And when he said these things,
he was taken from their sight, and they could see him no more" (Tob. 12:21).

"I have reached the end of my sojourn here;
it is fitting that I return to my Lord.
Praise God, and bless these days;
render grace to him for all that has happened;
now I must return to him and no longer remain. O dear
friends,
abide here in peace."
Then he disappeared like a bolt of lightning,
and they could see him no more, openly or in secret.
Each of them fell down
to the ground for three hours; their faces low,
they lay there stupefied, and then they said:
"Are our hearts made of rock, or of stone?
How is it that they have not been consumed
in thinking what he did for us by descending
below!"
Then did each one rise up
to bless God with renewed fervor;
but the old man remained kneeling on the ground.
His heart had been inflamed with great joy,
and he did not disguise in his words
how passionate he was with perfect love.
His mind raised up, with profound
and worthy prophecies he discoursed at length,
showing the grace God had placed within him.[59]
And after this consolation
he lived, his sight regained,
for another forty-two years, as the book tells us.
He saw the sons of his grandchildren,
and he lived in much happiness
for all of the time I have recounted to you.
He lived one hundred twelve years without vice,
and he was buried in Nineveh
with honors and in comfort.
For when it was ordained by God
that he lose the light from his eyes,
he was fifty-six years old;

59. Tornabuoni omits the rousing canticle spoken by Tobias in chapter 13, which prophesies
the future of Jerusalem.

For ten years he suffered from that burden
>during which time he saw nothing, as I have said;
>he was sixty-six when he
saw the light again, and I find that
>he prospered for the rest of his life,
>and he lived without any sin.[60]
And it happened that at the end of his life
>he called to his side his dear son Tobias,
>who came to him, not alone or
with one or two, but with seven sons!
>[They were] handsome young men, and the old man
>>said to them,
>"I now wish to tell you my final wishes:
Gracious boys, my mirror and my light,
>thanks to its great sins, this city
>is readying itself for destruction;
leave this inhuman country,
>where the word of God will not vanish
>but be fulfilled according to his will.
Your brothers who now dwell outside this land
>will return to the country of Israel;
>and their countries will be repopulated.
They will delight in all these things,
>for they fear God, and they will be happy
>as they throw the empty idols to the ground.
O my sons, keep yourselves pure of heart;
>give alms, practice justice, and perform sacrifices
>so that God does not hide his face from you.
Do not wait or remain here
>after you have buried your mother;
>leave this land, and its territories
and do what I ask you:
>bury my wife by my side
>in a single grave, within the city walls."[61]

60. Tornabuoni's (or the scribe's) math is incorrect, since the total should be one hundred and eight years, not "cento dodici." Why there should be a departure from the Bible here is not clear; Tob. 14:2 clearly states that Tobias "lived a hundred and two years" and regained his sight at age sixty after only four years of blindness, not ten.

61. "Claustro" can also mean monastery or cloister, or that part of the monastery where the cemetery was; it is difficult to know where, exactly, Tornabuoni intends for Tobias and Anna

And they heard his words;
>and when the mother of Tobias was dead and buried,
>he did not await the dawn of new struggles and outrage
but did what any wise and shrewd person would do:
>he took his wife, his sons, and his grandchildren
>and returned to his father-in-law, who bore him great
>>love.
And I want you to know, reader, he found him in good
>>health;
>Raguel possessed great riches
>and always devoted to God his every thought.
Just think how happy the elderly couple was
>when they saw their daughter and their descendants
>who had been born of her, with little or no price!
And for a good long time they lived together
>in health and great contentment, and when Raguel died
>he left to Tobias his house and his furnishings.
For he was his heir, and to him was given
>all of his house and possessions;
>all that had been Raguel's was bestowed on Tobias.
So worthy were his works
>that God enabled him to see
>his fourth and fifth generations.
He ended his life at ninety-nine years,
>and during all that time
>he never brought anyone a reason for displeasure.
And when he died at a ripe old age
>his descendants persevered
>in good works. And now to sum up:
Glorious God exalted him;
>in this world he made him gracious
>among men, so that everyone greatly loved him.
And at the end of his life he gave him true rest.

Here finishes the eighth and final chapter of *Tobias*.

---

to be buried. Tobias speaks only of the old man's request that his children "bury your mother by me in one sepulcher" (Tob. 14:12).

THE STORY OF JUDITH,
HEBREW WIDOW

INTRODUCTION

As readers of the Book of Judith know, this tale is anything but pedestrian in its treatment of its eponymous heroine—a heroine who first seduces, then slaughters the Assyrian general Holofernes in order to save her besieged town of Bethulia. When we first encounter Judith, in chapter 8 of the biblical book, she has been a widow for over three years, and she has spent that time in an upper room of her wealthy home mourning her husband. Yet she is also described as in Jth. 8:7 as "exceedingly beautiful," and as we will soon see, she is also extremely cunning. She thinks up, alone, a strategy for helping her fellow Israelites, who are literally dying of thirst, to overcome the persecutions of Nebuchadnezzar's unrelenting general. She betrays this strategy to no one, including the ruler of Bethulia, before she carries it out: "But I desire that you search not into what I am doing, and till I bring you word let nothing else be done but to pray for me to the Lord our God" (Jth. 8:33). Carrying out her plan demands a self-possession and cool-headedness that the Vulgate elaborates in some detail. She uses her beauty to impress Holofernes' spies, and Holofernes himself, with her strength and her wisdom; she coolly avails herself of a sword, tied to a bedpost, to decapitate the drunken general; she counsels her fellow citizens to place Holofernes' head on the city wall and to pursue the confused Assyrians. The book ends with Judith singing a canticle recalling both her feminine wiles and her strength: "She anointed her face with ointment, and bound up her locks with a crown; she took a new robe to deceive him. Her sandals ravished his eyes, her beauty made his soul her captive, with a sword she cut off his head" (Jth. 16:10–11).

This troubling narrative of female violence and deceit is ostensibly mitigated even in the Vulgate. In a prayer that Judith herself utters before she leaves for the Assyrian camp, her victory is said to illustrate nothing particularly virile or cunning about her but a great deal about the power of God: "For this will be a glorious monument for thy name, when he shall fall by the hand of a woman" (Jth. 9:15). Indeed, the following line of the prayer ("For thy power, O Lord, is not in a multitude . . . nor, from the beginning have the proud been acceptable to thee; but the prayer of the humble and the meek hath always pleased thee") lent itself to an interpretation that would become central in medieval readings of the book. Dante's *Commedia* is, in this light, emblematic of many moralizing treatments of Judith and Holofernes. The latter, depicted in the twelfth canto of *Purgatorio*, is treated along with others as a victim of his pride, while Judith, who dwells in paradise with Sarah and Rebecca, exemplifies humility and obedience. Judith is also seen in many commentaries as a double for the Virgin Mary; thus Jth. 13:18 was read as foreshadowing Mary's special status: "You are blessed by the Most High God above all other women on earth." But it is largely Judith's exemplary chastity during her widowhood that enables her to receive special favors from God, and she emerged in much medieval commentary as the incarnation of continence and chastity.[1] The liturgy of Mary's feast days in the medieval church was drawn extensively from the Book of Judith, and as Elena Ciletti notes, medieval art and theology consistently invoked this typology.[2] At the same time, writers did occasionally make a point of calling attention to more than Judith's "powers" of chastity. In the *Trionfi d'amore*, Petrarch speaks of Judith's ability to conquer Holofernes "con bel parlar, con sue polite guance" [with clever speech and rosy cheeks].[3] And in the *Morgante*, Pulci suggests that it was "lawful" for this "little widow" [vedovetta] to resort to treachery to save her fellow Hebrews.[4] (Like Pulci and Petrarch, Tornabuoni refers to Judith early in the

1. See, among other sources, Tartari, "Maestro della storia di Griselda e una famiglia senese di mecenati dimenticata," 45, and Capozzi's dissertation, "Evolution and Transformation of the Judith and Holofernes Theme."

2. "Key phrases from the Book of Judith were adopted by the church for the liturgy of Mary's feast days, and throughout medieval art and theology there are invocations of this typology" (Ciletti, "Patriarchal Ideology in the Renaissance Iconography of Judith," 42).

3. In a section in which Petrarch witnesses men succumbing to the passion of love, we see this scene: "Vedi qui ben fra quante spade e lance / Amor, e 'l sonno, ed una vedovetta / con bel parlar, con sue polite guance / vince Oloferne, e lei tornar soletta, / con una ancilla e con l'orribil teschio, / Dio ringraziando, a mezza notte, in fretta" [Here you see among swords and lances Love, and sleep, and a little widow, who with her clever talk and rosy cheeks conquers Holofernes, and she returns alone, at midnight and in a hurry, with her handmaiden and that horrible head, thanking God] (Petrarch, *Trionfi d'amore* 3.52–57).

4. "E lecito fu ancor la vedovetta / per tradimento al lume di lanterne / riportarne la testa d'Oloferne" (Pulci, *Morgante* 25.189).

poem as a *vedovetta*—a diminutive that perhaps takes away from the virile acts Judith will go on to perform.)

Pulci was by no means the only Florentine besides Tornabuoni to allude to Judith in his work. The scene with Holofernes is one of the most striking on Lorenzo Ghiberti's famous golden doors to the Florence Baptistery, and in the late 1460s Sandro Botticelli painted two small works illustrating Judith's victory over Holofernes—one of them a graphic depiction of the discovery of the general's body by his soldiers.[5] But perhaps the most famous Quattrocento image of Judith is the imposing statue by Donatello. The sculptor fashioned the Hebrew woman with sword raised above her head, standing astride Holofernes; it is clear from the deep gash in the general's throat that Judith has already struck him. Cast in the late 1450s and commissioned by either Cosimo or Piero de' Medici for the new Medici palace in Via Larga, Donatello's Judith acquired an overtly political connotation after Piero's victory over the mutinous Pitti faction in 1466. It was then that Tornabuoni's husband apparently ordered an inscription regarding the health of the res publica to be carved into the column that formed part of the base. Judith thus becomes symbolic of a civic identity linked with the health of Florence—and of Piero de' Medici.[6]

Tornabuoni no doubt began her own poem on Judith after Piero's death in 1469. One should probably not insist on a firm link between Donatello's statue, with its redefined symbolic status after the failed Pitti conspiracy, and Tornabuoni's *Judith*. If anything, Tornabuoni might be said to have returned to a more "medieval" understanding of Judith, one that explicitly associated the Jewish heroine with humility and the Assyrians with pride and overbearingness. Like Tornabuoni's poem, the Book of Judith does not begin with the heroine herself but devotes a full seven chapters (out of sixteen) to background material on Nebuchadnezzar and Holofernes, as well as the excruciating sufferings of the people of Bethulia. Chapter 8, however, opens with the intervention of Judith, and save for a brief segment

---

5. Ronald Lightbown notes that this picture and its companion piece, in which Judith is seen triumphantly leaving Holofernes' tent with her serving maid, were too small for *cassoni*; they were "small and precious pictures intended for close inspection" (*Sandro Botticelli*, 32). Capozzi suggests that art historical scholarship has occasionally interpreted the painting of the calm, even dreamy Judith returning to Bethulia as an allegory of Medici victory over their enemies; "Evolution and Transformation of the Judith and Holofernes Theme," 29–30.

6. An identity that Donatello's statue would lose in the intervening decades, when Cellini's much larger Perseus would upstage her. An earlier inscription had been framed in the discourse of humility and pride; see the introduction and the note to Janson's *Sculpture of Donatello*.

that recounts the attacks of the victorious Israelites after Judith's brave deeds, she never really leaves center stage. Tornabuoni is also extremely inventive in the elaborate way she stages introductory material and historical setting. In fact very little of her first forty stanzas is strictly biblical, as she rearranges the few suggestive passages about overweening pride in Judith 1–7 and chooses to create a compelling new story about Nebuchadnezzar's sudden lust for power after his lengthy contest with the unfortunate King Arsaphat, who merits only seven verses in the Bible. Given the preponderance of this story and its obvious interest to Tornabuoni, we don't see Judith until stanza 87, more than halfway through the poem. Moreover, whereas the biblical account ends with an impressively long "canticle" by Judith (Jth. 16:1–22) and a reference to her final days and the subsequent celebrations in her honor, Tornabuoni's Judith disappears in the midst of festivities that begin with the coming of Joachim from Jerusalem. The poem ends not with the account of Judith's death but with Nebuchadnezzar's rage that "a Hebrew woman" has killed his valiant general Holofernes. So much of the poem has focused on Nebuchadnezzar's greed ("it was not enough for him to conquer the world: / he wanted others to worship him as god"), that Tornabuoni's poem can be said to speak more about the pride and reckless ambition of kings than about the faithfulness of a Hebrew woman. At the same time, without Judith's initiative, Nebuchadnezzar and his strongest general, Holofernes, would have carried on unchecked. The fact that Judith's victory over Holofernes indirectly provokes Nebuchadnezzar's death may suggest that Tornabuoni is amplifying the powers of this "little widow."

Moreover, it is by no means obvious that Tornabuoni was willing to marginalize or downplay the more threatening aspects of Judith's "appeal," such as the way she deploys her femininity for gain and transgresses the normal boundaries prescribed to her. When Judith is first introduced in the Bible, we see her as a wealthy widow who has been shut up in her house ever since her husband's death three years before: "And she made herself a private chamber in the upper part of her house, in which she abode shut up with her maids" (Jth. 8:5). Dressed perennially in haircloth, Judith is portrayed as fasting "all the days of her life." When she hears that Uzziah has promised that within five days he will deliver up the city to the enemy, she sends for two of the elders, who come to talk with her, presumably in the enclosed space of her house; eventually Uzziah joins her there as well. Tornabuoni omits the details of Judith's reclusiveness, just as she mentions neither her constant fasting nor her wealth. We hear only of her "honest and virtuous life" and, more interestingly, her "manly heart" [animo virile]. When Judith learns about Uzziah's orders, she takes it upon herself to seek out the priests and the prince: "she rose up and instantly went out [usciva fuori], / going off to find her superiors." It is in a public place where she announces that God has placed a plan in her heart; in conspicuously homely language, she announces that this plan involves her "meddling" [framettersi] in affairs of state so that the prayers and offerings of the priests will be heard. She herself, she says, will be the "medium" [mezzo] through which the torturous events besieging her beloved city will be remedied. The Bible's Judith is far less forthright. She first instructs the elders that God is sending afflictions not to destroy his people, but "for our amendment" (Jth. 8:27), and she speaks in the subjunctive when she articulates her relationship to deity: "so that which I intend to do prove ye if it be of God, and pray that God may strengthen my design" (Jth. 8:31).

That said, Tornabuoni tends to give Judith's compelling speeches in the Bible short shrift. Her heroine is far less verbose than the Judith of the Bible, whose prayers go on for entire chapters. At the same time, even though she triumphs over selfishness, deceit, and pride, enjoys special closeness with God, and respects Jewish tradition and law, she is not an unproblematic heroine, given her manipulative use of her beauty. Tornabuoni in fact exaggerates rather than downplays the effect her looks have on the Assyrian men whose camp she invades. Unlike the innocent Susanna or the daughter of Herodias, she is calculating as she displays her attractions: "Judith curtsied before Holofernes / her countenance beautiful to behold, / and he gave her tender audience in turn, / lavishing caresses as though he were her lover." In her depiction of Judith as a valorous "little widow" with a "manly heart," Tornabuoni at the very least does not shirk addressing the many contradictions this compelling figure presents to her.[7] It is true that she fits easily into Tornabuoni's wide-ranging allegory about pride and its downfall, thereby enabling the author to call her at one point a "fearful widow" through whom "tanta superbia" has met its revenge (stanza 143). But she also threatens to escape from this essential flattening of her character, as Tornabuoni introduces subtle details such as her tending to her servant's dowry and brings in the language of the chivalric *cantari* to describe the "gran maraviglia" [the great marveling] that greeted Judith's valiant efforts and "virtuous work."

7. Ciletti argues that most Renaissance depictions of Judith downplay her threatening aspects. Although Tornabuoni may also do this, some details seem to escape the kind of "patriarchal containment" Ciletti argues for ("Patriarchal Ideology in the Renaissance Iconography of Judith").

HERE BEGINS THE STORY OF JUDITH, HEBREW WIDOW,
COMPOSED IN RIME BY THE MAGNIFICENT AND
VENERABLE WOMAN, MADONNA LUCREZIA, WIFE OF
THE MAGNIFICENT PIERO DI COSIMO DE' MEDICI

1. O Son of God, our good Jesus!
   O Son of Mary, virgin mother,
   your charity was so great that you
   descended to earth through elegant works,
   you left heaven to inhabit the earth below,
   disseminating virtues bestowed by your father
   on you, his worthy son:
   you made it possible for us to share in your kingdom.

2. Lord, I appeal to your charity,
   and pray that you help me tell a little story[8]
   that is very old, and please, do not deny me [such a gift]:
   I would like to recount the tale of Judith,
   who risked her life, as thus I read.
   She submitted herself to a narrow pass
   to escape the proud tyrant;
   she had the victory, he suffered harm and shame.

3. I found her story written in prose,
   and I was greatly impressed by her courage:
   a fearful little widow,[9]
   she had your help, and she knew what to do and say;
   Lord, you made her bold and helped her plan succeed.
   Would that you could grant such favor to me,
   so that I may turn her tale into rhyme,
   in a manner that would please.

4. How much the sin of pride angers you
   can be seen by us from numerous signs,

---

8. "Una storietta": not only does the term allow an end rhyme with "Iudetta," but it will resonate as an internal rhyme in stanza 3 when Tornabuoni introduces the word *vedovetta*, or little widow; see the introduction to this section.

9. "Essendo vedovetta et temorosa": Both Pulci and Petrarch speak of Judith as a "little widow" or *vedovetta*.

starting first with that audacious man
who was the handsomest in your triumphant kingdom.[10]
He did not know how to enjoy true peace,
he wanted to be a lord even worthier than you;
because he wished to be the greatest of all princes,
he was the first to know suffering in hell.

5. Thus did he lose that joyful glory
    that he has never been able to regain.
    This is what happens to all who revel in pride;
    similar things will befall them.
    He who goes about without reason
    and does not follow God is brought low;
    he who acts without reason finds—as one sees—
    that many things befall him that try his belief.

6. Whoever would like to tell of kingdoms
    made desolate through pride—
    kingdoms once of great nobility and worth—
    would need too much time to name them all.
    Because I wish to come more quickly to my conclusion,
    I will leave these things aside and follow instead
    the sayings and the worthy speech of our Lord,
    for he who humbles himself will be exalted by God.

7. And it suits me to go back a little in time,
    so that you will understand what I am going to tell you.
    There was a king who [wanted to] exalt himself,
    and with much boldness he built a city,
    and he believed he could conquer the entire world,
    such was his enthusiasm and his pride.[11]
    His name was Arsaphat,
    and he was crowned king of the Medes.

10. For another reference in Tornabuoni's work to Lucifer, see *Laude* 9. Nowhere in Tornabuoni's writings is the contrast between humility and pride underlined more forcefully than it is here.

11. Thus does Judith proper begin: "Now Arphaxad king of the Medes had brought many nations under his dominions, and he built a very strong city, and he called it Ecbatana." A detailed description of the dimensions of the walls and towers follows. There is no allusion here to his pride.

8. He had already taken over a great country,
   and such was his prowess that he seized many provinces;
   he was presumptuous and shrewd,
   a man of arrogance and pride.
   Nebuchadnezzar could tell the kind of man he was,
   and he said: "He has become too proud:
   he used to give a tribute to my father,
   but he has never wished to give a tribute to me."

9. And thus in his heart he decided
   to seek counsel from his barons;
   he quickly sent for them
   and concluded after long deliberation
   that he had been badly treated by the king of Media,
   alleging for this pressing reasons:
   for at one time Arsaphat paid tribute to his father,
   but he did not esteem Nabuc[12] enough to give the same to
      him.[13]

10. "And he appears to be vigorous and strong,
    and he fears no one of this world:
    but if you think this plan is wise, I will immediately go
       off
    to attack him with such fury
    that he will find out I am as ardent as he,
    and even more desirous of honor,
    and I will bring my soldiers with me, numerous and strong,
    and if he does not give me the tribute, he will die."[14]

---

12. Tornabuoni shortens the name for metrical purposes; she will continue to do so throughout the poem.

13. The story of the unpaid tribute is new with Tornabuoni, an excuse she creates in order to produce a far more dramatic story with regard to Nebuchadnezzar's character than that found in the Bible. Judith gives us a monarch who, as early as Jth. 2:3, is prepared to establish a universal kingdom: "And [Nebuchadnezzar] said that his thoughts were to bring all the earth under his empire." In order to develop a contrast between the initially pompous Arsaphat and the initially wronged Nebuchadnezzar, Tornabuoni omits such statements, choosing rather to have Nebuchadnezzar begin lusting for glory and dominion only after he has experienced the thrill of Arsaphat's submission (stanzas 25–26).

14. This stanza is a good example of Tornabuoni's hypotactic style, one she ostensibly learned from the *cantari*.

11. When they heard his intentions,
    the barons rejoiced and told the king what they thought:
    "Great lord, you are right to do this to him
    and to make him and all his kingdom fear you.
    We are all devoted to following you
    behind the banners of your kingdom;
    whoever will not obey your authority
    should lose both his property and his life."

12. When he saw they all agreed,
    he felt much gladness in his heart,
    and he instantly sent his ambassadors
    to Media and its king, and in haste he informed them
    of their embassy: if he wanted
    to live in a state of peace, Arsaphat
    should send a liberal tribute,
    just as he had sent one to his magnificent father.[15]

13. When they arrived in Media,
    at that strong city of Ecbatana (such was its true name),
    they came before the king with no other escorts.
    This Arsaphat, who was so cruel,
    saw them come within the gates:
    "Tell me the truth: Who are you?
    What do you come here to do? Tell me quickly
    who sent you and for what purpose you come!"

14. When they heard him ask to hear
    what each of them well knew, the messengers
    at once gave their response, and with vigorous voices:
    "Nebuchadnezzar wants his tribute!
    if you decide to obey him in this,

---

15. In Jth. 1:10, messengers are sent not to Arsaphat—he is already conquered as early as 1:5 ("Nebuchadnezzar fought against Arsaphat and overcame him")—but to the numerous nations surrounding Assyria, all of which refuse to honor the messengers ("But they all with one mind refused, and sent them back empty, and rejected them without honor," Jth. 1:11). Just what is refused is not specified. Tornabuoni will use the single verse about messengers and expand on it for several stanzas as she elaborates on the encounter with Arsaphat (see stanzas 13–18).

you will choose well and perform your duty;
now as before, you must give him [the tribute]
if you do not wish to suffer injury and shame."

15. When Arsaphat grasped their words,
    he replied to the messengers in this way,
    claiming that he will not pay the tribute:
    "Nor do I believe he shall ever have it from me.
    Do not let him think he can act like this,
    for I will no longer suffer such outrage!
    Mine is a city of great stature:
    I fear neither him nor any creature.

16. "[Go back] and say this to your lord:
    if I did not regard my honor so highly,
    I would make you die in torment,
    after great tortures and equal grief.
    [Instead] I will take vengeance on your effrontery;
    I will attack him with such fury
    and deliver him his tribute in such a way
    that he will repent ever asking for it."

17. When they had his response,
    the barons took their license to leave
    and returned to their lord without further delay,
    presenting themselves to him with this account:
    "Even though it is true that this journey did not harm us,
    nevertheless we knew great dangers.
    Lord, not only does he refuse to send tribute,
    but he will make you rue your request.

18. "He has a great city, built with strong walls,
    prosperous and wealthy.
    Such security does he gain from it
    that he fears no one, neither you nor your people."
    Nabuc said: "I will make him tremble;
    I will make him more cautious in his speech;
    I will make him feel my power
    and force him to cast aside his arrogance."

19. And he commanded that without delay
    all his army be made ready,
    and he wanted it sent toward Media
    to burn down the city and whoever was within
    and to lay waste the entire country.
    "I trust that I will cause him great grief;
    because he has sought my shame and dishonor,
    I will make the dogs tear out his heart."

20. As soon as the ambassadors departed,
    Arsaphat at once prepared his people:
    out toward the borders he sent them,
    and they were numerous, and strong, and bold.
    For his part, Nabuc was also gathering troops;
    they covered the land and all the shores,
    and his soldiers too were ardent and strong,
    and all of them cried, "To the death! To the death!"[16]

21. And so there began a vicious battle;
    all of the men were of such pride and daring,
    they came to blows without [an] order,
    and did not hesitate to slaughter one another,
    and many died at the hands of the rabble,
    who tore apart their bodies limb from limb.
    After the great battle and the fury of the fight,
    Nebuchadnezzar emerged victorious.

22. This cruel and pitiless battle was waged
    in that plain between the Tigris and Euphrates,
    and the land there was not uncultivated.[17]
    You could see that both those who had been lazy
    and those who had labored were covered in sweat;
    you could not tell if they were black men or white.
    The land was covered with their blood;
    Arsaphat has lost and is languishing quickly.

16. "Alla morte, alla morte!" See a corresponding moment in the *Morgante*, 11.102.4: "Rinaldo grida: Alla morte, alla morte!" cited by Pezzarossa in Tornabuoni, *Poemetti sacri*, 207n.

17. Thus does Tornabuoni return, if only briefly, to the text of Judith. Jth. 1:6 describes where the battle with Arsaphat was fought: "in the great plain which is called Ragua, about the Euphrates, and the Tigris."

23. And thus he was beaten and subdued
    by Nabuc, who clearly emerges his lord,
    and now he reveals little of his former boldness
    and this after such enormous effort!
    Had he at first only yielded up the tribute
    such struggles would not have happened;
    but because he challenged Nabuc's demand,
    he was beaten so badly that he lingered near death.

24. Nebuchadnezzar is triumphant,
    and Arsaphat is greatly humbled;
    and he went to the king without circumstance or pomp,
    bearing Nabuc a magnificent tribute.
    As history tells us,[18] he submits to Nabuc;
    he pledges fealty and swears that never again
    will he fall into such error but
    forevermore will be a good and faithful servant.

25. Hearing this, Nabuc was greatly contented,
    and he accepted his tribute and oath.
    But now I want to tell you of another thought
    that instantly came into Nabuc's heart:
    he desired to lay a siege so potent
    that all the lands around him would fear him.
    Not content with what he had, as you will hear,
    he ventured new wars and sought out new quarrels.

26. Before he had gained the obedience
    of Arsaphat, he was a great lord;
    and justly he punished Arsaphat's crime,
    and he ruined his honor.
    And because of this, he took far greater license,
    and up he rose, inflamed with pride,
    and it was not enough for him to conquer the world:
    he wanted others to worship him as god.[19]

---

18. "Dice la storia." Given that virtually all the details surrounding the confrontation between Nebuchadnezzar and Arsaphat are contrived, it is difficult to know which "storia" Tornabuoni refers to; all Judith tells us is that the Assyrian king "overcame" the king of the Medes.

19. The third chapter of Judith depicts a ferocious Holofernes who cannot be assuaged even by generous offerings: "And though [the people of the towns] did these things, they could

27. Nor did he bear in mind that his enemy had fallen
    because he too had suffered from excess;
    that Arsaphat became wretched, a mendicant;
    he lingered beaten, close to death, as I have said.
    Now listen carefully to what I tell you,
    and be sure to keep in mind this warning:
    for whoever leaves moderation so far behind
    merits only damnation and derision.

28. For him, one great victory was not enough;
    our appetite is never satiated.
    Thus he sought to usurp glory even from God,
    his mind blinded and full of presumption,
    King Nabuc completely lost his senses.
    Observe this strange and disrespectful work,
    and note that one cannot do worse in this world
    than try to equal or be greater than God.

29. He sent his ambassadors all the way to the Jordan,
    all the way to the city of Samaria,
    to places that were near and places that were far,
    so that each would yield to his dominion
    and agree that in all the world
    there was no greater lord or sovereign to be found.
    And from Jerusalem too he desires abundance,
    all the way to the mountains of Ethiopia.

30. Among these lands many were found
    who agreed to follow his command;
    they sent him ambassadors and gifts,
    judicious words delivered with thanks.
    The Hebrews, however, did not choose this course;

---

not for all that mitigate the fierceness of his heart. For he both destroyed their cities, and
cut down their groves." It is at this point that the Bible introduces the allusion, on which
Tornabuoni will expand at length, to Nebuchadnezzar's desire to be worshiped as a deity:
"For Nebuchadnezzar the king had commanded him to destroy all the gods of the earth, that
he only might be called god by those nations which could be brought under [his control]
by the power of Holofernes." It is safe to say that Tornabuoni attempts to introduce finer
nuances into her characters' behavior.

  This stanza is characteristic of Tornabuoni's paratacticism; lines 3–7 all begin with *et*
[and].

they began instead to gather provisions,
they worked to strengthen the walls of their lands,
because they feared he would attack.[20]

31. And with many prayers and petitions and with much fasting,
they asked the Lord not to deny them his aid
but to help them escape from the hands of the pagans
and assist them as he usually did;
they asked that through his love for them
he yield to their prayers and not fail to protect them
and to guard them from all shame and harm
and save them from the cruel tyrant.

32. With much devotion and humility,
the Hebrews turned themselves to God,
and all of them were of one mind:
to refuse to obey Nabuc, and in this they agreed
to remain firm in their decision.
His messengers they chased away
and gave them neither audience nor honor;
with a brusque dismissal they sent them away.[21]

33. Returning to their lord Nabuc,
the messengers delivered the words they had heard:
all except the Hebrews chose to obey him,
and only when they came to their country
did their embassy go unheard.
They told him everything at once,
how the Hebrews would not obey him,
"little esteeming either you or your people."

---

20. Once again Tornabuoni takes significant liberties with the biblical text. In Jth. 1:11 messengers are sent to all the places above. But when all the nations and towns refuse them the king "swore by his throne and kingdom that he would revenge himself on all those countries" (Jth. 1:12). Tornabuoni has Ethiopia, Jordan, and other countries agree to offer up tribute; the Hebrews alone resist. Judith 4 is the first time we hear of the Hebrews' resistance, and in this context it is articulated not so much in terms of principled opposition as of panic: "Dread and horror seized upon their minds, lest [Holofernes] should do the same to Jerusalem and to the temple of the Lord, that he had done to other cities and their temples" (Jth. 4:2).

21. Again, note Tornabuoni's innovations on the biblical text: there is no explicit mention of Holofernes' sending messengers to the Hebrews, save for the initial embassy in Jth. 1:10–11 that goes out to all the surrounding nations.

34. When he learned of the Hebrews' response
    and their utter disinclination to obey,
    Nabuc decided to send forth his army,
    and he sent for Duke Holofernes to come:
    "Prepare yourself at once, without delay;
    go to the west and do not fail,
    oppose those Hebrews who seem to be of such mettle.
    With every possible weapon, go forth and assault them.

35. "And by no means indulge in pity;
    destroy their lands and all their people.
    Whoever should persuade you to seek peace,
    do not listen to him for any reason.
    Commit indecencies and crimes, unleash harm and discord,
    anguish and punishment and great confusion:
    burn and rob and lay waste their country,
    since they have decided to take arms against me.[22]

36. "Why should they not know Nabuc,
    or his people who are so plentiful?
    Why should they not know how I tamed Arsaphat?
    I want Jehoshaphat filled to the brim;
    I will make them open their mouths
    in a way that they have never done,
    as they pray desperately to their God who is worth nothing,
    and whom I esteem no more than a fig.[23]

37. "Teach them all manner of torments and tortures;
    do not lead any to jail or take any away from there,
    but treat them so badly I will never have my fill."
    Holofernes answered Nabuc's command:
    "O my lord, I thank you for this,
    today you give me great consolation.

---

22. This stanza is copied almost verbatim in the Florentine *sacra rappresentazione* called *La rappresentazione di Judith hebrea*; see the introduction to this volume.

23. "A pregar loro Idio che non val nulla, / i' non lo stimo il valer duna frulla"; a *frulla* is something worthless, and the expression is familiar to the tradition of the *cantari*. It is worth noting that the end rhymes in this stanza exemplify Tornabuoni's experimentation with word endings, as she truncates the final syllables in "trabuc[ca]," "boc[che]," and "fat[to]."

I go so willingly to seek their destruction
that I will ask no other favor from you than this."[24]

38. Thus as soon as he received his commission,
Holofernes, Nabuc's ardent seneschal,
went out to gather infinite numbers
of horsemen and foot soldiers of every rank,
war machines and archers, and he was obeyed,
because his orders have come from the king,
and he is furnished with every possible weapon
to harm those who wish to contend with Nabuc.

39. Off they went with this equipage,
in numbers so great that the like was never seen.
Burning with courage and pride, they advanced
to attack all those who did not obey him;
they marched past the borders, and their first siege was,
as you will presently hear,
in the first lands they found before them:
Mesopotamia and Cilicia were laid waste.[25]

40. And so they traveled throughout that country,
seizing their lands as you hear,
lands that profited little from defenses,
since the enemy's number was countless.
Unable to sustain the attack,
their victims fled from every quarrel and brawl;
and yet another land sent its ambassador [to Nabuc]
and sought from him peace and goodwill.

41. They sent him presents and expensive gifts,
praying him not to treat them so cruelly,

---

24. In Jth. 2:5, Holofernes is given this order by his king: "Go out against all the kingdoms of the west, and against them especially that despised my commandment." No specific mention is made here of the Hebrews, who in Tornabuoni's text emerge as the only people to deny homage to Nebuchadnezzar.

25. Only at this point does Tornabuoni begin to follow Judith systematically, as she picks up with Jth. 2:14–15: "And he passed over the Euphrates, and came into Mesopotamia. And he forced all the stately cities that were there, from the torrent of Mambre, till one comes to the sea."

and they came before him with songs,
promising him they would all be faithful;
and if before they delayed, now they sought pardon,
because they were content to have changed their minds,
to obey Holofernes without deceit
and to give him tribute and all that he wanted.

42. Thus did Holofernes accept their tribute
as soon as he came into their lands,
and once he was within, he tore everything down
to its foundations: he destroyed their forts
and threw their gods to the ground, of whatever false sect,
so that none would ever be worshiped again
and so that in King Nabuc they would place their desires
and adore him alone as their deity.

43. For this was the command
of Lord Nabuc: all of the lands
that Holofernes took through siege
in these new wars through his might
must honor Nabuc's image, adorned,
and so they are forced into these conditions:
they must hold him in honor, as a god,
in all the lands where he is lord.

44. Now that each city and hill town
had rewarded Holofernes' lord with devotion,
the army raged toward the beautiful province
of the children of Israel.
And when the Hebrews saw that evil people,
as I said, they had recourse to God,
beseeching him to protect them from fury,
begging him to overlook the wrongs they had done him.

45. They lived in fear, they were greatly afraid
of Holofernes, who was so strong,[26]

---

26. Tornabuoni here returns to the biblical text cited earlier, Jth. 4:2, in which "dread
and horror" seize the minds of the Hebrews and turn them to praying and gathering provi-

and of the torments and violence
he would unleash once inside their gates,
and the way he would pillage and lay waste
their revered temple, condemning it to destruction
as he had done everywhere else:
he had plundered them all and left them in desolation.

46. To all their borders they sent their people
to block the passes so they could not fall
into imminent danger;
they made every place around them ready for the siege.
But their most diligent provisions were directed
toward God, for their hearts were made alert
through the intervention of their priests,
who were in Jerusalem, just and devout.

47. The altars they covered with haircloth,
and they offered generous sacrifice;
day and night they have absolutely no rest,
asking God to deliver them
from this martyrdom, and with fasts they observe
all the precepts that are due their office;
and whoever was of age uttered heartfelt prayers
with great devotion.

48. In this way did the sons of Israel
prepare themselves, as I have said,
in great humility and in much fear;
they attend neither to pleasures nor delight,
but they all ready themselves with weapons
in all those places where they least suspect attack,
guarding the passes to the mountain and the plain
from Holofernes, their savage enemy.

49. To Holofernes it was announced
that the children of Israel were making ready;

---

sions. This is one point where Tornabuoni's experimentation with the story gets her into some
difficulties, albeit minor ones, regarding her characterization of the Hebrews.

they had secured their city in every place,
and they were all sworn to resist him.
He marveled greatly at this news,[27]
and he called before him two grand dukes;
both of them had been lords of countries
that Holofernes had recently seized.

50. Each of them had once been lord
of lands that bordered on the country of the Hebrews.
One of them was from the family of Amon,
the other from Moab's, and they left their idols
behind out of reverence and fear
for Lord Nabuc, for neither wished to know
the sorrows that Holofernes could inflict
through torture and disdain.[28]

51. He said to them: "I want to be informed
about this people who wish to resist:
How strong are they? Of what disposition?
Tell me the truth and leave stories behind.
If you really want to know, I admire them,[29]
because usually people do not get in my way;
all the other places to which I have traveled
have yielded to me, ready to serve.

52. "These people who would challenge me:
What is the source of their boldness, their overweening
    force?
If I can—and I am sure that I will—
I will make them repent what they do,
I will inflict on this people such great penance,
that all of the world will talk of it."
One of these dukes, Achior by name,
responded to Holofernes, as you will hear:

27. "Di questo forte s'è maravigliato": a far cry from Jth. 5:2: "And he was transported with exceeding great fury and indignation" [Et furore nimio exarsit in iracundia magna].

28. Judith does not elaborate on the princes' reasons for surrendering.

29. "In verità i' n'ho admirazione / che questo intervenir già non suole": a touch of admiration that is missing in the Book of Judith.

53. "Lord, these Hebrews have their own god,
who is strong and just and powerful,
and it displeases him greatly when he sees evil done
and when his people disobey him,
and he castigates them, and he turns his back,
and he hears nothing of their prayers:
because this is a God whose goodness is so great
that he hates iniquity and holds it in contempt.[30]

54. "They were enslaved in Egypt for a long time,
dwelling within the hands of Pharaoh;
their god's power and his great virtue
led them out of there, and he won the battle,
and to ensure their salvation in these parts,
he gave them this land, the land of the promise,
the promise many years ago he made to their fathers,
and they have turned it into a rich and fertile country."

55. Then he said, "O Holofernes, I greatly fear
that you do not have sufficient respect for them,
you will fight them throughout the summer and winter.
I suggest that you must try to find out
if they have disobeyed their Lord who governs them.
If they have disobeyed him with lies,
you can quickly take their country and their lands,
but if they are in his favor, you will never win this war."[31]

56. Hearing this, Holofernes became enraged
and said, "O Achior, listen now to what I say:
I don't think you have understood,
since it seems you did not grasp what I wanted:

30. In Judith, Achior says nothing similar to the lines in this stanza; rather, he launches into
a lengthy history of the Hebrews that goes on for twenty verses. Tornabuoni telescopes this
history into a single stanza (54); she omits any reference to the many battles against their
enemies that Achior lists. In general, Tornabuoni downplays the fervent Hebrew militarism
that is such a crucial part of the Book of Judith.

31. "But if there be no offense of this people in the sight of their God, we cannot resist them,
because their God will defend them; and we shall be a reproach to the whole earth" (Jth. 5:
25). This final sentence of Achior's incurs the wrath of "the great men of Holofernes," and
they "had a mind to kill him." Tornabuoni omits the reference to Holofernes' companions
and moves instantly to Jth. 6:1, which describes the general's wrath.

Don't you remember what I commanded?
Evil is he who will not follow Nabuc!
I want you to worship him, with great reverence,
because he alone of all is supreme.

57. "O Achior, I want you to know,
and do be assured, there is no other god
whose worth I esteem more than a fly,
in whom we can place our hope or desire,
and whom to worship would not be a sin.
All of the gods have now been forgotten;
Nabuc is the only one who should be honored,
because of earth and heaven, he alone is lord.

58. "And now since it happens that I no longer esteem you,
and I believe nothing of what you say.
go to that city: there you shall be first
among that people who is so hostile
to ourselves and Nabuc, lord and god sublime,
so that you will know great sufferings
in the company of that people.
May they remain forever in sorrow, without hope."[32]

59. And thus did Holofernes command
his servants that they immediately take
Achior to the environs of that city,
because he counted as for nothing
his words, if well I discern them;
and he was obeyed without delay,
and Achior was led there in a great rage
because Lord Holofernes had given the command.

60. Hear how they led him away
to the city that stood prominently above,
while Holofernes remained encamped in the plain
and called out to Achior with a wicked laugh:

32. "Che sempre stia in doglia senza speme": a possible allusion to the fourth canto of Dante's *Inferno*, where Virgil speaks of his own lot as that of living in desire, but without hope ("sanza speme vivemo in disio," 4:42).

"If you return into my hands, as I imagine you will,
I will have all of my army mock you,
for you are a fool that did not know how
to enjoy the favors he has had from me."

61. Thus as they approached the city,
called Bethulia by name,
they saw an army emerge from within the walls,
and in truth the army had handsome men,
and they were all well armed;
in those days they were called *frombolatori*, or slingers.
When they saw Holofernes' men
(who were few in number), they came outside,

62. for they wanted to know who these people were
who dared to come so close to their city;
although their band was very small,
they certainly seemed to be from the enemy's side,
and they went along quietly, and they had no banner,
and it seemed as though they went in great haste.
When Holofernes had slipped from their sight,
they whispered among themselves: "Let's not wait any
longer!"[33]

63. Quickly then, they grabbed Achior,
and they harshly tied him to a tree;
and because they had no need to watch him further,
they left him and regained their path
and returned below to the spacious field
where they were awaited by their lord;
meanwhile, the men from that land had found Achior,
bound cruelly to the tree.

64. And then those slingers asked Achior
what he could tell them, and why he was there:
"Why are you bound in such bitter griefs,

33. Tornabuoni furnishes far more details of this scene than does Judith, which simply reports
that Holofernes' men "tied Achior to a tree hand and foot, and so left him bound with ropes,
and returned to their master."

and why do you suffer such mockery?"
and he answered: "Release me from these knots,
and for good reason: bound so tightly,
I can tell you nothing,
but if you untie me I will recount my story."

65. Then they quickly untied him
once they had understood his words,
and gazing closely at his face,
they saw he was someone from their region.
Had he remained there longer, he would have been dead:
each of them took great compassion on him;
they consoled him, and they led him to their city,
to which he could travel only with difficulty.

66. When he finally arrived at their strong city,
he was recognized as a great lord,
and the people came up to him within the gates,
caressing him and treating him with love,
and his faithful escorts went before him,
and they did him great honors,
leading him to the worthy palace
so he could recover from his discomfort.

67. And when he had rested a little, he said:
"Lords, I want to tell you the reason
why I was so constrained and bound
and why I was led here, as though to prison.
Holofernes had asked me questions,
he sought information from me about you;
and because I spoke the truth about your God,
I have known this evil torment.

68. "I spoke of the power of your God,
how he is just and full of charity,
and how much arrogance displeases him,
and how he takes great pleasure in humility.
You can see how ignorance
rules their general, how savage he can be;

he wanted me to worship a man of human flesh,
Nebuchadnezzar, barbarous and cruel.

69. "And making fun of what I had said,
he treated me with great disdain,
and he mocked me and was full of disrespect.
Hear what he said: 'I see you were not worthy
of our god, Nabuc, who is so perfect;
he will have all the world and make it his kingdom.
Now go to their city, without fail,
so that you will perish along with it!'

70. "And he sent me out, as you have seen;
see what favor and how many gifts
I have had from you, for you untied me.
Because of your kindness, I am still in this world.
It was my good fortune you were so quick to find me,
and I have back the life that had been abandoned,
and so I place myself thankfully within your hands,
so that I may be a good servant to you all."[34]

71. Hearing him recount these words,
everyone took great pity on him,
and they grieved strongly in their hearts,
for they did not wish to be led to these battles.
They wanted to be able to go
freely through the whole country as they always had done.
None of them wish to submit to such trials,
and of that tyrant they are greatly afraid.

72. On that day from the great city
of Jerusalem were sent to them
two priests, both men of much dignity,
accompanied by the prince Uzziah,
to bring the city help in this time of need.

---

34. The vast majority of this speech is Tornabuoni's invention, as are the expressions of pity
and consolation by the Hebrews. Clearly Tornabuoni is leading up to the moment in Jth. 14:
6 when Achior converts to Judaism; she describes his conversion in stanza 137.

They had been advised to come quickly
and to bring with them their wealth and sacred implements.
(They were descended from the tribe of Simeon.)

73. When they learned that Achior had come to them
because Holofernes himself had sent him,
they paid him great honor and did not refuse him,
and they kept him always by their side.
And the entire city saw to it
that fortifications did not lack in a single place,
because Holofernes was pressing them so forcefully
that they could not leave through any of the gates.

74. The city was well guarded and strong,
and it could not be taken in battle.
Holofernes had men who were trained in war
and they knew its craft very well;
and there was one among them who planned the following
and said: "I will cause them no end of grief,
I will cut off their water; thanks to my wit,
I have followed the signs of certain birds [and found the
     source]."[35]

75. To Holofernes he said: "I have found a means
of defeating them, and if you wish I will carry it out:
I will take from them their water, and my plan fulfilled,
to their chagrin they will die of thirst."
And Holofernes replied: "I praise our God for this,
I could have no greater pleasure
than to see them die so desperately;
if you can do this, I'll make you rich."

76. And as soon as he had this order
he left, taking with him several companions,
and once he had found the conduit
he quickly put himself to ruining it.
In one shot he dispatched the news to his companions,

---

35. The episode of the aqueduct occupies Jth. 7:6; Tornabuoni elaborates on it at some length
and makes cutting off the water the plan not of Holofernes, but of one of his ingenious soldiers.

so that everyone heard the promise:[36]
if they destroyed the duct, they would all be rich,
but none of them could break away before the work was
    done.

77. And when the aqueduct was shattered and destroyed,
    they made their return to Holofernes,
    and what they had done they recounted to him,
    and together all of them rejoiced
    because their plan had turned out so well;
    and so they rested peacefully for several days,
    believing they had taken all their water away
    because they had turned it from the duct.

78. It was true that this aqueduct drew together
    the vast majority of streams into one,
    so that into the city they no longer flowed;
    and all within were greatly troubled,
    so that their hope began to fail them.
    But their lamentations ceased when they found
    certain little springs
    with fresh and lovely water, just outside the gates.

79. Although the springs had precious little water
    to quench the thirst of all those people
    (for this was an enormous city,
    and in those days there was a greater multitude,
    since, to tell the truth, the love of the siege
    had brought many from Jerusalem,
    and their needs for water were great),
    yet with even so little, they defend themselves.

80. Holofernes watched to see
    how the people would manage in their great thirst,
    and as it happened, he was told

---

36. "Con que' compagni il mandò giù di botto / che ciaschedun la promessa sentia": Tornabuoni is indulging in figurative use of the phrase "mandare giù di botto" [to swallow, to send down the hatch in one shot]; here the phrase obviously concerns the promise the soldier has had from Holofernes.

they had found certain secret springs nearby,
and it was said to him:[37] "Go, and see them;
if you want to take this city, you will need to seize
this source of water too,
and then the city will instantly be yours."

81. When he learned this, he sent forth
many soldiers to guard the springs
so that the Hebrews can no longer go there;
he made his men take away this water from them too.
And he brought them into such dejection
that they no longer knew what to do;
they were no longer allowed to leave the city,
yet without water they could not remain within.

82. And for twenty days they lived in such a state,
there was no water anywhere to drink,
and they were dying of thirst; this people had nothing
with which they could refresh themselves,
and they no longer knew where to turn,
and reduced as they were to such extremes,
in their great thirst they began to say,
"Now, however, we all must die.

83. "Given the straits to which we are led,
it seems to us better to obey
that barbarian Holofernes than to continue in these torments:
if not, we will all die of thirst."
Once the priests heard their protests,
they answered their people with humble words:
"We want to ask of you only this favor:
wait just five more days to see what might happen.

84. "We know that this thirst burns and torments us,
and we all experience great suffering;
let us endure for just five days more,

---

37. "Sì hebbe a sapere" [he was given to know]: Judith is explicit about the source of this
knowledge: "The children of Ammon and Moab came to Holofernes" and told him about the
secret springs (Jth. 7:8).

and then let our Lord show us what we should do:
either we will implement your plan,
or God will aid us in our distress.
If he does nothing, let us make peace;
we will see if he will take pity on us."

85. When they heard the priests, they were content
to continue to suffer a little bit longer,
and they made offerings and vows to the Lord
so he would save them from their martyrdom.
Now take good note of my words:
see how the just Lord saw fit to exalt his people,
note in what manner he sent a remedy,
and see how they were liberated from that cruel siege.

86. The sons of Israel were racked
by harsh burdens, they lived in great fear of deception;
and as you will now hear,
their prayers were heard by God,
and he rescued them from harm.
You will witness his infinite grace;
he reveals his power to unbelievers,
and he gives victory to them who have faith.

87. In the city there was a young woman,
very virtuous and very beautiful too.
Judith was her name, and she was gracious,
noble and worthy, and possessed of every goodness;
she was valorous and had a manly heart,
hers was an honest and virtuous life.
For three years she had lived all alone as a widow,
and Judith did not seek another husband.[38]

88. Thinking about this siege and the constraints
in which her people found themselves,

---

38. Tornabuoni omits a good many details from Jth. 8:1–8: Judith's genealogy (one of the few genealogies provided for a woman in the Old Testament), her husband and how he died, her excessive reclusiveness and fasting (she has lived shut up in the upper part of her house for forty-two months), and her enormous wealth. But she also introduces one especially interesting detail, Judith's "manly heart" [d'animo virile].

this young woman fell into a quandary,
and she said to herself: "I would like to try
to see if I can come up with some remedy.
I will set out to prove if my plan might be useful,
and why not? otherwise, we are lost:
either dead of thirst, or subject to that pagan.

89. "If God wants to help his people escape,
he will put this plan into effect,
for he has placed in my heart what I must do:
through his grace he will give me such understanding
that I will know how to direct this plan
and have success." And after she spoke
she rose up and instantly went out,
going off to find her superiors.[39]

90. Judith took herself to the priests
and to the prince, Uzziah, and thus she said:
"May each of you note my words![40]
Through his grace, God has put it into my heart
to meddle in things so your vows will be heard,
and thus my Lord has promised me
that I might serve as the means
whereby our suffering might be alleviated and ended."

91. As they listened to all that Judith said,
the leaders were seized with a little hope:
"O gracious woman of such great worth,
such is our trust in both our God and you
that we believe you will save us from these evils
through your virtue and thanks to your courage;
tell us whatever it is we must do,
and gladly we will help as much as we can."

92. And she said: "Here is what I want from you:
tonight, you must be at the gates,

39. "Et presto usciva fuori": The biblical Judith has the rulers of the city come to her instead, and she speaks to them at far greater length than Tornabuoni's Judith does.
40. "Ciascun di voi le mie parole noti": a deliberate echo of the preceding line from stanza 85: "Or fa' che mie parole a punto noti."

the priests and the prince with his followers,
and you will utter devout prayers for me;
and once that is done, I will depart
with your blessing, as you will see."
Their hope renewed, they left in a hurry,
all bound for the gates, to wait for Judith.

93. Judith then returned to her house;
full of devotion, she entered her room;
she raised her mind up to her Lord
and began to utter this worthy prayer:
"Help me, God, in my going out,
so that I may be the liberation of your people;
help me, Lord, in this enterprise,
because you alone, my Lord, are my defense."[41]

94. As soon as Judith had finished her prayer,
she rose and began to make herself ready:
she washed both her body and her face
and made [herself] so neat and clean
that truly she seemed to be an angel;
in noble garments she dressed herself,
with precious perfumes she anointed her face,
and thus she seemed to have descended from paradise.[42]

95. And when the valiant woman tended to these things,
she called one of her handmaidens to her side

41. Once again Tornabuoni omits a considerable portion of Judith's discourse. In the Bible her prayer takes up all of chapter 9 (nineteen verses); Tornabuoni limits herself to a single stanza that in fact repeats almost nothing from Judith ("Aiutami, Signore, in questa andata, / ch'i' sia del popol tuo liberazione": in the Bible there is no parallel moment alluding specifically to Judith as the liberator of God's people). It is unclear why Tornabuoni should not avail herself of the opportunity to translate verses such as "Bring to pass, O Lord, that his pride may be cut off with his own sword" (Jth. 9:12) or "For this will be a glorious monument for thy name, when he shall fall by the hand of a woman" (Jth. 9:15). Is she anxious to downplay the militaristic overtones of the passage, or is she reluctant to sanction the biblical opposition between the humble *vedovetta* and God's overwhelming strength?

42. The Book of Judith makes a great deal more out of Judith's transition from widow to seductive young woman than does Tornabuoni: "She called her maid, and going down into her house she took off her haircloth, and put away the garments of her widowhood. . . . And the Lord increased this her beauty, so that she appeared to all men's eyes incomparably lovely" (Jth. 10:2–5).

and said: "Listen to what I tell you now,
do what I say, and do it with care:
you must bring enough food
to last us three days, excluding tonight."
This said, off she went to the gates
with this maidservant alone, and no other guide.

96. And when she arrived so richly adorned,
she made the priests who were gathered there marvel;
and as they beheld her great beauty,
they fell on their knees to beseech
the highest God to give her strength
and keep her safe until she returned;
and she wholeheartedly commends herself to him,
and then from the city she made her way.[43]

97. Judith came down from the mountain,
and when she walked out onto the plain,
she was seized by the spies of Holofernes,
and instantly they led her to him.
When Holofernes saw her, he was set aflame:
that ferocious heart of his became human,
and once he began to gaze at her lovely face
he could not take his eyes away from hers.[44]

98. Those knights who were in the service
of Holofernes all spoke among themselves:
"Let us linger here no longer to give them grief;
let us make peace with them at once!
Look at this woman: she seems a goddess.
If the others all resemble her,
then, our worthy lord, make peace with the Hebrews
so that we can stay here; we seek no other kingdom!"

99. Judith curtsied before Holofernes,
her countenance beautiful to behold,

43. "Et poi della cipta usciva fore": an echo of stanza 89, when Judith leaves her home to approach Uzziah and the priests: "Si levo su et presto usciva fuori."

44. The biblical phrase is suggestive: "Statim captus est in suis oculis Holofernes"—literally, Holofernes was caught in his eyes (Jth. 10:17). Tornabuoni avails herself of the Petrarchan language of love ("Come la vide fu la mente accesa").

and he gave her tender audience in turn,
lavishing caresses as though he were her lover.
"For what reason have you left your people
and ventured forth to us?"
Judith answered, and said, "O my lord,
I will tell you the reason why I come.[45]

100. "Holofernes, my most worthy lord,
I will tell you because you wish to know.
A sign has come to our people from God:
destruction draws near, and such is only fitting:
they who have taken the pledge [to be our priests]
are the very ones who have sold the sacred vessels
of the altar, vessels made of silver and gold,
only to gain things necessary for their lives.

101. "And now what they command us is far worse:
although it is forbidden, they want us to drink
the blood of animals, since they expect
no other remedy from any quarter,
and they have made a mockery of their God,
refusing to observe his commands.
And they are afflicted, and because of their hunger
and thirst they feel that they are already dead.

102. "Know that my God has sent me here
so I might reveal these things to you:
the God I will worship here with purest heart
and thus he commanded and imposed on me
this journey, that I come to you with love,
that I reveal everything and hold nothing back,
for it is up to you to show us the day
when he wants his people to pay the penalty.[46]

45. "O signor mio, / la cagion ti dirò perché veng'io." Note that Judith greets Holofernes
with the *tu* or informal mode of address, suggesting that she views him as her equal. Holofernes'
soldiers, on the other hand, use the more formal *voi* when speaking to him (e.g., stanza 75:
"se voi vorrete il metterò in effetto").

46. Once again Tornabuoni seems to neglect an opportunity to make Judith a more sym-
bolically charged character; the biblical text has her referring to herself as Holofernes'
handmaid (*ancilla*), a designation that would evoke parallels with, among others, Mary and
Susanna.

103. "The punishments he metes out are strong and harsh
when the sins they commit are similar to these:
first he torments them, then he follows with death;
in such matter are they treated by their Lord.
Thus I will let you inside the gates
of this ungrateful and unfortunate people;
you will seize Jerusalem within several hours,
because you will find it a godless place."[47]

104. Then Holofernes answered her:
"If you will do those things that you have told me,
you will see your god of such magnificent works
in the numbers of my followers;
these events are so marvelous, and of such great worth,
that you will find favor from Nebuchadnezzar
for this good counsel you have given me;
he is a grateful god."

105. Moved by all the love he bore her,
he turned to see his treasurer,
and he made a sign for him to come quickly;
willingly he came to his side,
and Holofernes said: "I order you:
place her who is like the rose of an orchard
here tonight among my treasures,
let her sleep there with her maidservant.[48]

106. "And, my wise treasurer, make sure she is given
splendid things to eat,
and let nothing be lacking to her,
and take care that no wish of hers is denied."
Judith heard him and said:
"I have brought with me my own food;

---

47. "I will let you inside the gates" [Allor ti mettero dentro alle porti]: one wonders if Tornabuoni is thinking of the *Aeneid*, book 2, in which the Greeks are allowed to enter the gates of Troy through the stealth of Sinon. One of the most famous (if unfinished) contemporary manuscripts of the *Aeneid* was made in the early 1470s for the Medici family, with illustrations by Apollonio da Giovanni and his workshop. The illustration of the siege of Priam's palace in book 2 is clearly based on the design of the Palazzo Medici on Via Larga, where Tornabuoni and her family lived.

48. This and the next eight stanzas adhere fairly closely to Judith 12.

I must not eat things given me by others
if I am to escape the wrath of my God."

107. Holofernes said to her: "But what is to happen
      when the food you brought with you is finished,
      what then will you eat?" And she replied:
      "I believe that I have brought enough.
      You have my word: I promise you in faith:
      this God of whom you hear me speak
      will show me so clearly what I must do
      that I know I will have from him great rewards.

108. "I ask of you this favor alone:
      leave me free to go outside the camp at night
      to worship him, so that I do not fall
      into disgrace before the Lord of Lords."
      And he responded: "Your wish is granted;
      now go outside and make sure you honor him."
      She thanked him and she took her leave,
      departing quickly to her chamber.

109. For three nights Judith went outside the camp,
      where she devoutly said her prayers,
      and with great devotion and with much care
      she washed herself in pure, fresh water.
      "Lord God, help me to be wise!"
      Sincerely she uttered this prayer,
      that she might assist her people in such cruel times
      and release them from these hardships.

110. The fourth day came, and Holofernes
      held a great feast for all his barons,
      and to his faithful servant Bagoas he said: "Go
      and bring me that Hebrew woman; with eloquent words
      tell her she should comply with my full wishes,
      and press her with good reasons
      so that she will come to my banquet to sit with me,
      because it is urgent that I speak with her."

111. His manservant Bagoas went to find Judith
      and said to her: "O young woman of goodwill,

while you linger here by yourself and so lonely,
you make my lord suffer.
Come dine with him, for he awaits you;
to stay here like this is not at all seemly.
Go to him now and have no fear;
he loves you more than any creature in the world."

112. Judith listened to his words
and showed that she was quite happy:
"Willingly will I come; I do not at all regret
what it is that he commands;
I want to obey him, all my life I shall do
whatever he wishes, so disposed am I
to honor his desire. Tell your lord I will be ready
as soon as I dress in my worthiest garments."

113. Bagoas returned to Holofernes
and told him Judith was coming of her own will,
and that she had gone to dress herself without delay:
"I think that even now she is on her way.
She has a face so pleasing and noble,
O lord, she is so elegant and lovely,
possessed of so many sweet manners;
I don't think she will ever wish to leave you."

114. When Duke Holofernes heard him say
that Judith was coming so willingly,
the worthy sire greatly rejoiced
and instantly called one of his manservants:
"Now go, bring me something to wear,
that short garment that fits me best,
in which I look most handsome." His beard and his hair
he cleaned, and he put on his fingers valuable rings.[49]

115. He awaited Judith in this fashion,
neat and trim and richly adorned,

49. This almost charming portrait of Holofernes in stanzas 114 and 115 is Tornabuoni's invention, as are the prayer that Judith utters in 116 and the subsequent greeting of Judith by Holofernes in 117 and 118.

and he wanders among his guests
saying cheerful and happy little words to all.
Throughout his pavilion he sprays pleasing perfumes,
and it was not for nothing that he did so;
and so with happy thoughts did he await her,
fervently desiring that she join him.

116. Judith, before she left for that place,
knelt down upon the ground
and with pure heart and with firm intent,
she turned her words to the true God,
words that were pious, full of strong affection;
then she rose up, unpreoccupied
with what was to come. She was so beautifully adorned
it seemed that all that she lacked were wings.

117. Along with her maidservant, she went off
to the pavilion of Holofernes, the lord,
and upon reaching him she knelt down before him
with a pleasing greeting and much reverence.
As soon as he saw her, he instantly rose
and with a few short steps he came to her side;
he took her by the hand with great gladness and said,
"Welcome, flower of all beauty!

118. "How well you have done this evening
in coming here to dine with us!"
She replied in sweet manner:
"Willingly I did it, and just to please you."
It was springtime, when all of our hearts
are inflamed with love, and Holofernes
wanted it to be springtime forever
so that winter would never come.

119. Thus did they go in to dinner;
they expected no others that night
besides the guests who had already arrived,
and Holofernes made a hearty welcome
to those who had come and those who were present.
Everything there seemed delightful to him,

he does not ask for love, but simply gives it,
everything seems to be lovely, within and without.

120. The evening's banquet was magnificent,
abundant with delicacies,
among them a wine that was so precious
to drink it gave one both appetite and thirst.
Do not even ask if Holofernes was joyous;
it seemed to him a thousand years before the guests would
leave
so he could remain alone with Judith,
who for her part remained apprehensive.[50]

121. Judith took care how much she drank,
and she said to herself: "I need to watch out!
See him sending down drinks without restraint;
he drinks with both his right hand and his left.[51]
This could now well be a sign of my good fortune;
divine grace will surely assist me now."
After he finished dining in great delight,
Holofernes began to nod off.

122. When they had eaten to their hearts' content,
the people were dismissed and took their leave
and having no suspicion of what was to come,
all of them returned to their quarters.
Holofernes took himself to bed,
because his eyes were heavy with sleep.
Down he threw himself into his ruin:
and divine power was the cause of it all.

123. He had hardly fallen into his bed
when very loudly, he began to snore;
his head was dangling off to the side

50. "La quale stava pur molto sospetta": a detail not found in Judith, where the heroine comes
across as more self-assured.

51. "E' se ne dà da ritto e da mancina": Pezzarossa sees an echo here of Lorenzo de' Medici's
youthful *Simposio* 2.102, "or gnene dà da ritto e da mancino"; Tornabuoni, *Poemetti sacri,* 41–
42. If the filiation Pezzarossa proposes is true—that Tornabuoni was influenced by Lorenzo's
writing—then 1474 would be the earliest that *Judith* could have been written.

so that it did not even rest on a pillow.
Judith then warned her handmaiden
to let no one through the entrance:
"And guard it well for reasons I will tell you;
if I succeed you will have from me great favors."

124. And with much reverence,
Judith fell to her knees and began to pray:
"Comfort me, Lord; be clement with me;
give me daring, strength, and victory.
O Lord of Israel, in your power and pity,
do not let us perish;
may your people escape from these dogs
and let the victory be through my hands."[52]

125. Once she had said her prayer
Judith rose, her heart resolved,
and in one hand she grasped a sword she had found
leaning against a column or the wall,
and so well did the young woman brandish it
it would have been fitting for a strong and sturdy man;
she struck him twice, with force,
and his head rolled away from his shoulders.

126. And after this the valiant woman
cut it clean, for there was little left to do,
and she took it carefully in her hands
and she gave it to her handmaiden,
and she said to her, "Say nothing";
and from the curtain encircling the bed,
she tore a piece of fabric and bundled into it
only the head, which she intended to carry away.

127. Then the young woman instantly departed,
making her way toward the city,

52. "Questa victoria fia per le mie mani": Judith is in some ways more equivocal: "Strengthen me, O Lord God of Israel . . . that I may bring to pass that which I have purposed, having a belief that it might be done by thee" [Et hoc quod credens per te posse fieri cogitavi, perficiam] (Jth. 13:7).

and her servant carried the head.[53]
They arrived at the gate, and she began to call out:
"Open up at once, and let us make merry;
now come out with clean hearts to thank
our great and omnipotent God,
for to us he dispenses his favor!"

128.   The gate was shortly opened,
for they heard that Judith had returned,
and the multitude of people came out
carrying torches, the young and the old;
all of them came quickly
to see the woman they so prized.
Said Judith: "Now may God be thanked,
for he has saved us from evil torments."

129.   And when she said this, that excellent woman
drew the head out from the curtain,
the head that she so quickly packed away
when she became Holofernes' scourge.
"Now let each of us devoutly praise
the divine Majesty with strong hearts;
he has given us an enormous victory:
you alone are God, you alone the Lord of glory.

130.   "You alone are the one who can do all things,
and all things come into being through you;
you alone have the power to give and take away,
and from you come all marvelous works.
O my Lord, how much I have to thank you
for your bounty, which you never conceal;
through my hands, you have given us victory,
you preserved me and returned me in safety.

131.   "From this siege you set us free,
from great dangers and from their fury,
from Holofernes, who to every misery
subjected us: he plunged us into suffering and grief.

53. This is the scene Botticelli depicts in his painting of a dreamy-looking Judith and her maidservant on the road to Bethulia.

We were without remedy, we found no succor,
either within our city or without,
but you, O Lord, you sent him to his ruin
and showed once and for all who is master."[54]

132. All the people gathered there to see
beautiful Judith, who inspired such trust;
they gaze at the head, which they still fear,
since the dead thing made them feel so afraid.
They showed it to Achior so he would find pleasure,
but when he gazed on the head, he was so overcome
that he fell down as though he were dead;
but soon thereafter, he regained his senses.

133. When he recovered, he said to Judith:
"Oh, how much favor you have had from God;
I believe that you are blessed by him,
and filled with every virtue.
I want you to take this cursed head,
and mount it upon the wall so it can be seen,
and then tomorrow morning when it is day,
they will see their loss and our disdain."

134. And they did exactly what Achior said,
placing that head upon the wall
so that by everyone it could easily be seen.
Then he said: "Make sure to arm your people quickly;
you will find their camp unprovided for,
and surely you can inflict on them grave harm."
Such counsel pleased Uzziah, and he gave his consent
and commands: "Hurry, everyone take up arms!"

135. More quickly than lightning they seize their weapons,
and instantly they go to assault the camp;

---

54. Once again Tornabuoni omits the biblical language implicitly contrasting Holofernes'
(and God's) strength to a woman's traditional weakness ("Behold the head of Holofernes . . .
and behold his canopy, wherein he lay in his drunkenness, where the Lord our God slew him
by the hand of a woman" [per manum feminae] (Jth. 13:19). Tornabuoni's Judith simply refers
to the work of her hands ("per le mie mani la victoria hai donata") with no reference to her
gender; the phrase echoes an earlier passage in the Book of Judith, "And he hath killed the
enemy of his people by my hand this night" [in manu mea] (Jth. 13:18).

the road from the city was so full of men
there are not more grains of sand on the shore.
Seeing them come, the enemy suffers,
this army of great strength and even greater dejection.
The head of Holofernes is upon the wall,
and in fury the Hebrews advance without fear.

136. And not knowing now what part to play,
since all of them see their numbers so scarce,
and they no longer have anyone to offer them counsel,
the Assyrians begin to take off in flight;
and they want to instantly leave that country
where they fear they will come into battle,
and they said: "Here come the mice from their holes,
out they come to ensure our dejection."

137. Achior saw these great events unfold,
and he said: "Surely this is the true God
who offers his grace to those whose hearts are sincere;
I too wish to taste their food,
I too want to become circumcised
and live according to their strict laws,
all that I want to do now is serve him;
as long as I live, I will honor him."

138. Bagoas, the manservant of Holofernes,
found out what had happened to his lord,
and in a loud voice he shouted:
"They have led us into chaos, and brought us great grief:
a Hebrew woman has brought such injury and shame,
my heart will never rejoice at anything again!
Nebuchadnezzar must have vengeance
on the Hebrew people and their Judith!"[55]

139. And instantly Prince Uzziah
set about sending letters out

55. The scene of the discovery of Holofernes' body was painted with chilling effect by Botti-
celli, probably in 1467–70. It is with this phrase uttered by Vaggio, "una donna giudea," that
in both the Hebrew and the Italian one might notice the pun at the story's center: the name
Judith is in fact the generic word for "a Jewish woman."

to all the nearby lands and cities:
they should come join him in this enterprise,
and help in catching that riffraff;
and he asked them to come armed, but without pride,
so they could win the day without risking danger,
and so that God would give them victory.

140. The people of Bethulia were so emboldened,
as were those of the neighboring towns,
that they chased their enemy all the way to the border,
where some were taken and others cut to pieces;
although they were many, they were so dejected
that from there they were easily routed.
When they had passed beyond the borders,
the Hebrews let some of those wretches go.

141. And leading a great number of prisoners,
they returned to their enemies' camp,
and there they found many possessions
because so many countries had been despoiled;
and these treasures that they gathered
had lent great dignity to their barracks,
and the pavilion of Holofernes was full of them,
and so were the others as well.

142. This booty of which you hear
was gathered together by orders of Uzziah;
it had cost him nothing to capture,
and he dispersed it among his barons,
and it took a month with no rest to do this work,
to give them what they deserved and himself as well;
but the things that were seized from Holofernes
were given to Judith, and everyone praised this.

143. The goods and the treasures of Holofernes
were given by Prince Uzziah to Judith
as eternal memory of her deed,
for she had cut his life so short;
thanks be given to God forever,

who allowed great vengeance to be carried out
through the fearful little widow,
such pride brought down by such a lowly creature.[56]

144. Judith clearly merited
that great and generous treasure,
she remembered her handmaiden
and happily gave some of it to her:
"Now here, I don't want to be ungrateful to you,
for you helped me and you were so prudent";
and she gave her bountiful treasures,
with which she could marry well.

145. From the city of Jerusalem
the high priest traveled without stopping,
by name Joachim; he could not rest until he saw
the valorous Judith, and he could not refrain
from praising her virtuous works,
how dexterously she carried them out,
together with the priests in his train,
who followed him into the city of Bethulia.

146. And when they had visited her, each one,
and she had made them all marvel greatly,
they made Bethulia their resting place
for several days, feasting and taking pleasure,
always praising God for such good work
and blessing her with happy faces,
asking God to preserve in true love
this woman of such valiant heart.[57]

---

56. "Tanta superbia ad questa sì vil cosa." The "vil cosa" here is the "vedovetta temorosa," the fearful widow who lays such "superbia" to rest. There is a possible echo here of the inscription on Donatello's *Judith*, "caesa vides humili colla superba manu" (see the proud neck being severed by the humble hand); the introduction (p. 47) discusses this further.

57. Thus does Judith disappear from a story that continues to focus only on her in the Book of Judith: Jth. 16:1–21 is her lengthy canticle to the Lord, and lines 22–31 describe the holocausts and victory celebration and Judith's last days; her perpetual chastity is also stressed. Tornabuoni omits any mention of this, returning instead to focus on Nebuchadnezzar's swift demise. Perhaps Tornabuoni was drawing on a passage in Daniel 5, in which Daniel tells King Belshazzar about his father: "But when his heart became proud and his spirit hardened by

147. When he learned of all that had passed,
     Nebuchadnezzar was crushed; he lamented
     the defeat at the hands of the Hebrews,
     which had brought him into such trouble,
     and enraged he said: "Not even a sixth
     of my men are dead, but the death of my
     valorous Holofernes is bad enough,
     for a better captain I never have had."

148. And he departed from Egypt with more men
     than the worthy [Holofernes] had gathered,
     to vindicate the harm he had suffered;
     they had been martyred at the hands of the Hebrews.
     But the great and omnipotent Lord
     never forgets those who serve him well,
     and he did not want Nabuc to have so much power
     and sent him a dark and heavy penance.

149. The enraged Nebuchadnezzar
     wishes to turn upon the Hebrews,
     but a strange sickness came upon him
     that afflicted his whole body:
     every limb was stricken,
     and he was able neither to sit still nor go,
     neither to ride his horse nor do anything at all,
     so strange and terrible was this disease.

150. And it was necessary for his barons
     to carry him on their shoulders
     or find special litters to accommodate him;
     still, he took from this mode of travel
     little comfort or solace,
     and he had to turn back and was brought
     to Damascus without delay, where
     because of his grave sickness Nabuc finished his days.

---

insolence, he was put down from his royal throne and deprived of his glory; he was cast out
from among men and was made insensate as a beast" (Dan. 5:19–21).

151. When he died, he was buried
in the kingdom of Persia
by his barons, with much honor; thus his
cruel appetite met with a fitting end.
May you, omnipotent Lord, be thanked,
who drew me out of the sea to the shore,
and I am now in harbor, where my heart
offers up to you my weak and unpolished rhymes.

THE STORY OF
QUEEN ESTHER

INTRODUCTION

There are more manuscript versions of Esther surviving from the medieval period than of any other biblical book.[1] Clearly it has continuing relevance for Judaism as an etiological narrative that explains the origins of the festival of Purim. For medieval and Renaissance Christians, however, one must find other rationales for its popularity. One possibility is that it is a dramatic example of the *de casibus* literature that was so popular in the Middle Ages, as it starkly contrasts the rise and fall of wicked princes with the corresponding exaltation of a faithful and once lowly people. One recent scholar has also seen an instance of wisdom literature in this story of a young Hebrew woman who, with the aid of her uncle, marries the Babylonian king Ahasuerus and dares to become the savior of her people.[2] Like the other biblical stories Tornabuoni turned to, particularly Judith and Susanna, it gives us the story of a male leader who is overcome by sin—in this case the wicked Haman, right-hand man of the king—and whose demise enables the triumph of a woman and her people. Rebuffed by Esther's uncle, Mordecai, Haman sets out to persecute and murder all the Jews, enslaved by the Babylonians after the fall of Jerusalem. But Mordecai's own fidelity to the Babylonian king, and his ability to persuade his niece to take her life in her hands and admit to the king her Hebrew origins, sets the stage for Haman's fall and the Jews' deliverance from persecution. The biblical text ends with the Hebrews turning the tables on their would-be persecutors, and the feast of Purim celebrates their slaughter of those who had been instructed by Haman to kill *them*.

1. Carey A. Moore discusses the importance of Esther for both Jews and Christians during the Middle Ages (Esther, Anchor Bible, xxiii–xxx).
2. "According to Werner Dommershausen, Esther is 'veiled Wisdom Theology'" (quoted in Esther, Anchor Bible, xxxiv).

Tornabuoni downplays this violent aspect of the text, partly, it seems, so she can focus on the story's heroine. Such a focus is consistent with the Greek version of the book that Jerome used for the Vulgate; the Greek Esther has passages not in the Hebrew version, and Jerome placed them at the end of Esther and thus out of sequence. Two passages in particular portray Esther in far more detail, allowing readers considerable insight into her dilemma as the wife of a king whose deputy is hostile to her people: her fervent prayer to God once she learns that Haman has ordered the murder of the Hebrews (Esther 14:1–19) and the dramatic delineation of her appearance before the king to plead for his mercy when she asks that the Hebrews be spared (Esther 15:4–19). Importantly, Tornabuoni chooses to integrate these passages directly into the story line where they belong, thus organizing her narrative along chronological lines, unlike Jerome's version in the Vulgate. Tornabuoni also elaborates on both of these passages, as well as on a number of earlier moments in the text—embellishments that suggest another reason for her choice of *Esther* as one of her *storie sacre*. For the Book of Esther begins with the Babylonian king Ahasuerus or Artaxerxes (Xerxes in the Hebrew version) married not to Esther but to another woman, Vashti. He hosts a lavish banquet for his many guests from all over the kingdom and asks that Vashti appear "with the crown set upon her head, to show her beauty to all the people and the princes, for she was exceedingly beautiful" (Esther 1:11). But Vashti, for some reason that Esther does not make explicit, refuses to come,[3] and at the behest of his seven wise sages, Ahasuerus divorces her and looks for another wife.

Eventually the king chooses Esther out of a large harem of virgins from all over his kingdom. What occupies only the first nine lines in the biblical book—the initial description of the feast—becomes almost two chapters in Tornabuoni as the Florentine author lingers lovingly over the furnishings and draperies of the palace and the garden.[4] More important, the scene

3. See the suggestion of recent feminist scholars of the Bible such as Lillian Klein, who, following rabbinical commentary, argues that Ahasuerus's command that the queen come before him and his guests risks degrading her to the status of a concubine. Hence Vashti "is faced with a dilemma: whether to relinquish her claim to honor through abandoning her modesty and appearing in a forbidden masculine space, or through defying her husband's authority" ("Honor and Shame in Esther," 155).

4. As Orvieto has suggested, Tornabuoni may owe much of her detail to the lavish description of Venus's palace in the first book of Poliziano's *Stanze*, as well as to the depictions of the many pavilions described by Pulci in the *Morgante* and in the *cantari* tradition more generally (25–26). This passage was apparently one that many other translators of Esther also amplified at length. Bach observes that the setting of the banquet in the first chapter of Esther occasioned a number of elaborate retellings in medieval Jewish commentary; hence she notes that "medieval readers fill[ed] the gaps of description of the Persian palace with *medieval* details. . . . [They] dream[ed] up increasingly exotic decorations: elegant billowing canopies, crenelated

with Vashti becomes the occasion for extensive moralizing by Tornabuoni, as she counsels women to submit to their husbands and speculates on Vashti's eventual fate: "Women, learn nothing from this queen: / be prudent, and listen to my words / with great care and discretion. / And if you do not think that what I say is right, / consider Vashti; I myself would guess / that much wretchedness befell her." Such a direct and explicit address to a female audience is nowhere to be found in the biblical source.

Yet such attention to women's "prudence and discretion" is not, in fact, borne out by the rest of the story, for Esther's uniqueness consists in her willingness to *disobey* what she believes to be royal custom and approach her despotic husband without being summoned. Even as Tornabuoni paints a convincing picture of her anxiety as she goes into the palace—as in the Vulgate, she must lean on her handmaiden for support—we also receive a glimpse of her coy strategizing. Thus, after she nearly faints she "turns to the king with a sweet laugh. / And she said to herself, "Now I will have vengeance: / O my Lord, teach me how to speak; / so I will know how to utter words that will persuade." The biblical Esther petitions the king twice, once for the deliverance of her people, then again asking him to revoke the letters Haman had sent out. Tornabuoni's Esther petitions him yet a third time when she asks that Haman's ten sons be hanged too. Thus even if Vashti must serve as a counterpoint of the disobedient wife, Esther cannot be seen as her exact opposite, particularly in Tornabuoni's retelling. She too disobeys; she simply does so more strategically.

And she does so, of course, not for her own purposes, but for her people, as Tornabuoni emphasizes as well. Tornabuoni's *Esther* takes far greater liberties with the biblical text than do her other Old Testament poems. One of the most telling additions occurs when Esther informs the king that she knows about Haman's order to slaughter the Hebrews. Up to this time she has kept her Hebrew origins a secret; now she must reveal them. In the Bible, Ahasuerus shows no curiosity about Esther's request that he rescind the order; he is primarily concerned with learning who has lied to him about the Hebrews' supposed wickedness. Tornabuoni is far more intent on creating a psychological portrait of the king, making him curious—and perhaps compassionate—enough to ask Esther "Why do you petition me / for these people, and care so much that they suffer?" Esther's reply is a fitting climax to a scene to which Tornabuoni has carefully led us—indeed, we are a mere two chapters away from the poem's end: "It is

---

curtains covering the ceiling, curtains suspended by purple silken ropes tied to marble pillars set into silver wheels" (*Women, Seduction, and Betrayal*, 91n). One wonders whether Tornabuoni may have known of such interpretations, described, as Bach notes, by Barry Walfish in *Esther in Medieval Garb*.

fitting, my lord, / because I am Hebrew, and one of their people. / Not to plead on their behalf would hardly be just. / . . . / I too am implicated in this cruel sentence; / I too must die, in the same way / that all of the Hebrews must die." In having Esther openly acknowledge her real identity, Tornabuoni highlights the courage of her heroine before a king whose favorable reaction to her petition is by no means assured. He in turn recognizes the magnitude of what she has done when he responds: "Much do I praise you, / for not allowing this evil deed to happen; / it gives me great joy to learn you are one of them."

Tornabuoni's boldness in the poem is evident in more places than these suspenseful exchanges between the king and queen. Far more than in her other *storie sacre,* she refers to the grace she has been given to compose her "operetta," or little work. God himself commends her poetry in the poem's second chapter when he instructs her to take up her singing again in his name, and the end of the poem is almost jubilant in acknowledging its success: "I thank you [Lord], and I bless the hour / that you revealed to me this fantasy; / you inflamed my heart with fire for this little work. / And you came with me as a companion, / as you promised, and I was ever content; / and you constantly showed me the way." Such an expression may simply be a sign of Tornabuoni's relief at finishing what is her longest poem; by the same token, it conveys a sense of confidence that is not always apparent in her other works.

If Judith and Susanna were to have a singular "renaissance" in Florentine Italy, Esther was not; there are far fewer plays and artworks based on her than on the other two Old Testament women who were the subjects of Tornabuoni's poetry. (Such would not be the case for a later century, however; Handel's first English oratorio was his *Esther,* composed in 1718 and revised in 1732.) At the same time, one of the most important works based on the story of Esther during the fifteenth century had its provenance in Florence, from the workshop of Filippino Lippi; several panels detailing the central events in the Esther story, probably painted about 1480, survive in European museums. Moreover, one must not overlook the numerous pairings of Esther and the Old Testament heroine Judith throughout the medieval and early modern periods.[5] New Testament typologizing tended to interpret them both as paradigms for Mary, in that they are said to prefigure Mary's own deliverance of her people. They were paired most dramatically

---

5. Citing several patristic works dating from the first several centuries C.E., Moore notes that "allusions to the bravery of Judith and Esther are mentioned in the same breath," and Augustine lists Esther, Judith, and Tobias side by side (Esther, Anchor Bible, xxviii).

in Michelangelo's Sistine Chapel, where they illustrate divine intervention: Esther and the treacherous Haman (who is portrayed as being crucified) are balanced against Judith and Holofernes in two of the lunettes in the cloister vault.

The Mariological potential of the story may well be one reason Torna-buoni chose to include *Esther* among her poems, although she does not exploit that potential as fully as she might have. Mary is invoked only in the proem of *La vita di Sancto Giovanni Baptista*, the one work in which Mary appears as a character. Nonetheless, Tornabuoni deliberately links Esther to the role of handmaiden or *ancilla*, a word Mary uses to refer to herself in the Gospel of Luke (and that Tornabuoni uses in *The Life of Saint John the Baptist* and in *Susanna*). And Tornabuoni's choice to accentuate Esther's self-sacrifice for her people with her frank admission of her Judaism strengthens her links to Mary, who likewise submits to the needs of her people and her God.

HERE BEGINS THE STORY OF QUEEN ESTHER: HOW SHE LIBERATED HER PEOPLE, THE HEBREWS, FROM THE HANDS OF THEIR ENEMIES. COMPOSED IN TERZA RIME BY THE MAGNIFICENT AND NOBLE WOMAN MADONNA LUCREZIA, WHO WAS WIFE OF THE MAGNIFICENT MAN PIERO DI COSIMO DE' MEDICI

[*Preamble*]

I call out your name, O glorious Lord,
    because you are the authentic guide.
    Who follows you finds true repose.
In you my mind trusts, and I hope
    you will assist my feeble talents
    as I compose in rhyme this entire story.
As I set out to speak of this work,
    I would like to color it as I've designed it
    in my heart, and in a manner that will please.
Lord, if I were to have from you this favor,
    I would not number it among the least of things
    for which I have beseeched you and received from you.
But there is little I could have that is greater
    than what you have given me as my destiny,
    even though my verses are so poor.

In the name of Jesus, human and divine,
    I will begin, and in him alone I hope,
    and trust that he will not abandon me
as I tell of that great king, Ahasuerus,
    and his wife, whom he held in such esteem.
    Niece of Mordecai, a most just and holy man,
she was called Esther, and was wiser than the king's first
    [wife].
    And as I will tell you in my rhyme,
    she liberated her people from death,
from the hand that was so powerful and strong,
    that sought to kill the children of Israel.
    But God protected them from that fate.
And I will sing of Queen Vashti, who withheld herself
    from her husband and was disobedient,
    whence she deserved the shameful things that befell her.
Oh how sad she was, and mournful,
    because she had not obeyed her lord.
    But when repentance comes too late, it is of little use.

                        Chapter 1

King Ahasuerus was highly regarded;[6]
    he was king of India, lord of Ethiopia,
    one hundred and twenty-seven provinces were his,
and he possessed riches in abundance;
    and he ruled with great fairness,
    and he was liberal with his wealth.
And in the third year of his reign,
    he wanted to gather his barons together:
    "I mean those who are valiant,
so they will better understand my words."
    Thus he commanded, and put his mind
    to wherever he had jurisdiction,
and he extended his order even
    to the farthest reaches of his kingdom,
    so that no one would feel cheated.[7]

---

6. After this rather long preamble, Tornabuoni launches into *Esther*, which opens with this account of Ahasuerus's kingdom and wealth.

7. The remainder of this chapter embellishes on the description of the two banquets with which Ahasuerus feted, first, the great princes of his kingdom, and second, the citizens of his

It was springtime, when the world dresses itself again
   in fresh greens; the day grows longer,
   and evening fades more quickly.
This worthy lord does not conceal
   his liberality; he would make it felt
   in all places, even beyond the sea.
In Persia he began to put his words into works,
   and he invited to a magnificent banquet
   all of the barons that I mentioned above.
The time and the place were confirmed,
   and so he ensured that everyone could have
   whatever appealed most to his appetite and tastes.
Because I think you would like to know
   the number of days they feasted and the foods they ate,
   I will tell you; they were there for one hundred and
      thirty![8]
And just as he had done in Persia,
   so did he do the same in Media,
   throughout all his great and magnificent kingdom.
As I have said, the guests lacked nothing,
   they had choice foods of every variety
   and they took great delight in much besides eating.
It's a good idea for me to return
   to the city where Ahasuerus held his court:
   it was called Susa, its true name.[9]
And because describing to you the beautiful
   decorations is so much work,
   I will call again on my faithful guide

---

city of Susa. Even the biblical text supplies a surprising amount of detail about the palace of Ahasuerus and the orchard in which he holds his banquet—we hear about the hangings in the garden, the beds, and the golden cups the guests drank from. But Tornabuoni expands a mere four verses into 156 lines of poetry.

    Several scholars have recently commented on all or part of this extensive passage; see Paolo Orvieto's introduction to Tornabuoni, *Istoria della casta Susanna* and Martelli's "Lucrezia Tornabuoni."

8. "Trenta furono et cento, puo vedere": The Bible says that the guests dined for 180 days; additionally, the feast is held in only one place. It is not clear why Tornabuoni would have deviated from the text on these details. Martelli suggests the possibility of scribal error (*Femmes écrivains en Italie au Moyen Âge et à la Renaissance*, 81).

9. Tornabuoni now turns her attention to the second series of festivities Ahasuerus organized (Esther 1:5: "And when the days of the feast were expired, he invited all the people that were found in Susa, from the greatest to the least; and commanded a feast to be made seven days in the court of the garden, and of the wood").

so he can give new force to my words, which come so
   slowly, in the hope that he will conduct me to harbor
   and send my sails a fresh wind.
This worthy lord, for his pleasure
   had a garden in the city,
   or rather I should say a comely and fertile orchard.
And to enter it, one took a straight path
   that led through a graceful loggia
   made of costly and precious stones.
It had been built by many fine sculptors;
   its alabaster columns were perfectly straight,
   each one ornate and beautifully carved.
Half of them gleamed in porphyry,
   the other half in serpentine;
   to look at them, you would think they were emerald.
The walls that encircled the loggia
   were so beautifully made with elegant stone
   that midnight almost appeared to be day.[10]
The floor in truth
   was so resplendent with fine jasper
   that it was a great honor to behold.
The ceiling of the loggia
   was made of such polished, shining sapphire
   that to think of it can only astonish;
it seems not the work of humans, but gods;
   and there were stars in the ceiling
   cast in gold, and set in a sea of ultramarine,
and their rays and their fire were so sparkling
   that to gaze on them dazzled the eyes;
   I wish I could tell you how beautiful they were.
Now to proceed with my description:
   it remains for me to speak of the decorations,
   and I will say as much of them as my desire can
      attain.
For there is much left for me to recount,
   such as the wonderful tapestries hanging in the garden
   that lent it such elegance:
Draperies of silk, of silver and fine gold,

10. Martelli sees here an echo of Poliziano's *Stanze* (1:95): "Che chiaro giorno a meza nocte accenda."

spun of many patterns and diverse colors,
some white and green and others alexandrine,[11]
and they were embroidered with roses and flowers
in such subtle fashion, with such mastery,
that never had such worthy handiworks been seen.
The white and red roses that one could see
were so artfully displayed on a green backdrop
that to mention it will seem almost to lie;
and real roses could not compete with these, and
the same could be said for other flowers in that work,
the violets, the fleurs-de-lis, and the green fronds.
The cords that suspended these drapes
were threaded here with gold and there with silk.
Now I will move on, without delay,
inside the palace, where my memory tells me
there were bedrooms and sitting rooms just as
priceless and beautiful as all that I have recounted;
but to speak of the dwelling place of the king
and how beautifully it was adorned
would require more intellect than I possess,
and my wit is practically spent;
so my mind rests here, thoughtful
of what to say of the building's structure:
The girders were made of ivory, on top of which rested
the platform, and the roof was wrought in ebony
and it appeared a lovely work.
The golden couches were also enameled
with pearls and precious gems, so one
was thrown into a stupor to see such furniture.
And because the king wished the banquet to be noble,
he asked that the table be adorned
with vessels for drinking and utensils for eating,
all made of precious and valuable stones,
diamonds and emeralds of great worth
and other costly and impressive jewels.
Thus he made all these preparations
to honor his barons
and to demonstrate his magnanimous heart.

11. "Alexandrino" refers to the purplish color of a highly prized velvet that was made in Alexandria; the note is in Martelli, "Lucrezia Tornabuoni," 82n.

And he rested neither night nor day,
>and the decorations were so splendid
>that I seem not to tell the truth in describing them.
And after this, that excellent king
>had everyone invited, from the greatest to the least,
>the flower of his people, as I have said:
"Let everyone come eat! And all are permitted
>to ask for whatever would best suit his taste."
And thus the king ordered those who spoke for him:
And if there is someone who wants to take
>something from his treasures, to him it may be given;
>let him take as much as he desires;
and for seven days let nothing be denied to anyone.

Chapter 2

I have finished speaking of all the decorations
>in the palace and the garden, both inside and out,
>but now I will turn my song to the banquet itself.
If you will help me with your valor,
>O my worthy guide, your tracks will keep me
>from going astray onto a dubious path.
I ask, Lord, that you inform my words,
>for without you I lack all power
>to tell my story: and if I am not inspired by you,
my intellect sleeps. May you awaken me
>through your kindness;
>with you, I burn; without, I am made pale.
I know that before I arrived even halfway
>I would tire myself out and would need to sit down
>if I did not have you as my companion.
And it seems that you tell me "Do not fear,
>take up your singing again in my name,
>and you will have from it honor and great pleasure;
proceed with your verses and talk about
>how the lords and citizens whom I recounted
>in the first canto with such sweet style
were all in the garden with fresh May-branches;[12]

---

12. "Tutti eran nel giardin co' freschi mai": the "maio" (also called "maggio") was a flowering branch that a young man would cut from a tree and carry about during the Mayday celebrations, eventually bringing it to the door of his *fidanzata* or sweetheart. Angelo Polizano's "Ben

among flowers they walked through the grass and little
   fields,
among songs and music they knew many pleasures."[13]
Everywhere, young men went about
   with dishes, as had been ordered,
   and they were just like angels, they looked so lovely.
Each one was seated at the table
   according to his rank;
   the great king presided over them all.
And he could see everything all around him,
   and he happily encouraged his guests to eat,
   and often he invited them all to drink.
Everywhere you could hear instruments playing
   of every kind, an infinite number,
   it stuns me simply to think back on it all.
And to make his guests even more contented
   the king chose singers who could please them all
   with sweet melodies and skillful harmonies,
and they lingered in great happiness, sampling
   infinite dishes and savoring their aromas;
   don't ask if there was anything there that displeased
      them.[14]
Similarly, in her own rooms, the queen
   bestowed comparable honors on the women,
   both those from the court and those who came from
      without.[15]
Day and night in the palace she entertained
   the women and young girls, all richly dressed;
   neither old women nor serving girls were excluded.

---

venga maggio," a ballad on which Tornabuoni based several of her *laudi*, sings of the May
festivities and their rites of courtship.

13. It is difficult to know where God's address to Tornabuoni should end. Here seems to be
the logical place, but arguably the entire canto could be "his," just as he seems to suggest that
he was the one who sang in canto 1 ("dira' come / Signori et cittadin' ch'i' racontai / Nel
primo canto con dolce ediome"). The manuscript, of course, has no quotation marks for direct
discourse.

14. Martelli calls attention to echoes of the *Morgante* and the *cantari* tradition with this phrase:
"Non domandar se roba vi si spaccia," noting several moments in Pulci that begin with "Non
domandar" (i.e., "Non domandar quel che facea Rinaldo" [Don't ask what Rinaldo was doing],
7.59.5; etc.; "Lucrezia Tornabuoni," 83n).

15. With this stanza, Tornabuoni finally returns to the text of Esther: "Also Vashti the queen
made a feast for the women in the palace" (Esther 1:9).

And they had such sweet manners, and were so adorned
    with pearls and necklaces of gold
    that they all seemed a magnificent treasure.
Although she was surrounded by beautiful women,
    Vashti, the queen, was so nobly dressed
    that she seemed to be a sun among stars.
With much nobility and great riches
    that woman, proud of heart, honored the others,
    offering them solace and much pleasure.
The seventh day was almost over;
    the king was happy and greatly contented
    by food and wine. At that time (and this is true)[16]
he had seven eunuchs called to him
    by their masters, and to the ones he most trusted
    he spoke in this manner:
"Go to the queen, and for her guides
    I choose you, Mauman, and you, Barath.
    Join her in feasting, and may each of you find pleasure
      there.
Arbona and Athazas, and Adagath
    and you, Alogath, go quickly,
    let no one remain here, and you Zarath, go too
and tell Vashti not to argue with you,[17]
    but have her come here, dressed in her regal vestments,[18]
    for she is the only thing missing from my feast.
Let her come that I may gaze on her gentle face,
    and so that each of my barons can see her too,
    for no one desires anything else!
Delay no longer; now make your move,
    take with you companions skillful and well-mannered,
    bring no one with you who is unpolished or uncouth;

16. It is not clear why Tornabuoni needs to insert the parenthetical insistence on veracity: could her readers be wondering if eunuchs really existed in the Bible?

17. With this line, Tornabuoni anticipates Vashti's refusal; there is no parallel line in Esther.

18. "Bring in queen Vashti before the king, with the crown set upon her head, to show her beauty to all the people and the princes, for she was exceeding beautiful" (Esther 1:11). As Klein comments in "Honor and Shame in Esther," "Rabbinic commentary has interpreted that command to specify that she wear only her royal crown and appear naked, and gives her credit for refusing." Tornabuoni avoids the implications of nudity by translating the explicit "posito super caput ejus diademate" as "con reali vestiti."

but may they all be of the signorial class,
>   and may they honor her with instruments and music;
>   let each of you be reverent and humble,
for with her lovely customs and her graciousness,
>   she is of all other women the flower,
>   and I love her greatly, with all my heart."
The eunuchs left their lord and went to his wife,
>   and they made their embassy to her,
>   but she responded in a strange and disrespectful
>   manner.
Before she had even drawn a breath,
>   she refused to come, and gave them no reason;
>   and so the group was sent back to the king
to report to him her intentions,
>   that in no way whatsoever would she join him.
>   The king underwent a great change;
in a great rage he began to say,
>   "What obstacle can there be to her arrival?
>   Does she stay away from us out of anger, or pride?
We do not know her purpose;
>   but we know very well how *we* must respond
>   if it is not her wish to come here.
Truthfully, these are strange goings-on
>   if the lady I love and to whom I pledge my faith
>   does not obey me and sends me unkind words,
as everyone has seen.
>   She is taking too much license;
>   and I must do without her.[19]
Still, I want to be patient.
>   Who can tell me how the seven wise men
>   will counsel me in their prudence?
They are experts and grave masters of the law,
>   and they will know well what to do,
>   because they hold the keys to every form of knowledge.
I will do precisely what they tell me,
>   since they are dukes from Media and Persia;
>   I know they will not fail in their counsel.

---

19. The enraged speech of Ahasuerus is an embellishment on the terse biblical verse, "Where-upon the king, becoming angry, and inflamed with a very great fury . . ." (Esther 1:12).

Because of this controversy regarding the queen,
   I seek their advice;
   they must speak well so it can be quickly dispersed."
So taking this into consideration,
   they examined carefully what had happened,
   and for six of them, one perturbed face gave the
      verdict.
"Each of us thinks in himself
   that the queen has offended not only
   the king, but all the princes gathered here;
the people will speak at length of the mockery and grief
   that has befallen the authority
   of our King Ahasuerus, who comes from such great
      stock.
And thus would arise a great heresy,
   for women will refuse to obey their husbands,
   and men will be unable to govern their wives.
All the women will speak with passion
   of this rebellious queen, and they all will say,
   'we will make our husbands timid and meek.'
The king has every right to be disturbed by such news,
   and thus if he wishes,
   let her never come into his presence again.
Rather, let him make this command, bold as it may sound,
   known throughout Persia and Media,
   that Queen Vashti no longer pleases the king.
And therefore I say, let everyone know
   that she may no longer come into his presence,
   since she has given him such an affront.
Let him find another wife, more to his liking,
   one who will be better, more obedient,
   who will hold her lord in far more respect.
And may this also be announced to all people:
   'All wives and any women who wish to marry
   must be courteous, wise, and respectful,
so that their husbands have no reason to leave them.'"[20]

---

20. The Latin text is more forceful, and Tornabuoni omits the final line of the mandate insisting that "the husbands should be rulers and masters in their houses" ("esse viros principes ac majores in domibus suis," Esther 1:22).

Chapter 3

Through your grace, O Lord, I have told
    how the king and the barons were angered
    and how the queen did not wish to come:
Seven eunuchs had sent for her,
    and they were wise, faithful, and shrewd,
    and still she refused to come to the banquet.
After he received good advice and sage comforts,
    the king was content that she no longer be his wife,
    [because] she had wronged him so.
Women, learn nothing from this queen:[21]
    be prudent, and listen to my words
    with great care and discretion.
And if you do not think that what I say is right,
    consider Vashti; I myself would guess
    that much wretchedness befell her.
Now let me return to what I spoke of before;
    let me follow the work I have begun
    as I proceed to polish my verses.
His wrath spent, the king begins to remember
    his gentle Queen Vashti,
    and he almost repents of having left her.
His wise sages, whose minds were divine,
    knew that the king was sorry for what happened,
    and they sought remedies for this evil.
They knew the appetite of their lord,[22]
    and thus one began to suggest that they
    search throughout his kingdom, from one shore to
        the other,
for beautiful and illustrious virgins,
    and that they be sent to their lord so he
    could know them all and content himself.[23]

21. "Donne non apparate da costei / State prudente et . . . / . . . udite e detti miei": One of the rare moments in which Tornabuoni addresses a specific group of readers, as opposed to the more general "Udite" or "Non domandar."

22. Tornabuoni here makes explicit what the biblical text refuses to say; in Esther, the king's servants must simply intuit the king's "appetite."

23. "Et mandisi chi sappi tutto apieno / Si chel signor senabbi acontentare": The biblical "to know" is understood here; again, Tornabuoni makes the passage more explicit than it is in Esther.

"Let Hegai, the eunuch,
   governor of all the king's women,
   have custody of all the virgins;
let the chief places be well searched,
   and let all of the women be seen
   so that we can redeem this evil and shame.
And then bring them before the king
   so that he may take one who satisfies him,
   one who is gentle and constant and mild.
Let her be given the crown of the first queen,
   and may she tranquilly take her place."
   At this, the king raised up his head;
he was greatly pleased, and so he commanded
   that what the wise men said be carried out:
   they should begin to search without delay.
In the city of Susa, and in the district nearby
   there lived among others a Hebrew,
   son of Giamo, as I find it written,[24]
by the name of Mordecai,
   who left Jerusalem when the city was undone
   by her evil sins.
Born of a noble tribe, he had been living
   in Jerusalem with many others when Jemini
   went into Babylon, as one may read;
and he was seized through the authority
   of Nebuchadnezzar, and with his brothers
   he was placed for some time in prison.
And out of Jerusalem went boys and old men
   during the time of the transmigration,
   and Mordecai was among them, for he too was seized.
He was a just man, and with honorable intentions
   he raised a young and beautiful girl
   who was to liberate her people.
She was a comely virgin,
   the daughter of his very own brother,
   and Esther was her name.

---

24. Tornabuoni's source is unclear; Esther 2:5 makes Mordecai "filius Jair . . . de stirpe Jemini."

Her beauty made her seem immortal;
 she had neither mother nor father,
 but she was fortunate to have an uncle of great
  worth.
Upon hearing that the king
 was searching for beautiful and noble young women
 so that he might take one who pleased him,
Mordecai went along with his niece
 and gave her to those who were looking
 and it did not seem to them a wasted effort.
Now understand carefully the substance of what
  I say:
 Esther was led among a company
 of fair virgins, all possessed of pure hearts,
into the guardianship, the custody and care
 of the eunuch Hegai, who would govern them,
 and whose sole desire was to serve them.
The king's eye was drawn to Esther,
 and her looks pleased him more
 than those of any other woman he had seen.
Gazing at her in great delight,
 he had her dressed in such worthy clothes
 that she could almost seem the very goddess he
  conceived.
Seven handmaidens he gave her as servants,
 chosen from the royal house,
 so they would minister to her needs
and look after her and care for her in such a way
 that she might be pleasing to the crown
 and stand out among the crowd.[25]
Prudent Esther never revealed to anyone
 who she was, nor did she speak at all
 of her people.
Thus had she been commanded by her uncle
 that she tell no one of her family,
 that she conceal such things from everyone.

---

25. The exact meaning is unclear ("Et che lachavin fuor del generale"), but the sense seems to be that Esther is meant to stand out from the "general" crowd of women.

Mordecai would always walk just outside the palace
where gentle Esther dwelled, to see
what would become of her.

Now it happens that I am so unused to singing
that it's hard for me to put these words in order,
and easily I would remain confused,
O my sweet Lord: without your help
I could not follow this [divine] speech,[26]
and thus I wish to call on you again, O Lord,
that I might raise myself up with my verses,
and through your grace arrive at the desired end,
where I would like to go.
In well-wrought style, I would like to talk about
those virgins that had been gathered together
and in what manner they were sent before the king.
For six months they were anointed with various unguents,[27]
and they spent their time in leisure, as they liked;
they were contented in all that they asked.
And when these six months had passed,
the king ordered that must go to him,
one at a time, so that he might contemplate them.
And they could not return to him
if the king did not request them by name;
and thus he set about to scrutinize them.
The day came when it was Esther's turn.
She wanted to go before the king unadorned
and in her natural beauty present herself to him.
The others wanted to make themselves up,
but Esther was beautiful and graceful,
and she had no desire to adorn herself further.
Hegai, whose thoughts never rested,
dressed her up because he loved her,
and in his heart he said, May he make this one his
bride!

26. One must assume that "questo parlare" refers to the Book of Esther and that Tornabuoni
seeks God's guidance to "seguir" the Bible with fidelity.

27. "Sei mesi con unzione et ozio state / Eron"; such is Tornabuoni's translation of the rather
difficult Vulgate: "For six months they were anointed with oil of myrrh, and for another six
months they used certain perfumes and sweet spices" (Esther 2:12).

In the month that is called Tebeth,
    the tenth month, she was brought
    to the bed of the king, and he contented himself with
        her.
He took her as his bride and crowned her
    in the place of that disobedient woman
    as queen of his realm,
and having done this, he wasted no time
    arranging the wedding feast and the great banquets
    to which all of his barons
throughout all his lands were invited with much joy;
    he wants them to come to make them glad,
    they who had been forced to leave another time in
        dismay.[28]
Then he showered all of those young women
    with expensive gifts and presents,
    so that they would have dowries and be able to wed,[29]
and Mordecai came in with the other guests
    to see what now would follow;
    from the door of the palace he watched intently.
Esther had still not spoken
    of her people; she had said nothing,
    for Mordecai imposed upon her such fear
since she had been a young girl,
    and even now that she was queen she obeyed him
    as if she was still nursing or lying in the cradle.
Mordecai was standing by the door one morning
    when he heard two eunuchs arguing;
    they harbored thoughts of cruelty and violence.
They were doorkeepers and servants;
    they were making plans to kill the king,
    and Mordecai witnessed their great presumption.
He went immediately to the queen and
    made known to her this news,
    and Esther was fearful and thoughtful.

---

28. One assumes that Tornabuoni is referring here to the banquet held earlier, when Vashti refused to come before the king.

29. Such solicitude for the other women of Ahasuerus's harem is not in the Book of Esther.

And in person she went to the king,
  letting him know what was to happen;
  and the king, finding truth in her words,
commanded that the two be hanged;
  and so that all people would forever
  remember what had come to pass, he ensured
that this revealing and important event
  be registered in the sixth of his books,
  so that it would not be forgotten.
He orders Mordecai to remain
  there in the entryway, before the door,
  so that diligently he should guard it,
and Mordecai praised God for his happy fate.

Chapter 4

Having discovered the evil deed
  of those two ingrates, the king saw to their punishment,
  and both were swiftly hanged.
And they deserved such deaths,
  having sought to deceive and betray their king;
  and truly they failed miserably in their plans.
Mordecai, his eye always watchful,
  roamed about the palace
  and was content to see Esther,
and as I said, she had not revealed
  that he was her uncle; no one even knew
  they were related.
Through this was born, as I will recount,
  a setback for the Hebrews, a grave blunder
  that almost brought about the deaths of many people.
For twenty-two years the noble Ahasuerus
  had ruled the land in peace;
  and everyone bore him much love.
Among his barons one especially pleased the king
  by the name of Haman,
  and he was bold, and daring, and proud.[30]

---

30. "Ardito, superbo et aldacie": words used elsewhere in Tornabuoni's works when speaking of evil figures, such as Lucifer and Nebuchadnezzar.

He had been elevated by Ahasuerus
    to such a high post that none besides the king
    was honored more in the realm than Haman.
And so everyone complied with what he said,
    from the greatest lords to the least, and those in between,
    and he was obeyed in good faith.
[But] Haman was proud and harbored deceptive thoughts,
    and he wanted all men to revere him,
    from all the provinces and lands.
Mordecai, who was a man of great prudence,
    did not respect Haman at all,
    and he refused to listen to him.
To Haman it was said, "There is only one man
    who does not bow down and revere you,
    and he does not wish to obey you in any way."
Haman thought hard about altering this;
    he saw what was happening, and it disturbed him,
    and he began to mutter to himself,
and questioned some of the servants around him,
    asking what family Mordecai was from
    and why he did not honor him as did all the others.
They answered him that he was a Hebrew;
    he had been at the court for some time
    and he does not worship our god.
Haman was outraged when he heard this news.
    and he began to turn his thought
    to how he might bring about Mordecai's death.
(As I said above in my song,
    the Hebrews had been dwelling in that country
    since they were not able to stay in their lands.)
Haman took counsel with himself as to what should be
    done,
    and he said, "Perhaps I can make this man repent,
    so that he will no longer dishonor me."
With such thoughts, he went quickly to the king
    on the appointed day, and he said to him
    such words as you shall shortly hear.
He begins to speak, and he does not pause
    to deliver this false speech, which would send
    great confusion among the Hebrews.

"O my lord, your kingdom,
    your territory and your lands are full
    of people who cause us great trouble.
These are the Hebrews, who in those wars
    with cruel Nabuc were led away
    into Babylon in harsh chains.
Now they are here and they feel so at home
    that they have no desire to obey your laws,
    in fact, they scoff at them, the ingrates!
I have thought upon this at some length;
    you have no need of people like these,
    who could easily destroy your kingdom.
I long only for your honor and I want to be helpful;
    and I think that if it seems [best], O lord,
    to raise yourself up out of this dream,
then I will add to your great treasures,
    ten talents of gold will I give you
    if this people is cast into oblivion."
The king answered without delay
    that Haman's will should be done,
    and the Hebrews should be razed from his land.
Then Haman, full of cruelty,
    said, "Lord, let me take your ring
    so they will believe that what I write is the truth.
I will sign the letters with your seal,
    so they will obey me and believe my words,
    and so they will murder them all in one blow.[31]
And no trace, no seed
    of these obstinate circumcised ones will be left,
    nor will any basis for their crimes remain."
The king answered him with grateful words
    and said that Haman should have whatever he
        needed.
"Treat these things as yours, and I give them to you.
And carry out your will in all these things
    in such a way that these offenses will be purged,
    and I will take great pleasure in seeing them done."

31. "In un drappello": literally, "in a squad."

Then Haman went to call the scribes of the king,
    and this happened in the first month [of the year].
    The letters contained the following words:[32]
Haman commands that a decree be sent
    throughout the kingdom, to all princes, vicars, and
        judges,
    and says that it is done in the name of the king.
Bitter words are contained therein,
    bitter words for all the Jews,
    as I will narrate more fully below.
Thus precisely on the thirteenth day of that month,
    in the month they call Adar,
    they would inflict bitter death on all the Jews.
This had to be done, without delay,
    so that at the time that had been appointed
    not a single Hebrew should remain alive, not a one;
old men and children and young boys,
    mothers about to give birth, and young women ripe
        for marriage:
    such was the decision of the king.
Haman himself took these decrees and made
    the couriers hurry from province to province,
    those who make their way in every season.
And so it was ordered that on a single day
    the Hebrews, far and near, would be killed,
    and in Susa as well these things were decreed
and this edict was displayed,
    sealed with the secret seal
    so that everyone could see what it contained.
Haman had ascended to new heights,
    and anyone who could flatter him did so,
    and they honored him, calling him blessed.[33]

---

32. Here Tornabuoni alludes to one of the apocryphal passages Jerome placed at the end of Esther, without giving it to the reader in detail (see chapter 13). Tornabuoni condenses seven verses into four stanzas, while adding evocative details ("mothers about to give birth, and young women ripe for marriage").

33. The passages that refer to the flatterers of Haman, as well as to his "great audacity," are Tornabuoni's.

These are all true things of which I speak;
   I speak of Haman and his great boldness,
   Haman, for whom these troubling things seemed so
      playful.
He possessed such arrogance
   that he cared not for a single creature;
   he led the dance in the way that he chose.
As I said, he went about in high spirits,
   he spent his time on amusements and sumptuous
      banquets,
   and he had the ear of the king and all the court.
But all of the Hebrews were dejected
   and those who lived in Susa grieved in great sadness,
   and they all lived very much in fear,
and day and night they cried out their laments.

Chapter 5

And when Mordecai saw and understood
   what had been ordained for the Hebrews,
   he too was seized with terrible fear.
In loud voices they called out, "Woe to us,"
   and they tore at their clothes
   and went about crying, "miserere mei" to God.
They covered themselves with ashes,
   poured them over their heads, and wore garments of
      sackcloth
   as they prepared themselves for such outrage.
In the great palace could be heard
   the bitter cries of all the people,
   pale and lifeless with fear.
(The king had proclaimed a ban,
   that any man who was covered with sackcloth
   could not enter into his court.)[34]
And already in every province,
   in the cities, in the villages, in every home,
   the sad and evil news had spread.

---

34. This apparently insignificant detail is out of place in the text at this point; it becomes meaningful only later in chapter 5, when we learn that Mordecai was unable to come into the presence of Esther himself to make his appeal. The line is taken from Esther 4:2.

Whence each Hebrew burns and consumes himself
   in laments, in grief, in fasting and prayer
   and goes into a sweat at the thought of death.
They prayed to God that he not withhold
   the help that he was wont to give them
   and with which he so closely knit them to himself.
And Mordecai began to pray as well,
   turning to God his worthy prayers
   and asking that he assist his people.[35]
"Omnipotent God, I pray that my words
   will reach you, and ask that you rescue us
   from this great affliction.
You alone are God, you alone are without fault,
   and if you choose to help us now,
   we can be liberated from this curse.
Lord who helps us escape every [danger],
   take away from us this judgment;
   from such falsehood you can save us.
You made the heavens for our benefit,
   the land, the sea, and all that dwell within it;
   I pray that you rescue us from this martyrdom.
You dwell at the center of the heavens,
   and all things must obey you;
   to you I turn to speak with reverence.
Your power cannot be concealed,
   and nothing can be hidden from you.
   You know why I did not wish to revere Haman.
I abstained from honoring him,
   and it is not out of pride
   that I refused to adore that arrogant man;
I speak truly, my Lord;
   for the sake of my people I would kiss his feet,
   but I reserved worship only for you,
and since I know that you see all things,
   and since I must honor you, I would not want to err
   by worshiping only a man; and I know you believe me.

35. What follows is another apocryphal passage that Tornabuoni interpolates in the text
where it rightfully belongs; Mordecai's prayer, which Tornabuoni translates with surprising
fidelity, is in Esther 13:8–17.

Nor do we wish to worship another god.
    Liberate your people from this cruelty;
    in your pity, do not abandon us.
Now they wish to consume your few heirs,
    this little portion of your legacy;
    help us Lord, in your goodness.
Preserve your heirs, O Lord,
    whom you brought with much effort
    out of Egypt when they rebelled against Pharaoh.
We are your people, we are your friends;
    raise us up, O Lord, give us you help,
    so that all people may always say
that you saved us from this martyrdom,
    turning our mourning into happiness;
    through your charity, bring us solace.
Open our mouths and make us bold,
    so that we may always praise you, Lord,
    so that our lips are not sealed in bitterness."
And so loudly did Mordecai cry out
    that all the maidens of the palace
    heard his laments.
They went with great haste to the side of the queen,
    together with the eunuchs who served her,
    and reported this news to her in much fear:
how everything was being made ready
    to persecute the Hebrews, thanks to the command
    of Haman, who wanted them all to die.
When she heard this, the queen lost her beautiful color,
    and she became white and pallid,
    as someone who is carried off to the grave.[36]
With what force remained to her, she tore at her garments
    and asked that she be covered with sackcloth;
    this was not given to her, and this alone she lacked.
Sighing mournfully, she called upon Hathach,
    whom the king had given her as her guard,
    that he might serve her at all times.

---

36. A detail Tornabuoni adds. The Bible has "And when she heard it she was in a consternation" [Quod audiens consternata est] (Esther 4:4).

With piteous words she beseeched him
    to go and find Mordecai, only to learn
    the reason for his tremendous cries,
and thus off went the eunuch to see
    Mordecai and found him in great suffering,
    fearful of his impending death.
Wailing loudly, he recounted at length
    how Haman, spurred by envy, had declared
    that all the Hebrews must suffer and be killed,
and he would confiscate all their goods,
    and Mordecai gave Hathach the decree that was
      written
    and so that everyone would be able to read it,
it was nailed onto the gate of the palace.
    He instructed him to say to Esther
    that she should not hesitate to go to the king
and spare no words in beseeching him
    to save Mordecai's people from death,
    and Hathach should return to tell him everything.
Hathach reported his words carefully to Esther
    and told her all that Mordecai had said;
    so important it was that he relate everything well:
how Haman, for dishonest gain,
    wanted to do things so harmful to the Jews,
    how she should go at once to the king
to tell him these things without delay
    and prevent such cruel deeds from being carried out.
    Whence she answered, "Oh my, my heart!
Go, tell Mordecai that it grieves me greatly
    that I cannot do what he says, nor can I be swift;
    if I have understood Ahasuerus's word,
the king has commanded that whoever enters the palace
    without being summoned shall lose his head;
    and this applies to men and women alike.
But it is true that he has reserved the right to enter
    to whomever he shows his scepter of gold;
    this person may call on him and be honored.
Let not Mordecai think that I am inattentive to his
    words

or that I am negligent in my love for them;[37]
for I count my life to be worth nothing.
But because [the king] has not called me for thirty days,
　　tell him that I don't know what to do;
　　I have uttered and exhausted every counsel."
When Mordecai heard these things he said,
　　"Do not think of your own well-being, queen;
　　if we die, what good will it be that you escaped?
God will send you great punishments, Esther,
　　if you are silent about these things;
　　divine goodness will help us, not you.
I am sure that if you do not want
　　to plead on our behalf, we will be saved
　　by some other means, and you will repent of it.
Up to now, God has always saved us;
　　thus he promised, and Abraham was his witness.
　　If you help us, we will be exalted."
Seeing that Mordecai was so irate, Esther
　　sent him word that he and all the others
　　should devoutly pray to God,
and to make him receptive to their pleas,
　　for three days they should go without eating,
　　cover themselves with ashes, and sing plaints and grieve.
Devoutly they should pray to God for her,
　　that he might give her grace to know [what to do];
　　and thus she is willing to humble herself.
And once this was done, without fear
　　she would go, and break the command,
　　and then they would see if she would die,
and thus she resolved to herself to carry out this plan:
　　she would die for the sake of her people,
　　and Mordecai was content.
They prayed with clear and simple words,
　　devoutly they utter their pleas,
　　and their prayers take on wings,[38]
as they do what Esther asked them to do.

---

37. "Non creda mardoceo chi mi stanchassi / Perlamor loro"—-for *their* love; it appears that Esther is being extremely careful in speaking of her love for others who are presumably different from herself.

38. "Le prece han porte": literally, their prayers are carried off.

Chapter 6

The queen, seeing the danger
    that had befallen her people, also
    has recourse to God, as she humbly weeps.[39]
From her beautiful eyes come plentiful tears;
    from her mouth piteous words, and she speaks
    with a pure heart: "O God, in you I have placed my
        hope.
Liberate your people from this great fury!"
    Thus weeping, she removes
    her regal vestments in sorrow,
and accompanied by her ladies-in-waiting
    and dressed in a simple hairshirt,
    she went about the palace, grieving,
and where once she had used
    various unguents that usually remain
    fragrant for many days and nights,
now instead she began to pour ashes on her head,
    humiliating her body
    by fasting and saying devout prayers.
And she went about to all the places
    where once she had found solace and pleasure; now
    she weeps uncontrollably and prays to God in her
        heart.
"O glorious God, do not deny
    us your aid; Lord, give us some remedy
    make yourself known among the pagans.[40]
I labor, my Lord, in much suffering and distress
    and now I am faced with my ruin.
    Please, Lord, liberate us from this cruel siege.
So many times, when I was but a child,
    I heard from my father that you rescued
    your people from cruel punishments.

---

39. Once again, Tornabuoni brings one of the apocryphal passages that Jerome placed at the end of Esther into the narrative itself; this long evocative section on Esther's mortification and prayer is from chapter 14.

40. While once again Tornabuoni is curiously faithful to the prayer she finds in the Vulgate, she does omit a telling detail at the very beginning, when Esther refers to herself as a "desolate woman [adjuva me solitariam] who has no other helper but thee" (Esther 14:3).

According to what our ancient writers have said,
    you saved us from the hands of the pagans,
    great things were shown to Pharaoh on their behalf.[41]
But little caring that we were meant
    to be your heirs forever,
    or that we went against your law,
we sinned, committing great falsehoods;
    so you gave us into their hands
    and took away from us our liberty.
Here we live among their empty idols,
    and many times we are forced
    to humble ourselves before them and do them
        reverence.
Lord, you see that even this is not enough,
    they torment us always and want to deprive you of
    your glory and render you helpless.
They would like to destroy
    your noble temple and most worthy altar
    so that we would have to worship their idols.
Turn their iniquitous and evil counsel
    against them and destroy them,
    and show everyone that you are God.
The man who began this was full of envy:
    may this flood reverse its course and drown him;
    may this poison destroy his people.[42]
And as for me, make the tongue in my mouth
    pregnant with perfect words; may they surge forth
    like a rich vein of water from a spring.[43]
And may I succeed in uttering my words
    in such a way to the king that these great burdens
    be lifted from us and my wishes heard.
Change his heart, the heart of a lion,
    transform it so that deception
    falls upon the bodies of our enemies.

41. The stanza is an addition of Tornabuoni's.

42. This is exactly what will happen in the course of the poem. In a story without God's direct and visible intervention, we will soon see how Esther herself enables this "poison" to infect Haman and his people.

43. Once again, the homely simile is an addition of Tornabuoni's.

Reveal your power and send judgment
   so that this people can know
   that we are the ones you want as your friends.
You know, Lord, that I took on this glory
   against my will; I consented to this
   only to obey my uncle.
I wanted to go about without any ostentation,
   and I did not want to please [Ahasuerus]
   if it meant losing, Lord, the memory of you.[44]
The banquets of Haman never made me happy;
   never at his meals was I content.
   Always I did these things in great fear.
I have always been timid and shy;
   I would not have been happy as queen
   had I not kept my mind, Lord, fixed on you.
O God of Abraham, O God of strength; you know all
     this.
   Hear, O Lord, our prayer, the prayers
   of all of us who hope that you will save us.
And I, with all my people, bind myself to you,
   promising to follow always in your steps;
   do not deny us what we ask.
Be with us, Lord, in our company,
   for with you we will go without fear,
   secure from every villainy."
And once she had uttered this prayer,
   and the third day having come to an end,
   she felt herself consoled in her heart.[45]
Her eunuchs and handmaidens came to her side,
   and each one attends to comforting her,
   and they brought to her the noblest
garments that she usually wore
   when she wished to appear every inch a queen;
   without delay she dressed herself in her clothes,

44. For what are no doubt obvious reasons, Tornabuoni declines to translate with precision the following passage: "Thou knowest my necessity; that I abominate the sign of my pride and glory, which is upon my head in the days of my public appearance, and detest it as a menstruous rag, and wear it not in the days of my silence" (Esther 14:16).

45. Tornabuoni now brings into the text of Esther the apocryphal passage from chapter 15, clearly one of the most dramatic moments of the story.

and they attired her in her regal insignia,
> draping her in rubies, pearls, and infinite treasures
> so that anyone who saw her would be thunderstruck.
Dressed in this way, she concealed her grief;
> she was royally dressed, adorned, and graceful;
> she well knew it was the right moment to give her
> > all.[46]
There went with her two ladies-in-waiting,
> one who could support her and sustain her,
> another who attended to her rich garments.
She had never appeared so beautiful;
> and on this day she seemed to have come truly
> to this world from paradise.
She went off to the king, pretending to be cheerful,
> concealing from him and everyone else,
> her great sadness.
Not even her beautiful eyes betrayed her sorrow.
> The king was seated on his throne,
> and with his barons he was enjoying his wealth,
he was spending time in amusements and pleasure,
> there in his palace with a worthy gathering,
> when looking about him, he happened to see Esther.
He called his Esther to his side
> and held out to her the scepter of gold;
> with reverence, Esther knelt before him.
Instantly she took the scepter and kissed it;
> but as she gazed at that terrible face
> she fell on the ground, and this was her solace:
for as she lay, almost dead in the arms
> of her ladies-in-waiting
> (and it appeared to all that she was undone),
the king's heart was suddenly transformed,
> the heart that had earlier been so ferocious;
> he instantly rose from his throne
and began to speak to her with humble voice.
> "What is wrong, Esther?" and opened his arms.
> "This command was not meant to harm you!"

46. "Dar le soie": to be generous, to sacrifice herself.

And saying this, he kissed her face:
    "Doubt not; have no fear;
    chase away every suspicion and doubt,
and mark my word, for you must know
    that this commandment does not affect you.
    You will not die but live, sure of what I say.
I am your brother; take my crown, Esther,
    and now let loose your words."
    She took the crown and made a rock of her heart.
"Speak to me a little"; thus he reasons with her,
    and she hears his sweet words,
    and then she answers in this fashion:
"I saw your face resplendent
    like the sun; I heard the sound
    of sweet words that [come] from paradise."
He gazes at her beautiful eyes
    and clutches her little white hand tightly;
    and Esther turns to him a sweet laugh.
And she said to herself, "Now I will have vengeance:
    O my Lord, teach me how to speak,
    so I will know how to utter words that will persuade."[47]
Ahasuerus took her [aside] to ask what she wanted
    and said, "Petition me for whatever you will;
    speak in safety; I will not deny you.
If you wanted half my realm,
    as soon as you asked for it, you should have it,
    and my people are witnesses to your request."[48]
And the queen spoke to the king,
    saying, "My lord, I will request something of you,
    since I have found such benevolence in you.
What would you say to entertaining yourself
    at my palace and coming to dine? I invite as my guests
    you and Haman; and when I see you,

---

47. The thought expressed in this terzina is not found in Esther. Tornabuoni boldly elaborates on Esther's disguised cunning, despite her apparent fear of being in the presence of the king.

48. There is a clear and perhaps intentional similarity to a corresponding moment in *The Life of Saint John the Baptist*, when Herod tells Salome in the presence of worthy lords that he will give her half his kingdom as a gift (see stanza 134).

once you have dined at my banquet,
   I will make my wish known."
The king responded that he would willingly come,
and he cheerfully accepted the invitation.

Chapter 7

Having promised Esther that he would
   dine with her the following day,
   the king put behind him all of his wrath.
The queen returned to her palace
   and there she began to entertain hope,
   ordering a sumptuous and magnificent feast.
Haman, who was as arrogant as ever,
   found Mordecai sad and grief-stricken;
   but Mordecai still did not change his ways.[49]
Haman was terribly angered and said, "Never will I rest
   as long as I come to this door and see
   that presumptuous Mordecai.
It seems that his only goal is to be lord,
   and he is even slow to honor the king;
   he seems to value no one [other than himself]."
He returns to his house, suffering great torments
   because he had not been revered,
   but he does not reveal his anger.
Rather, his heart burning in pride,
   he begins to tell all his friends
   how great he is and how much wealth he has,
he talked about how the king esteemed him,
   he spoke of his beautiful children and wise wife;
   of all this he boasted at some length.
"And all my wishes are always granted;
   whatever I ask of the king is fulfilled;
   and whoever meddles with me learns his lesson.
I go tomorrow to the banquet
   to dine alone with the king and his queen;
   see how important I am, see how highly I rank!

---

49. With this passage, Tornabuoni returns to the earlier sections from Esther; the allusion to
Haman's anger at Mordecai is in Esther 5:9.

And yet with all this, I will still be unhappy
    as long as Mordecai remains at the palace door;
    but I hope to see his ruin.
Now may my soul soon find comfort,
    because the day of his sentence approaches,
    when I will see him and his people go to their deaths."
His wife said to him, "Take things into your own hands:
    tomorrow morning before you go to the banquet,
    punish this obstinacy of Mordecai.
Have a beam prepared; let its length
    be fifty cubits; make him hang from it,
    and no longer go about so dismayed.
And thus you will go to the banquet in peace."
    This advice pleased Haman a great deal;
    he boasts to have favor before the king.
He had the beam built, that great danger,
    so imposing were the gallows that he made,
    that all the Hebrews viewed it with downcast brow.

It was night. The king went into his chambers,
    but he was unable to sleep,
    so he called for his chancellor to be with him.
He also requested that he bring with him
    the book that he was accustomed to having,
    and thus he fetched it, wishing to obey.
This lord always carried with him
    a book in which he took care to record
    the people who had benefited the court;
such things the king did not wish to forget,
    and thus he was a just and worthy lord
    who wanted to reward those who had been of service.
As I told you, the book was brought before him,
    and as he read it, the king discovered the treachery
    that Mordecai had already divulged to him:
the grave crime of the eunuchs
    that Mordecai revealed, and how their treason
    had been punished and prevented, thanks to his virtue.
That great lord, King Ahasuerus,
    asked now what reward Mordecai had received,
    what honor or gain he had won.

A counselor then inquired,
  and the response was that in fact he had gained nothing;
  he had reaped no pleasures from the court.
And then by chance, Haman came in,
  entering the court just then, to beseech the king
  for the hanging of Mordecai.
The king called to him to request his counsel,
  and he asked him, "Tell me, what should I do
  for someone who has long deserved to be honored?
How should his lord exalt him?
  What kind of reward does he deserve?"
  Haman turned to his lord with ready words.
That he is the man of whom King Ahasuerus speaks
  he is certain, and he began to say
  openly what he thought:
that such a man should be dressed in royal vestments,
  he should wear the king's crown, and go about on his
    horse,
  and travel all throughout his land,
so that he might be seen by all the people.
  Having performed works so worthy,
  he is owed the highest honors, second only to the king.
The king said to him, "Go now to Mordecai
  and do to him precisely what you have said;
  if you do not, I will treat you with great disdain.
And make sure that you carry this out quickly;
  do what you have advised, nothing more, nothing less."
  Haman departs, full of shame and vexation,
and all that the king had commanded him
  he brings to pass, without delay,
  and he goes about in grief, his eyes downcast.
This was the testimony God wants to give [Mordecai],
  revealing that his prayer had been heard
  and that quickly he would raise him up.
Because of this, Haman was greatly shamed,
  and weeping he returned home in haste,
  full of jealousy, and gripped with fear.
He told what had happened to his wife,
  he recounted it also to his friends
  as best as he is able to put it.

"If the Hebrew Mordecai has had
    such honor from the king, I will
    never be able to come before him again!"
And while they were speaking of these things together
    and were still discussing what to do,
    several of the eunuchs appeared before him.[50]
And they said, "Haman, you are wanted
    at the banquet of the worthy queen;
    the king awaits you, you must not delay.
The queen has taken care to have prepared
    special foods that she knows
    the king will very happily sample.
And everything has been arranged just so,
    to give the king pleasure in all things besides
        eating,
    so that he will want to hear her request.
The king has already gone willingly today
    to make his dear wife happy,
    and he wants his counselor Haman with him."
So he went off to see the king's wife,
    and she immediately rose when she saw him,
    and came toward him with her great train.[51]
This was a beautiful gathering of ladies,
    noble and richly jeweled, all of them lovely,
    each one was from an esteemed house.
The king was also there, with his cortege,
    and as he watched the women enter,
    he told some to remain, others to depart,
but when he saw the most beautiful flower of all,
    the king was left speechless by the light
    flashing from her eyes or, should I say, her two stars.
He is stunned and struck by wonder,
    just as someone too much in the sun is dazzled
    by the rays on which he fixes his gaze.

---

50. Tornabuoni elaborates on the eunuchs' request that Haman join Esther. Esther 6:14 merely says that "the king's eunuchs came, and compelled him to go quickly to the banquet which the queen had prepared."

51. The remainder of this chapter represents Tornabuoni's improvisations on the beginning of Esther 7: "So the king and Haman went in, to drink with the queen."

He takes her by the hand, and he joins
  his graceful companion.
  She wears an elegant garment;
at her throat, a precious stone,
  whose value was impossible to surmise.
  Her face was cheerful and joyous.
The hour had now come to dine,
  the king and queen sit down at the table;
  Haman is to sit close to them.
And everyone eats, their appetites inflamed;
  they dine on those morsels, perfectly prepared,
  and Haman does not dream of the judgment to come.
Here one would need rhymes better suited than mine
  to recount the infinite number
  of dishes and treats laid out before them.
Still, it seems to me that the best decision is
  not to be tedious; better not to waste time
  even summarizing such a magnificent banquet.
I will not mention (although one might easily imagine)
  all the wines that were suited to each dish;
  they take away one's thirst and set the heart on fire.
The king was happy, his heart expansive;
  he partakes in these great comforts,
  and is given to taste of neither acorns nor water.
Once all the dishes had been removed from the table,
  he listened intently to the sounds of sweet songs
  that appeared to come from the legions of heaven.
With much sweetness he gazes
  at the face and bearing of his gentle queen,
  who truly seems worthy of the gods.
"O my dear lady, in faith, this morning
  I have known such great pleasure;
  you seem to me none other than the morning star.
And thus I ask you: now make known your wish;
  as I told you, I am ready
  to furnish you with every pleasure."
She spoke to him in words graceful and humble
  and answered him, saying, "O my sweet lord,
  I thank God that I have found such grace in you."

And on her knees, with words that were pious and sweet,
    she revealed to him the cruel things she had learned
    and made known to him her wish,
almost weeping over such great treachery.[52]

Chapter 8

The queen knelt before the king to tell him
    all that she wanted him to know;
    the king took her now and urged her to rise.
He has her sit alongside him,
    saying to her, "You may reveal to me in safety
    all that you desire. Speak without fear;
tell me, queen, speak to me freely,
    because if you asked for half my kingdom
    you would obtain it, by the word of our living god."
To which Esther, with expressive words
    and weeping piteously, replied,
    "Since you have granted me such privileges,
the favor, my lord, that I ask of you
    is that neither I nor my people must die;
    for fear we live in trembling.
We have spent our days in trials and troubles,
    suffering cruel tortures, knowing little
    of pleasure or joy,
and the tears flow like rivers from our eyes.
    We will all be overcome by fear,
    if you, O lord, will not grant us your favor,
if you will not listen to us, lord,
    and learn of the false crimes of which we are accused.
    But if you heed our word, we will be uplifted.
It would have pleased God more if you sent us
    outside your country as servants and slaves,
    rather than expose us to the death reserved for us here.
Such things would have been mere games to us,
    and we would not have minded the weariness,
    the hardships and work, even if they were heavy.

---

52. Thus does Tornabuoni enhance the suspense, as we are made to wait until chapter 8 to know in full the king's reaction to her request.

But I will tell you who first began
   and ordained this falsehood, and who made himself
   an enemy to my people.
He has received your favors with hatred,
   O lord, you who have been so gracious to him,
   this man turns against even you in his cruelty."
Enraged, Ahasuerus replied:
   "If what you say is true and this man has such power,
   I will indeed make him grieve."
Prudently the queen replied:
   "I will show you this great enemy:
   there he is, lord, in your very presence.
Haman, your counselor, is the man of whom I speak,
   who out of envy and great avarice
   wanted to turn my people into beggars."
Said Ahasuerus, "But why do you petition me
   for these people, and care so much that they suffer?
   Why reveal to me the iniquity of Haman?"
And she answered, "It is fitting, my lord,
   because I am Hebrew, and one of their people.
   Not to plead on their behalf would hardly be just.
I want you to know this, my lord:
   as I told you, I was born of Hebrew parents,
   and Mordecai is my uncle.
I too am implicated in this cruel sentence;
   I too must die, in the same way
   that all of the Hebrews must die."[53]
The king answered, "Much do I praise you
   for not allowing this evil deed to happen;
   it gives me great joy to learn you are one of them.
In faith, it grieves me, and weighs on me,
   that all of you have suffered such hostility,
   and that I have not understood the truth.
I will make sure that everyone will see
   how unhappy I am at what has been ordered,
   and I will punish whoever strays from his duty.

---

53. There is no such question in the Bible. Tornabuoni is far more explicit than the author of Esther about the queen's loyalty to her people and her willingness to articulate her own

I want everyone to know who this evil man is!
    For he will serve as an example to all people,
    and I never want to lay eyes on him again.
Now then, let our love revive you,
    and make you happy. Your people will be treated
    compassionately by me."[54]
Haman was there, and he could hear
    what Ahasuerus was saying to his wife;
    and he was about to faint from grief,
and he could barely manage to raise his eyes
    to gaze up at the queen or Ahasuerus:
    his shame was such that he kept his head low.
The king, enraged by terrible thoughts,
    rose up in great anger and disdain;
    first he had been happy, now he became cruel.
He went into the garden, a beautiful place
    full of trees and tasty fruits,
    and here he calculated how to punish Haman.
Haman rose up as well, with plaints and weeping,
    hoping to go to the queen to make his petition,
    and his eyes were wet with tears.
Knowing of the great wrath of the king,
    he threw himself on his knees before Esther instead;
    but the king saw Haman and began to suspect him,
and so he turned back and stared at him at length,
    asking to whom he had given his company,
    with whom he had been uttering strange words and
      sighing.
To his barons, he says it was not enough

---

compromised identity before the king. Esther 7:3 is the most direct reference to Esther's Hebrew identity: "If I have found favor in thy sight, O king, and if it please thee, give me my life for which I ask, and my people for which I request. For we are given up, I and my people, to be destroyed, to be slain, and to perish." Tornabuoni translates these lines as well, albeit taking considerable liberties.

54. This speech by Ahasuerus is also Tornabuoni's innovation, an addition that makes him a more compassionate and thoughtful monarch than he is in Esther (and incidentally, far less similar to another monarch Tornabuoni wrote about—King Herod). In Esther, Ahasuerus's only response to Esther's petition is a question regarding the identity of the wicked man: "Who is this, and of what power, that he should do these things?" (Esther 7:6).

for Haman to do what he had already done; now
he seeks to violate Esther the queen!
The king hurls no other words at Haman;
the servants see him so out of temper
that one eunuch spoke to him as he was wont
(he was greatly trusted by the king,
and his name was Harbona,
and he had informed him of the ways of Haman).
He speaks now to him, "Holy crown,
evil Haman had built for Mordecai
a pair of gibbets," and he tells him this.
"May you heed what I say: they are fifty cubits high,
and on these, my lord,
he said that he wished Mordecai to hang:
Mordecai, who saved you from great distress
when he revealed the treachery of your servants;
he has always been faithful to you in his heart."[55]
The king became so violent on hearing this
that he said to his loyal servant,
"Now may he hang!"
Since he was so wicked to him, and so cruel;
since he has committed such evils
and has tried to render the sweet honey bitter;
since he has uttered falsehoods to me
by claiming that the Hebrews were so scandalous,
now let him taste the fruit of his evil.
Go instantly, without delay,
and do to him what he wished to do to Mordecai:
let him be the one to die.
For he is the one who is wicked and cruel,
he is the one who is full of presumption
and suffers from envy and has such pride.
Now hurry, put this evil man to death,
let him hang on his own gibbet,
and let it be done instantly, without delay."
Unmeasured in his grief, Haman

---

55. The rest of this chapter elaborates on the following two verses: "And the king said to him: Hang him upon it. So Haman was hanged on the gibbet, which he had prepared for Mordecai. And the king's wrath ceased" (Esther 7:9–10).

wants to try speaking with his lord,
 but he was prevented by the king's servants.
"Oh, woe is me!" he cried; "what use to me now are my
  sons,
 or my wife, or my friends, or my relatives?
 Thanks to me, they will now fare badly.
It it fitting that I know such torments,
 for I wanted to make others suffer,
 and now the winds have shifted direction.
It is fitting that I die in great shame
 and that my cursed plan fall on me alone,
 since I sought to see evil come to others."[56]
And thus they took him away and did not pause,
 and quicker than lightning they strung him up,
 and his gibbet was adorned with himself.[57]
Upon him alone came all the pain,
 and true enough it is, that he who throws stones
 will find them thrown back before he can breathe.
His friends, his sons, and his sorrowing wife,
 who shortly before had lived in such honor,
 now find themselves in one instant wretched and low.
O vain world, you are full of error,
 so few things in you are stable and secure;
 so quickly does gayness turn to grief.[58]
Blessed is he who is shielded from your blows.

Chapter 9

Thus did the proud Haman swing from the gallows,
 suspended, as I have said, in great violence,
 his skin and his nerves distended.[59]

---

56. Tornabuoni also attempts to humanize Haman by giving him this final confession; in the Bible, he has no chance to speak.

57. "Et la suo forcha fe di se adorna": possibly an echo of Dante's "Io fei gibetto a me de le mie case" [I made myself a gibbet of my own house], the final line of the Florentine suicide whom Dante and Virgil address in *Inferno* 13:151.

58. Perhaps another Dantesque reference, this time to *Inferno* 26:136, in which Ulysses laments the overturning of his little boat: "Noi ci allegrammo, e tosto tornò in pianto" [we were glad, but soon our joy turned to grief].

59. This gory depiction of Haman's death and the townspeople who talk together "in bassa vocie" is original to Tornabuoni.

The people were stupefied, gazing at him in fear,
  speaking together in low voices,
  asking themselves, Why Haman's sudden death?
What could it mean that the king so swiftly
  had him killed and exposed to such shame,
  subjecting him to such a cruel and ferocious end?
Some respond that he was too proud,
  that he desired to do too many things himself;
  that he was arrogant, insolent, and thoughtless.
And when this was done, the king did not wait
  to give all the substance of Haman, his great treasure,
  to Esther, his queen.
And in turn the queen, without delay,
  gave all these things to Mordecai, her uncle;
  the jewelry and vases of silver and gold.
"My lord has fulfilled my desire
  to see this deceiver dead";
  and she went about thanking God.
Now the king turns his attention to Mordecai,
  and to render him merit he tells him:
  "So that you know the great love I bear you,
take this ring, and let it be witnessed
  by all of my people";
  and he spoke so that everyone would hear.
"The worthy office that Haman once held,
  I now give to you, to honor you;
  I know I can trust you and that you will do well.
I am greatly disturbed by the vice of pride;
  I would like to be generous everyone,
  to those in my kingdom and to all humankind."
Upon seeing the liberality
  of that magnanimous king,
  Mordecai said, "Now, God, I know of your bounty.
You have sent your help to us so swiftly
  that I know you would never deny
  anyone who hopes and trusts in you.
Yet another time you freed us
  from the trials and labors of Egypt,
  showing us that we are your people."

Then he turned to face his lord;
    he took the ring and accepted the worthy office
    and thanked him with a happy heart.
"I ask my lord that he give me the wisdom
    to govern so that it please each man
    and let me never depart from your plan."[60]
But the queen, her desire still unfulfilled,
    gazed into the king's face,
    and readies herself to speak with him again.
On her knees, she spoke with pious words;
    weeping, she beseeches him sweetly:
    "I want another favor for my people;
I want you to revoke the fraudulent plans
    of Haman the proud so that my people will not die;
    please remedy this at once, and with care.
Without delay, may you send out
    letters throughout your entire country,
    and do it now, without wasting any time.
Haman, ever ready to harm our people,
    wanted all the Hebrews, everywhere, to die;
    I want you to write so they may be protected."
Answered the king: "Esther, so well have you exhorted
    me"—
    and touching his crown with his hand, he went on—
    "that now it will be done: now you can be consoled."
He showed to her his kindness then,
    when he touched the crown. It was a good sign;
    he heard what she requested,
and he continued: "I made Haman hang from the high
    beam
    because he bloodied his hands
    with your Hebrews that now have been made so
    worthy.
Write on my behalf to every village, town, and city,

60. Mordecai's prayer to God and his graciousness before the king are not in Esther; we learn, moreover, only later in the narrative that Mordecai was so elevated by the king (Esther 8:15). No doubt Tornabuoni moves this scene up in order to accentuate the contrast between Haman's fall from power and Mordecai's concomitant rise to the very position Haman had held.

to every place in the mountains and plains;
    send to them my command, sovereign and majestic.
May the earlier order be reversed
    and sealed with my most secret of seals;
    in such manner let this word be spread;
and may the letters be sent out at once,
    my intentions sealed within them,
    so that what I say can be made manifest to all."
The queen and Mordecai instantly had the scribes
    of Ahasuerus come before them,
    and in this manner the letters were written.
He[61] began to speak to them with great passion;
    on behalf of the great king, they told the scribes
    what to write to make his wishes known.
One hundred twenty-seven provinces had to be warned,
    so that princes, rectors, and vicars, all
    would understand this latest command.[62]
"Greetings and good cheer, dear friends,
    you are welcomed and loved by us;
    may you listen carefully to what follows.
I want all of you to be advised
    about one who was an ingrate (despite our great love);
    now learn how his falsehoods were discovered.
This man raised himself up in pride,
    and he cared little for his companions,
    desiring that he alone be honored.
And for his part, he wanted a decree to go out
    heralding him as worthy of all things,
    such a slave was he to his envy and pride.
With a mind that was presumptuous and blind,
    he maliciously accused
    a man deserving of highest praise,

---

61. In the Bible it is clear that Mordecai does the speaking: "The letters were written, as Mordecai had a mind, to the Jews" (Esther 8:9). Tornabuoni's Italian, however, leaves it unclear whether Mordecai or Esther recites the letter ("A parlar comincio con grande ardire / Per parte del gran re"). The rest of the line—"fecion narrare / Che ciascheduno intenda il suo disire"—gives us "fecion," which Tornabuoni generally uses as the third-person plural: it is possible that here *both* Esther and Mordecai are dictating.

62. The letter is taken from one of the apocryphal passages; the entirety of chapter 16 is devoted to the text.

using lies and fraud to make his case,
 and so before us he made us believe
 that the false was true; but now he enjoys nothing.
He claimed one thing for another
 and we believed he spoke the truth;
 and we trusted him because we thought he was loyal.
But things were quite the reverse, and we now call him
 accursed and false, and full of every vice,
 and we seek to erase him from our memories,
and make him a stranger to ourselves.
 Now you may know who this malefactor is,
 he who lost the serene state he once had:
it was the son of Hammedatha, the traitor,
 evil Haman, cruel, heartless, and savage;
 his wicked heart was full of violence.
A stranger, he came from Macedonia,
 an alien to the blood of the Persians.
 And he was gifted in deceptions;
he adopted new manners, fooling us with his looks.
 We showed him compassion,
 calling him father, but he acted foolishly.
He did not know how to be liberal and kind;
 and once he was adored as second only to the king,
 he quickly turned his heart to wickedness.
Elevated in arrogance and pride,
 he sought to deprive us of this great kingdom
 and gave all his thought to our death.
Mordecai, the Hebrew of whom I now speak,
 he sought to kill, along with his people:
 Mordecai, who saved us from death by using his
  wit.
With false accusations and traps
 he sought a grave martyrdom for them all,
 as he devoted his every word to lies.
I now want to compensate gracious Mordecai,
 known to us all, and Esther, my wife,
 for all the suffering they have known.
As my words will further show,
 Haman plotted their deaths; he imagined
 that neither you nor I should have dominion,

but believed the Macedonians, few though they were,
    would be able to resist us, and
    from us they could quickly recover Persia.
Now that we have had a chance to observe
    this Hebrew people, we wish to save them
    from undignified death; we wish to raise them up,
for so we imagined, and so we have found,
    that they are worthy of every favor,
    for they observe our precepts and our laws.
And let us never tire in honoring them,
    esteeming them, and doing their pleasure;
    and let them profit from the disgrace of Haman.
They have been the disciplined children of God,
    the guardians and protectors of our realm;
    since our ancestors' time they have kept us safe.
Now understand this well in your hearts:
    that cursed man sent to you letters;
    I revoke them and cancel their errors.
Be attentive and hear what I say:
    I want you to know that after deliberation
    Haman was hanged, in shame and contempt.
This was carried out in Susa because of his false deeds;
    let no one ask if this was our doing:
    for God awarded him this end for his sins,
and it was carried out through divine power,
    which rendered a fitting reward
    to one who had acted with such great presumption.
Now to the command that I give you:
    the Hebrew people are permitted to observe
    their own laws, in which each of them is expert,
nor may they be prevented from worshiping as they see fit.
    And the Hebrews may carry out vengeance.
    against the evils prepared for them.[63]
And let these days always be honored
    when their laments turned into happiness
    when we numbered their feast days among our own.

---

63. A reference to Haman's instructions. Unlike the biblical account, Tornabuoni's does not dwell on the details of the Hebrews' attack.

With great solemnity and ceremony,
    and in perpetuity, I command these things;
    and I want them to take place at once.
Who does not observe this, may he know violence
    from the knife and may he be punished with fire,
    and let this law be universal.
And many men and women will be burned and destroyed;
    all things, even their beasts will be plucked out,
    so that these decrees can be stabilized.
And always be ready
    [to carry out] our mandates, and may no one wish
    to deviate from these commands,
and for eternity, never violate them."

Chapter 10

The letters were written and packed up,
    and sent out on their quick courses,
    sealed with the most secret of seals.
And resting neither day nor night,
    the couriers traveled as quickly as they could;
    obeying their lord and expecting great gifts in return;
they could not rest at all: they had to prevent
    the cruel and evil fate of the Hebrews;
    the Hebrews should not be led to death!
And without fail, they arrived before
    the messengers that Haman sent out;
    on horseback and on foot, they arrived where they
        should.
Thus did the news spread everywhere
    that the traitor Haman had been hanged,
    and Mordecai had taken his office.[64]
And this happened in the month they called
    Adar, for such is its Hebrew name;
    in our language it is called *febbraio*.

---

64. The five stanzas above vividly portray the dissemination of Mordecai's and Esther's command as well as the news of Haman's death; they elaborate on Esther 8:10: "And these letters which were sent in the king's name, were sealed with his ring, and sent by posts who were to run through all the provinces, to prevent the former letters with new messages."

Now Mordecai had attained a worthy state;
    he was royally dressed in great honor,
    but the king gave him even greater tokens of his power:
He wore on his head the crown of valor
    that the king awarded those who held that position
    and which represented their great lord.
He celebrates, taking great solace and joy,
    and he dwells in happiness, eating well.
    To their enemies, this seemed no small thing.
And with volatile and suspicious thoughts
    they watched the Hebrews become exalted
    throughout all the provinces and cities,
they saw them become highly regarded
    and reverently obeyed;
    thanks to Mordecai the Hebrews were honored and
      feared.
Mordecai governed with prudence,
    doing his job with diligence and discretion
    throughout all the land.
Then the Hebrews, without delay,
    seized their enemies and did to them
    what they had wanted to do to the Hebrews.
In Susa alone, where the king dwelled,
    there was such a slaughter
    that at least five hundred died and were made
      miserable.
But Esther still is not contented,
    and she kneels before her king to pray once more
    that he bestow his favor and grant her wishes.[65]
"Haman had ten sons; make them hang,
    and then the vendetta will be complete
    and then my heart will finally be at peace."
The king answered her and said such words
    that it was clear that her will would be done:
    and it was carried out quickly and with dispatch.[66]

---

65. Tornabuoni adds this additional request on Esther's part. In the Bible, Ahasuerus asks Esther if there is anything else she desires ("What askest thou more, and what wilt thou have me command to be done?" Esther 9:12).

66. The Italian is most evocative: "cosi fu fatto infuria, inchaccia, enfretta."

And he permitted even greater license;
  besides the sons of Haman, three hundred others died,
  and the great bloodbath was seen by all.
The Hebrews were shrewd in all that they did;
  they touched nothing of the plunder,
  since its owners had met such a dismal fate.
In all those lands, only a single one
  failed to follow the command;[67]
  thus was the vendetta carried out, brutal and dark.
And once the dead were numbered and the count was
    made,
  seventy-five thousand had gone to their deaths
  where Ahasuerus had his kingdom.
And once these violent works came to an end,
  it was time for joyfulness, for feasting;
  in the past two days, they had not held court,
and everyone put on new garments
  (all the Hebrews, I mean); they dressed in noble garb,
  their hearts were filled with happiness.
Their days of lamentation and grief were at an end;
  in each city and village the orders were given
  to take part in rejoicing and delicious feasts.
With cheerful hearts, each Hebrew gave one another
  a portion of his happiness;
  Mordecai had given this order to all.
Thus did they chase away their grief,
  on the fourteenth and fifteenth days of the month;
  as it is recounted, and they regained their strength.
The festivities were open to all
  during these days, and great solemnities were held
  because God had heard their prayers.
They sent to those who lived in poverty
  great quantities of alms
  as a sign of their charity,
and to render thanks to God, to show

67. "In tutte quante le terre, sol'una mancho che non seguisse l'ordinato." A curious detail;
Esther 9:16 says: "Through all the provinces which were subject to the king's dominion, the
Jews stood for their lives, and slew their enemies, and persecutors"; there is no mention of a
place where the slaughter was not carried out.

they would always remember
the victory they had gained over their enemies.
"Throughout all the territory and surrounding lands,
    let there always be a memory of those days
    when they were liberated from their judges."
The king dressed himself in rich and ornate garments,
    and gladly he went to honor them
    with trumpets, drums, cymbals, and horns.[68]
The queen took great comfort as well.
    She bowed down low, and raised her eyes to heaven
    and felt in her heart great rejoicing.
And Mordecai, with exceptional forethought,
    ordained that on this day henceforth one must always
    exalt the divine majesty.[69]
So that others would always think back on this day,
    Mordecai considered what should be done,
    and he had these events written down so that people
        would read them.
The books recount how the governments
    of the kingdoms of Persia and Media
    were never wanting in their honor for God.
The king took his realm and placed it in
    Mordecai's hands, to do as he pleased;
    his every yes, his every no, would have to be accepted.
And thus my speech passes from one thing to the next;
    at times one needs to remove
    one passage and put another in its place.
My poor fantasy struggles to speak
    of the honors that were given to Mordecai;
    I do not lie when I say he was second in the realm.
In the presence of the king, it was made known
    that he was revered and esteemed
    by Persians and Medes, and by every Hebrew.
The people were all pacified,

---

68. Tornabuoni is explicit about the king's participation in the festivities; the Vulgate is not, declaring that "the Jews undertook to observe with solemnity all they had begun to do at that time" (Esther 9:23).

69. Curiously, in the Bible such "forethought" is Esther's as well. See Esther 9:29: "And Esther, the queen . . . wrote also a second epistle, that with all diligence this day should be established a festival for the time to come." One verse later, the day is spoken of as that which "Mordecai and Esther had appointed." This is a reference to the origins of Purim.

and the balance that he held in his hands was just,
 and no one knew dismay in any part of the kingdom.
Mordecai rendered worthy favors to God;
 and remembering a dream that had
 given him great consolation, he said:
"I was sleeping one night, and I saw
 a little fountain, very small,
 which quickly grew to become a great river.
This was Esther, who as a young girl
 was poor and dwelled in lowly estate;
 God raised her up and she became queen.
Then two dragons went to the extreme pass;
 one was Haman, and I was the other,
 and we were engaged in a great struggle.
The people whom I saw prepared
 to finish off an evil race
 were the Hebrews, just and pious.
And the sons of Israel, amid great suffering,
 prayed to God with devout hearts,
 and their just Lord raised them up
and freed them, and he imparted to them his vigor
 to reveal his power, and show his great sign
 that he is Lord of all things."[70]

Through grace, my fragile boat
 has been led to port from every dubious pass,
 and my scheme is satisfied, at least in part.
I thank you, and I bless the hour
 that you revealed to me this fantasy;
 you inflamed my heart with fire for this little work.
And you came with me as a companion,
 as you promised, and I was ever content;
 and you constantly showed me the way.
No longer slow, but with lively steps
 and without a trace of weariness, I come to the end,
 and my mind is glad.
And here I rest and come to a close.

70. This dream is the first of the apocryphal passages placed at the end of Esther (10:4–13). The dream is as close as we get to any kind of divine intervention in a story that has depended largely on *human* initiative and prayer.

THE LIFE OF
SAINT JOHN THE BAPTIST

INTRODUCTION

The life of Saint John the Baptist shows Tornabuoni at her most original, as she makes twenty stanzas out of the single verse in Mark suggesting that Salome and her mother Herodias were responsible for the saint's beheading. But Tornabuoni's poem was certainly not the first time John's fate was treated so richly. As the most prominent of Florentine feast days, the Feast of Saint John the Baptist (June 24), had long been an occasion for dramatic representations of the Baptist's life and death.[1] Then as today, the feast day was marked by processions, banquets, and plays, culminating in a fireworks show that the entire city attended. (On at least one occasion, the celebrations of 1475, it was considered remarkable that the buildings in the Piazza della Signoria did not go up in flames.)[2]

---

1. The feast day of the Baptist seems to have provided the initial impetus for the genre of the *sacra rappresentazione* in Florence in the fifteenth century. Some of the earliest dates for plays in Florence associated with liturgical feast days are the late 1430s, when during the Ecumenical Council of 1439 plays were performed for the Feast of the Annunciation and the Feast of the Ascension. An anonymous Greek visitor, however, notes with bewilderment the number of spectacles performed for the Feast of Saint John the Baptist: he speaks of plays of the Resurrection, of the Nativity and the visit of the Magi, and of the miracles of Saint George. Although these early attempts may not be full-fledged dramas, it certainly seems that by the mid-1450s numerous comparatively lengthy plays were performed after processions and parades. Such performances were especially grandiose when visiting dignitaries were in town; hence in 1465, when the son of King Ferrante of Naples and his sister-in-law Ippolita Sforza were in Florence, they spent several days at the house of Piero and Lucrezia and were entertained by the "gran festa di S. Giovanni"; in June 1473 when Eleonora of Aragon was visiting, seven plays were performed. Newbigin has a succinct historical summary of important documents and dates; see her introduction to *Nuovo corpus di sacre rappresentazioni fiorentine del Quattrocento.*

2. Piero Cennini, writing after the fireworks in 1475, calls attention to the display and then adds, "mirabiliter ardet nullo inferente incendium" [it was a marvel that the (fireworks) burned

One can surmise that Tornabuoni herself must have been present at many such spectacles in Florence, in which the Medici played a not insignificant role.

Given the importance of this civic occasion, it is no surprise that a number of Florentine *sacre rappresentazioni* about John survive. Of varying length and quality, like Tornabuoni's poem they all elaborate in innovative ways on the Gospel and apocryphal accounts of John's life.[3] One of Florence's most industrious writers of *sacre rappresentazioni*, and one who was closely tied both to the Medici family and to the pious archbishop Antoninus Pierozzi, was Feo Belcari, who composed a *Rappresentazione quando Santo Giovanni Battista essendo fanciullo fu visitato nel diserto da Gesù Cristo* [Play about when Saint John the Baptist, while still a boy, was visited in the desert by Jesus Christ]. The play features an episode popular in the apocryphal literature, the young boy's decision to leave his parents and live in the desert—an episode that Tornabuoni takes up as well. Another contemporary play, *La rappresentazione di Santo Giovanni Battista quando fu decollato* [Play of Saint John the Baptist when he was beheaded], first performed in August 1455, dwells on the final days of John's life. Unlike Tornabuoni's *Vita*, which is a true "biography" of the saint insofar as it begins with the prophecy to Zechariah when he is praying in the temple, the play opens with John already baptizing in the desert, where he is visited by Jesus, the Pharisees, and Herod (called only "il Re" [the king]). In the intense dialogues, first between Herod and his wife, then between his wife and stepdaughter (neither of whom is given a name), we see character developments that will also to some extent characterize Tornabuoni's poem. But the writer of the *sacra rappresentazione* minces his words far less than does Tornabuoni. Herod's wife calls John "un romito tutto pien d'errore" [a hermit full of sin], a phrase that might have struck a chord in mid-fifteenth-century Florence, and Herod refers to his wife as "the worst of whores" [pessima meritrice scellerata] and curses his dancing stepdaughter with far more vehemence than Tornabuoni's Herod. In a close worthy of Mozart's *Don Giovanni*, Herod's wife is swallowed in a violent earthquake ("la terra s'apre ed inghiottisce la Reina"), whereas Tornabuoni's

without causing a fire]; he also notes the vast crowds gathered in the Piazza della Signoria ("frequenti populo in platea Priorum") to see the show. Cited in *Tems revient*, 105.

3. The apocryphal Gospel of James provides details about John's life as an infant and a cousin of Christ, and it served the author of *The Meditations on the Life of Christ* as an important source. Many narratives also circulated about the early life of the Baptist, most famously the stories included in the late medieval *Legenda aurea*, or *Golden Legend*; other evangelical accounts include that of Domenico Cavalca, a well-known fourteenth-century Dominican who influenced, among others, Saint Catherine of Siena.

Herodias goes mad, gruesomely depicted as tossing the Baptist's head like a tennis ball as she descends into insanity.[4]

Tornabuoni's own *storia sacra* of John presumably has no connection with the performances of *sacre rappresentazioni*, even though in all likelihood it was inspired by this tradition. (At the same time, it is interesting that after the plague of 1478 the festivities for the city's patron saint were suspended, to begin again only in 1488. If Tornabuoni's account of John is from the late 1470s—and stylistically it seems superior to the other *storie sacre*—it may have been written for a private Medici celebration of the Baptist's feast day.)[5] Still, her retelling of the Gospel tale, with its considerable embellishments and details, shares in the lively dramatization of events that the New Testament relates in only the starkest of terms, and it is possible that she may have been influenced by the earlier play, particularly in her depiction of Herod's wife.[6] Even where she seems to be doing no more than translating some of the most famous passages of the Gospels—Mary's annunciation scene, for example, or her meeting with Elizabeth—we are treated to telling details about domestic life that reveal Tornabuoni's sure-handed ability to transform biblical narrative into memorable verse. The angel's remarks to Mary are delicately and joyfully phrased: "Think how much gladness will be yours! / Unknown till now, nor shall it be known again." Shortly afterward we see Mary "setting out into the mountains" to Elizabeth's home, where Elizabeth, whose "veder sottile" [subtle sight] makes her aware of the movements of the young John in her womb, addresses her cousin with "'Who am I, that the mother of the Lord / comes to my house, only to visit me? / I have such joy, and yet my heart is fearful; / I feel my own son bowing in reverence / to honor his noble maker. / And blessed are you, who believed in those things / God gave you to understand.'" Such moments are not so much departures from Luke's Gospel as poetic retellings. Far more innovative are Tornabuoni's scenes of the Baptist's early life. Particularly touching is his departure from his parents and his relief on entering the desert, after he has yearned for so long to leave

---

4. The text of the play can be found in *Nuovo corpus di sacre rappresentazioni fiorentine del Quattrocento.*

5. Nonetheless, it seems that Lorenzo himself took no great pride in honoring the Baptist's feast day; thus in a notorious letter Tornabuoni's favorite poet, Luigi Pulci, reprimands Lorenzo for failing to enlist the talents of Florence's citizens in organizing the festivities; see the letter of May 6, 1472, in Pulci, *Morgante e lettere,* 979.

6. See stanza 102 of the poem and the accompanying note for the speculation that Tornabuoni was in fact dependent on an earlier account such as *La rappresentazione di San Giovanni Battista quando fu decollato.*

the familiar surroundings of family and home to which he senses himself unsuited: "So gracious and comely was John / that whoever knew him bore him love, / but he often chose to remain thoughtful and alone, / and he told no one what he carried in his heart. / He would say to himself: 'Here I linger, doing nothing; / I must take myself away from here, / where I live with ease and am well cared for; / my home must be in the desert.'"

The tale of the Baptist's entanglement in court politics occupies only one-third of Tornabuoni's poem, but the characterization of the two principal female participants in this section make it by far the most dramatic part of the *Vita*. Tornabuoni seems to be at pains to rescue Salome (never so named) from the denigration to which she was often subjected, making her purely a puppet of her mother's evil plot. Pawn of a woman who hated John because he condemned her supposed adultery (she had married Herod after leaving his brother), Herodias does all she can to turn the king against the Baptist. Failing in such tactics, she next uses her daughter. The story is to this point strictly biblical; Mark 6:17–20 informs us:

> For Herod himself had sent and taken John, and bound him in prison, because of Herodias, his brother Philip's wife, whom he had married. For John had said to Herod, "It is not lawful for thee to have thy brother's wife." But Herodias laid snares for him, and would have liked to put him to death, but she could not. For Herod feared John, knowing that he was a just and holy man, and protected him; and when he heard him talk, he did many things, and he liked to hear him.

The rest of Tornabuoni's story, however, unlike that of the *sacra rappresentazione*, derives from a single biblical verse: "And Herodias's own daughter having come in and danced [for Herod's birthday banquet], she pleased Herod and his guests. And the king said to the girl, 'Ask of me what thou willest, and I will give it to thee'" (Mark 6:22).[7] The Florentine play depicts a Herod bound by his "barons" to keep his word after his stepdaughter asks (at her mother's urging) for John's head. In this the author of the *sacra rappresentazione* follows the Gospel account: "And grieved as he was, the king, because of his oath and his guests, was unwilling to displease her"—or as

---

7. We find an almost identical passage in Matt. 14:1–12; in all likelihood it was modeled on the earlier text of Mark. Luke refers both to the imprisonment of John (Luke 3:19–20) and to the fact of his beheading in a passage about the apostles' mission: "Now Herod the tetrarch heard of all that was being done by [Jesus] and was much perplexed, because it was said by some, 'John has risen from the dead.' . . . But Herod said, 'John I beheaded; but who is this about whom I hear such things?'" (Luke 9:7–9). Mark's account is by far the most detailed and is presumably the chief source for Tornabuoni's story of John's death.

the Greek literally means, "would not break faith with her." With Tornabuoni, however, the matter is less clear. On the one hand, Herod is not so much bound by his word in the presence of his vassals as he may be literally seduced by an unwitting and innocent young girl, who in turn has been placed in a compromising position through her obedience to the queen. Even, and perhaps especially, when she is ignorant of her erotic powers, the young woman possesses an unsurpassed ability to poison men's thoughts against their will. As Alice Bach has recently commented in her study of biblical women: "The young girl is fulfilling her mother's wish to have the troublesome Baptist silenced, not her own."[8] Tornabuoni heightens this tension when she originally suggests that the young woman had been influenced by the Baptist's teachings: "She had even begun to follow / the true light of the true faith / at the time her father went to see John at the river; / she had been honest and respectful, / she feared infamy, and was not shameless."

Yet the fatal dance can also be seen as only the final step of a plot in which Herod and his scheming wife Herodias have long been entangled. Unlike her daughter, Herodias is the femme fatale who conspires shrewdly to have John killed. Respecting, as in the biblical version of the story, women's traditional absence from their husbands' feasting—an absence that continued into Renaissance Florence—Herodias must work behind the scenes to effect her plan to silence the Baptist and pay him back for her mental anguish. In an unnerving moment before Herod, she berates her husband: "'Why on earth do you listen to this critic, / this barking dog who has riled up the entire nation? / See how he esteems your honor when / he has already broadcast [your sin] to all the people! / If this John really felt for you true love, / he would have advised you to take a different path, / but he wants to appear a great saint." As in *Susanna* and *Tobias*, once again we see a concern with *onore* or reputation, and it is this concern that motivates Tornabuoni's queen. Herod's role in this plot is less clear, as will be seen. Is he truly angered by his stepdaughter's request, or is he merely concealing his complicity, as he does in the *sacra rappresentazione* and a long commentary tradition summarized by Jacobus de Voragine in the *Legenda aurea*?

> [Herod] wished to please his wife but feared to lose the allegiance of John's followers. What he really wanted to do was to kill John, but [he] was afraid of the people. Indeed, both Herodias and Herod longed to find an opportunity to get rid of John, and they seem to have arranged secretly between themselves that Herod would invite

8. Bach, *Women, Seduction, and Betrayal in Biblical Narrative*, 230.

the leading men of Galilee to a banquet in honor of his birthday, and would have Herodias's daughter dance for them, after which Herod would swear to give her anything she asked for, and she would ask for the head of John. On account of this oath he would have to grant her request but would pretend to be saddened because he had sworn. . . . So the banquet is held, the girl is present, she dances for the company, everyone is pleased, the king swears that he will give her whatever she asks, she follows her mother's instructions and demands the head of John. Two-faced Herod feigns sadness because of an oath—because, as Rabanus says, he had to do what he had sworn to do. But the sadness was only on his face. In his heart he was delighted.[9]

What may seem to be Tornabuoni's inability to create a consistent portrait of Herod might in fact be a sign of her artistry: she has managed to conceal even from her readers Herod's "two-faced" nature, leaving us uncertain as to the extent of the king's complicity in his wife's scheme.

A juxtaposition between the superficial frivolity of life at Herod's court and the seriousness and asceticism of John, dedicated to fulfilling the prophecies and serving as the forerunner of Christ, furnishes the real contrast of the story.[10] Tornabuoni elucidates this contrast implicit in the brief Gospel account, and in so doing she underlines John's own resistance to the various "festive" norms that had characterized her other poems: the lavish banquets at which Esther makes her pressing supplications to the king; the lush garden in which Susanna enjoys her noontime walks; the festivities in *Tobias* when children are regained. Notably, John avoids the social worlds of all of these figures (and, one might add, of Tornabuoni herself. When Galeazzo Maria Sforza visited Florence in 1459, he wrote a letter to his father describing the performance of a song by one Maestro Antonio about the mighty deeds of the Sforza family, followed by a dance in which Tornabuoni's daughters, Lucrezia and Bianca, took part).[11] As in a touching scene from a fresco cycle in the cathedral in Prato, painted by Fra Filippo Lippi in 1466, John disappears into the desert when he is only a young boy,

9. Jacobus de Voragine, *Golden Legend*, 2:133.

10. This is Bach's point (232). Whether one can argue that the Gospel story may then serve as a critique of a similar story line in Esther, another biblical book Tornabuoni versified, is not entirely clear. Bach suggests that the Gospel writer may have linked the two banquets in which two women were supposed to dance before relatively uninspiring kings; that Herodias's daughter complied whereas Vashti did not, she says, "leads one to speculate about an undercurrent of parody in the gospel account of Herod's banquet" (233).

11. See the account in Maguire, *Women of the Medici*, 67.

leaving behind his frantic parents; they send their servants out to look for him, and he agrees to come home only to say good-bye. As he returns to the desert, where he believes he has been called to spend his life, his parents sadly watch him depart: "Willingly would they have accompanied him: / they wanted to live together, with all of their family." John's haste to perform penance and prepare himself to announce Christ's coming marks him as an extreme version of the other protagonists in Tornabuoni's stories; like them, he is moved by a deep sense of responsibility to his people and his God. But he has little of their anguish and occasional hesitation regarding his ministries in and outside the world; and to this extent he emerges as the only true "saint" of Tornabuoni's works.

Given the Baptist's centrality in Florence, it would be impossible to delineate all the possible artistic influences on Tornabuoni's work.[12] There are many tondos showing the infants Jesus and John with their mothers, as well as numerous gaunt Baptists. It is probably the great fresco cycles of the Baptist's life, themselves inspired by the apocryphal and Gospel narratives, that have most in common with Tornabuoni's work. Particularly in Filippo Lippi's paintings of the Baptist's life in nearby Prato, works Tornabuoni might easily have seen, one witnesses not only the tender parting of parents and child but the Baptist's desert solitude, Zechariah's writing his son's name on a slip of paper, and Herod's banquet, complete with a tentative Salome, her eyes on the richly decorated floor, and an imperious Herodias receiving the Baptist's head from her daughter's hands. Tornabuoni's poetic narrative of the complex interpersonal dynamics that characterize this story, far more detailed in its many apocryphal versions than in the New Testament one, is a highly compelling treatment of the well-known events of John's life and deserves to be included among some of the most interesting poetic accounts of the Baptist from the Renaissance.

It is also Tornabuoni at her most sophisticated, leading one to suspect that she may have written it after the other poems. Nowhere else is she quite so free with enjambment; in over twelve instances, she creates an almost seamless transition from one ottava to the next. She is also far less insistent about using formulaic phrases to introduce spoken discourse; whereas in her other works often one or two lines are taken up calling attention to conversational exchange ("Udendo que' baroni quella risposta" [*Judith* 17.1]; "Udendo e sacerdoti questi motti / risposono ad costoro"

---

12. Ernesto Livorni's unpublished essay "When Death and Birth Conjoin: The Worship of St. John the Baptist in Renaissance Florence," presented for the Renaissance Society of America meeting in March 2000, is an important contribution to our understanding of the relationship between the iconography of the Baptist and the Medici.

[*Judith* 83.5–6]; etc.), Tornabuoni often leaves out such fillers altogether. Their omission enables dialogue to move at a more natural pace and allows her to develop more supple and evocative lines. Finally, that Tornabuoni not only draws on biblical accounts but feels free to incorporate popular and pseudoevangelical writings and representations of John as well may suggest increasing confidence in her ability to bring together a range of materials as opposed to relying on a single text. To this extent, *La vita di Sancto Giovanni Baptista* is less a translation than an imaginative retelling of the life of Florence's patron saint—a saint to whom Tornabuoni professes her devotion in the poem's last lines as she dares to envision her *storia sacra* enhancing his reputation on earth: "By virtue of his delightful works / and through his grace, I will be able to boast / of having told the story of his death and of his people, / [so that] through me and others devotion to him may grow!"

HERE BEGINS THE LIFE OF SAINT JOHN THE BAPTIST,
COMPOSED BY MADONNA LUCREZIA, WHO WAS WIFE OF
THE MAGNIFICENT MAN PIERO DI COSIMO DE' MEDICI

1. In the name of the omnipotent Father
and the Son who is high wisdom,
and the Holy Spirit's ardent fire:
I pray that through divine clemency
I may be granted grace and diligence enough
to tell the tale and do reverence to the honor
of the glorious John the Baptist,
and may my vision suffice!

2. And because I want to speak of this worthy saint,
I also pray to the true Mother of God
that she help me find good matter[13] for writing
and enable me to succeed in my design:
I would like to complete the entire work.
Guide me, Madonna, and give me the skill[14]

13. See Dante's proem to *Paradiso*: "Veramente quant'io del regno santo / ne la mia mente potei far tesoro, / sarà ora materia del mio canto" [Nevertheless, as much as I, within / my mind, could treasure of the holy kingdom / shall now become the matter of my song] (*Paradiso* 1:10–12).

14. The Italian is *ingegno*, which can be variously translated as wit, skill, or intellect; cf. another Dantesque proem, that of *Inferno* 2: "O alto ingegno."

to draw it all together, and put it into rhyme,
so that it may be worthy of honor and esteem.

3. Through the mouth of the prophet Isaiah,
the Lord God spoke: "Hear me, O coastlands,
O peoples far and near, attend to my way.
Since the time of the ancient struggle
in the womb of my Mother,
I was called to do pleasing works:
to make ready the way of the great Lord,
sent ahead of him to be his precursor."[15]

4. John the Evangelist speaks of this saint,
the living light of the world,
in whose word nothing is confused:
this light was sent by God,
and his name was John the Baptist,
he who came before that true light
and prepared the way for him by preaching
and administering holy baptism.[16]

5. In his blessed speech, Jesus spoke
of that happy John: never had woman given birth
to one who was greater than he,
nor was there any prophet more acceptable to God,
and he is called more than a prophet.[17]
You know who has spoken of him:
prophets and evangelists [have spoken] in his honor,
and the final one to do so was his Lord.

6. Observe, readers, the divine Majesty;
take note of the affection with which he speaks

---

15. See Isa. 49:1: "Hear me, O coastlands, listen, O distant peoples: The Lord called me from birth, from my mother's womb he gave me my name."

16. The ottava invokes another passage from Isaiah, one that virtually opens the Gospel of Mark: "Behold, I send my messenger before thee, who shall prepare thy way, the voice of one crying in the desert, 'Make ready the way of the Lord, make straight his paths'" (Isa. 40:3).

17. The reference is to Matt. 11:11: "Amen I say to you, among those born of women there has not risen a greater than John the Baptist; yet the least in the kingdom of heaven is greater than he." The same passage will be echoed in stanza 114, when Jesus speaks of John after his arrest.

of the great prophet John and his great worth.
Well do I know my ignorance and my presumption,
O Lord, you who know the truth:
I have taken on this [work] out of my
devotion to the gracious and worthy saint,
in whose honor and praise may my song reside.

7. I realize that this enterprise is too weighty
for one who knows nothing about making poetry,
and that I will be corrected
by those who do understand.
But I hope they will use discretion,
seeing how my mind burns—as I have said—
with constant devotion for him,
and not for anything else: thus love makes me bold.[18]

8. In his Gospel[19] Saint Luke recounts
that at the time of the powerful King Herod
there lived a priest from the family of Abijah,
a zealous man of much excellence.
His name was Zechariah,
and his heart was turned to heaven;
his prayers were just and devout,
and he worthily fulfilled his office.

9. The priest Zechariah had a wife
whose name was Elizabeth,
one of the daughters of Aaron, and with her husband
she walked a straight and narrow path;
the two were just and their minds pious.
Their souls were fixed on heaven,
they never gossiped or complained,[20]
and they always glorified their Lord.

---

18. "Cosi lamor mi fa prosumptuosa": an interesting phrase, given Tornabuoni's attacks on presumptuousness elsewhere in her poems (e.g., in the eighth stanza of *Judith*, where she observes that Arsaphat was "prosumtuoso molto" and was a man of "molta aroganza").

19. Tornabuoni here turns to Luke 1:5, which initiates the account of Zechariah's vision at the temple. Tornabuoni follows the chapter fairly closely, up to the prophecy of Zechariah after John is born, albeit with interesting additions that will be noted.

20. "Né mai di nulla cosa mormorando": a detail not found in Luke, and one that interests Tornabuoni elsewhere, as in *The Story of Devout Susanna*.

10. And although they had been together a long time,
    they had not been able to have a son;
    she was sterile and had never given birth.
    Elizabeth was not distraught
    because she had no children, nor did she complain,
    provided she was able to please her Lord,
    and both she and her husband stood always ready
    to serve him and obey his commands.[21]

11. It so happened that at this time Zechariah
    had to celebrate the sacrifice in the temple
    as was his custom, and so he journeyed
    to his usual destination.
    With pious thoughts, he arrived at the temple
    at the chosen hour to perfume it with incense;
    and all the people with great devotion
    waited outside to say their prayers,

12. and in that very hour of which I speak,
    Zechariah was attentive at his prayer,
    when look! All at once,
    on his right, he saw a vision,[22]
    a man who said to him: "Fear not;
    I am an angel, sent to you
    from the great dwelling place to announce
    that God wishes to give you a wonderful son."

13. When he saw him, Zechariah was disturbed;
    the angel said to him: "Do not be afraid;
    the son who will be given to you
    will be full of truest wisdom;
    he will be of such excellence
    that never was such a one of woman born,
    and you will call him John,
    and he will bring respite to your long suffering.

21. Tornabuoni continues to stress the couple's piety; Luke 1:7 simply has: "But they had no son, for Elizabeth was barren, and they were both advanced in years."

22. "Da lato dextro vide visione": the Vulgate alludes only to the presence of an angel "standing at the right of the altar of incense" (Luke 1:11).

14. "This son who will be born of you
    and your dear spouse Elizabeth
    will make many people glad at his birth,
    for he is chosen by God and will be great in his sight.
    Let his food be bitter
    and his diet constrained;
    he shall not drink of the wine that may make him drunk,
    and he will be sober in his eating.

15. "The Holy Spirit shall completely fill him
    in his mother's womb,
    so that he will convert the sons of Israel
    and direct their thoughts to our joyful Lord,
    and teach them to walk in the living spirit.
    And through the power of Elijah
    he will turn the hearts of fathers
    and sons alike to serve God

16. "and make ready for him a perfect people,
    because this is the will of the Lord."
    Zechariah replied, and as it is said,
    he displayed great fear in his speech:
    "How shall what you say come to pass?
    Neither my wife nor I has the strength
    [to have children], we have been elderly
    for some time, so that I can put no trust in what I hear."

17. And the angel answered him: "I am Gabriel,
    the angel that stands before God the Father.
    And he has sent me to you with this gift,
    to announce the things that I have heard
    from him who is seated in the highest throne.
    But since you have not believed what I said,
    now I tell you this: You shall not be able
    to speak of these things until you behold them."

18. The people outside awaited Zechariah,
    all of them wondering why he delayed;
    then he came out, and wanting
    to make his way home, he set out.

He made gestures to them, but he said nothing
because there was nothing he could say;[23]
they knew only that he had seen a vision
and that he was unable to talk.

19. I see that the Evangelist says
he returned to his house, where his wife conceived
a son,
but she hid [the fruits of] her desire for a good five
months;
this is what I find and understand.[24]
She said: "It is God who has brought this about;
he has taken away my shame and raised me up,
and among women I shall not be the least,
because my Lord is pleased to do this to me."

20. In the sixth month God sent to Galilee,
to a town called Nazareth, Gabriel,
an angel of his kingdom;
he sent him to that virgin who was promised
to a man named Joseph,
of the worthy house of David,
and she was a virgin by the name of Mary.
Hear how the angel welcomed her:

21. "Greetings from God, you are full of grace,
and the Lord God is with you everywhere.
Blessed are you, luminous light;
you are the light and fire of all women."
Hearing him address to her this kind
of salutation disturbed her not a little.
"Mary, please, do not fear my words;
you have found great favor with God.

23. A typically homely example of Tornabuoni's style: "Nulla non dicia / perche niente non
potea parlare."

24. "Ma ella sì celava il suo disio / ben cinque mesi, così truovo et piglio": a colloquial transla-
tion of "and she secluded herself for five months" (Luke 1:24). Jacobus de Voragine is more
explicit: "She then hid herself for five months, because, as Ambrose says about this, she felt
some shame at having a child at her age, fearing that she might seem to have indulged in
lustful pleasure despite her years" (*Golden Legend,* 1:330).

22. "Here in your womb you shall conceive,
    and the mother of God will be you alone,
    and in the fullness of time, you will give birth
    to a son, and you shall call him Jesus.
    Think how much gladness will be yours!
    Unknown till now, nor shall it be known again;
    this worthiest of children who is to be born
    will be called the son of the Highest God,

23. "and to this glorious and worthy child,
    God will give the seat of his father David,
    and he will reign with true wisdom;
    he will rule forever, with all his legions,
    and his reign will have neither equal nor end."
    Mary responded: "I am not able
    to be a mother. Now how can this be, since I
    have not yet desired to know any man?"

24. "The Holy Spirit," the angel said,
    and the power of God will overshadow you,
    and you will know great sweetness, rejoicing, and song
    on the day that the son of God is born.
    And Elizabeth, your cousin,
    who has been barren for so long,
    will in her old age give birth, an incredible birth;
    know that nothing is impossible with God."

25. As soon as she understood what he said,
    she answered him humbly, and with reverence:
    "I am his handmaiden"—so ready was she to speak—
    "let what you have just revealed
    so clearly and so openly be done to me."
    The angel swiftly departed, and Mary went off too,
    setting out into the mountains,
    to the home of Zechariah.

26. Entering their household, the humble virgin
    gave Elizabeth a worthy greeting,
    demonstrating her gentleness
    and seeking to show her the gift she had received.

Elizabeth, filled with the Holy Spirit,
with keen awareness[25]
sensed that her son within
was performing great honors to his worthy Lord,[26]

27. and this holy speech thus followed:
"Who am I, that the mother of the Lord
comes to my house, only to visit me?
I have such joy, and yet my heart is fearful;
I feel my own son bowing in reverence
to honor his noble maker.
And blessed are you, who believed in those things
God gave you to understand."

28. Hearing Elizabeth say these words,
Mary in turn began to speak in this fashion:
"My soul magnifies the Lord,
and my spirit exalts in God
for holding his humble handmaiden in his regard:
He is my way and my salvation.
All the generations
that shall ever be will call me blessed

29. "because of the wonderful things he has done to me;
he is powerful, and his name
is holy, and his mercy
will endure for all generations.
Those who fear him and trust in him
will be strengthened in their arm and their body.
He will disperse the proud and make them humble,
and he will bring great honor to the lowly.

30. "And he has cast out the mighty from their thrones,
he will fill the hungry with good things,
and he will leave the rich unsatisfied.
He will raise up the son[s] of a Nazarene,

---

25. "Veder sottile," or subtle sight, which might also be translated as "sixth sense."
26. One of many examples in the poem where Tornabuoni refuses to enclose a passage within the strict boundaries of the ottava; see the introduction to this section.

who bear in mind the memory of his mercy;
he has remembered us, and he comes for us
just as he told your father Abraham he would,
and Abraham's seed, that now is ours."

31. Devoutly they all listened
    to the sweet words that she speaks,
    and all who are there do her reverence,
    believing her to be the genetrix of God.
    Blessed are they who can serve her,
    and whoever touches her is content.[27]
    With holy Elizabeth she remained
    for almost three months, and then she returned home.

32. But while Mary still dwelled
    at the house of her dear, sweet relatives,
    Elizabeth's time was completed,
    and her hour arrived; with sweet labors
    she brought forth her son at dawn.
    Just imagine how delighted and content they were!
    The first to touch her son
    was lovely Mary, with happy brow.

33. She took him and carried him joyously
    to his mother, and she began to say:
    "Our lord manifests his mercy
    to those who choose to follow him,"
    and she spoke to them with modest demeanor.[28]
    The eighth day arrived, and they went
    to circumcise him, following the custom of the law
    in those days, so as not to delay,

27. Tornabuoni adds this tender response to Mary's Magnificat; especially interesting is her use of the word "genetrix" to denote Mary's role as mother.

28. The scene with Mary is also not biblical, although it is a favorite one in medieval commentaries and prayer books; see in particular the following passage from the fourteenth-century *Meditations on the Life of Christ*: "When her time had come Elizabeth gave birth to the son whom our Lady lifted from the ground and diligently cared for as was necessary. The child loved her deeply, as though he understood her, and even when she gave him to his mother he turned his face to the Lady, delighting only in her" (24–25).

34. and they wished to call him Zechariah,
    the name of his father, as you have heard.
    Hearing this, the mother cried: "Let it not be so!
    John shall be his name, and you must obey."
    They responded: "There is no one of your clan
    who is called John; let us go ask his dear father
    to put an end to this quarrel,
    because in such affairs, we should not trust the mother."

35. They went off quickly to find Zechariah,
    asking him what name he wished for his son,
    and asked that he let them know through gestures,
    since he was unable to tell them with words.
    And as was usually the case,
    Zechariah made them surmise through his motions
    that they should bring him some implements
    with which he could write. And thus he wrote,

36. "Let John be his name," and as he wrote,
    suddenly his mouth was opened, his tongue untied;
    and he began to speak, praising God,
    and thanking him, and all of them heard him,
    and all of them were seized with fear.
    From everywhere the people gathered,
    saying among themselves: "Who would have thought
    that this child would be the Messiah?"

37. Father Zechariah spoke with much love
    of this boy, his strong and glorious son;
    he was filled with amazement
    and the Holy Spirit, who amplified
    his voice and opened his perfect heart
    that had fed on such good food.
    And thus he began in this way
    to speak and to magnify his Lord:

38. "May the God of Israel be blessed,
    and forevermore the visitation
    that he made to his people, as he

lovingly sent forth to them their redemption;
he has depleted the power of their evil enemy
as we were all heading to our ruin;
he has directed his strength to our salvation.
Now all the prophecies shall be fulfilled!

39. "This child is from the house of David:
thus he spoke through the mouths of his saints,
and they are all prophets, and they prophesied truly;
he released us from the hands
of our enemies and their followers,
and he would have this be our task, to be merciful to all,
to bear in mind his testament,
the promise he made to father Abraham

40. "when he told him he would give himself to us.
Thus liberated from our enemies,
we will serve him without fear,
so that we might become the perfect friends
of God and never see again
the dark places and the sorrowful slopes.
And you, my son, who now are born,
prophet of him who is called the Most High,

41. "you will go before the face of God
to make ready the path for your Lord,
you will bring your people desire and joy
and bring forgiveness to the sinner
who has lived for so long in shadows and forgetfulness;
you will guide their hearts toward true love,
and you will win the war against the enemy
who has been so bold, and procure for us the way of peace."

42. Then when Zechariah had finished his wise
speech, he turned to his son;
he laid his hands on him to bless him,
and to his mother he returned him;
and he watches him with greatest delight,
gazing as long as he possibly could.

His mother had been awaiting him with joy,
and when she held him again, she gave him her
   breast.[29]

43. Nourished by the Holy Spirit,
    the boy grew to be great in virtue,
    and when he was still young
    he went out into the desert to seek his health.[30]
    There he remained, and there the prophecies
    were fulfilled, and when the time was ripe,
    John revealed himself to Israel
    and made manifest to all his worthy works.[31]

44. So gracious and comely was John
    that whoever knew him bore him love,
    but he often chose to remain thoughtful and alone,
    and he told no one what he carried in his heart.
    He would say to himself: "Here I linger, doing nothing;
    I must take myself away from here,
    where I live with ease and am well cared for;
    my home must be in the desert."

45. Then one morning he stole away
    without telling anyone, departing alone
    through the gate; his thought and his plan
    were to go to the desert without a guide.
    And once in the desert, he said to himself:
    "This air and this place bring me comfort,
    here I will stay alone as I please;
    I enjoy living among wild beasts and birds."

46. He went about gathering flowers,
    saying on the threshold of the desert:

29. With this stanza, and until stanza 65, Tornabuoni moves away from the Gospels into popular legends on the life of John, inspired in part by the final verse of Luke 1: "And the child grew and became strong in spirit; and was in the deserts until the day of his manifestation to Israel."

30. "Per trovar salute": spiritual health is probably also implied.

31. This stanza is a résumé of what is to come in the next twenty or so stanzas; stanza 44 returns us to the adolescent John.

"May God be praised that I have left and[32]
come to a place where I can gain some worth.
And I seem already to hear these magnificent choirs
praising their Lord with expert song."
Thus as John goes about and speaks to himself,
the hour arrived when he usually ate.

47. So immersed was he in contemplation,
and in talking things over with himself,
that he did not realize it was time to eat,
and the sun was already beginning to set;
then looking all around him,
he saw some things that were good to eat,
like chestnuts and apples, locusts and acorns,
and a fountain that poured forth clear water.

48. When he had gathered these little things together,
he sat down near the fountain
among fresh herbs and flowers,
and he regrets having delayed for so long.
And while he was saying these things to himself
he looked up, and he saw coming from far off
the messengers that his father had sent,
and his mother had also sent them to find him.

49. "For a while I must return
to the home of my father." Zechariah and Elizabeth
had everywhere searched for him,
awaiting him until the hour of their dinner,
and then they called him until their voices were hoarse,
and then they began to suspect what had happened:
Could this possibly be true of their son,
that he would go into the desert alone?

50. They called some of their faithful servants
and said to them: "We cannot find our son,

---

32. "Lodato Idio ch'i' sono uscito fuori": there is an echo here of Tornabuoni's *Judith*, stanzas 89 and 96, in which Judith goes out first from her room and then from the city ("usciva fuori") to fulfill her fate as the liberator of God's people.

and we are disconsolate;
we no longer know where to search.
Go, make yourselves ready to look for him;
see if he has gone to dwell in the desert,
and if you find him, bring him back with you;
do not return home without him."

51. And off the servants quickly went,
and it seemed as though God taught them what to do.
After they had searched in many places,
they found John still seated at the fountain.
And he said to them: "Who sent you here?
What were you hoping to find among these stones?"[33]
"We are sent by your dear father,
so that we can take you to him and to your mother."

52. Absorbed as he was in contemplation,
John was troubled to hear their words,
and he said: "Since that is their wish,
I will come, to obey them.
But I will return here at once,
as soon as I have had their blessing,
because I wish to stay here in peace,
since this is what my Lord wishes."

53. And he got up and went with them,
returning to his home,
and when he arrived, his mother and father
embraced him, saying sweetly,
"Son, why did you want to leave us?"
He spoke to them with passionate words:
"It is clear that I was sent by God
so that I could spend time in the desert.

54. "I have come home to obey you,
O father and mother, but with your permission

---

33. "Che volete trovar fra questi sassi?" The question will be echoed later by Jesus in stanza 113 when he asks the crowds what they expected to find when they sought out John in the desert ("Che andasti / voi ad veder nel profondo diserto?").

I will travel again into the desert,
and I will stay there and undergo harsh penance,
so that I may speak of it to the people.
Please, do not let our parting seem hard;
I would like your benediction
so I may go off to my consolation."

55. "O son, what words are these that you say?
Why do you wish to abandon us so quickly?
Will this celebration endure for such little time,
this feasting we make for your return?
The request you make of us is hard, O son;
why do you wish to leave us?
O son, do not put us through these trials;
please, stay with us, and may God bless you!"

56. "I have told you and I tell you again
why I was sent into the world:
so that I may go, a mendicant, into the desert,
and live cheerfully in a state of penance.
Let me tell you yet again:
I must go alone into the most obscure
place that there is. Please rejoice with me
that I go to fulfill God's commands.

57. "O father and mother, I wish that it was
in my power to do your every pleasure;
I know that my departure will bring you pain and
      grief;
because I go, you will know great sadness.
But it is most fitting that I obey God."
Hearing him utter words so sincere,
both his parents marvel
and they answered their son:

58. "Sweet son, oh my! to what dark life
do you now choose to commit yourself, so alone?
Won't you be afraid of the beasts?
On what will you live, dear son?

You will sleep on the hard ground!
Think how much grief this would bring any parent,
to be so deprived of such a son.
We can only remain here without consolation."[34]

59. "Leave me to go where my desire leads me,
to do the will of my Lord.
If you only knew the pleasure and delight
that God sends me every hour of the day,
you would already have thanked him for me:
you [will] see me here and there in your hearts."
Hearing him speak with such passion:
"Now go, and may you be blessed by God."

60. Then his mother embraced him, holding him close,
weeping plentifully as she said: "Sweet love,
you are in years very young,
but since it pleases our great God to do this
[and since] I know well that he holds you blessed,
in good faith I give you my blessing too."
Father Zechariah wept and moaned
and could only gaze at his son with pitying eyes.

61. John took leave of them both,
making his way back into the desert,
and his mother and his father, grieving greatly,
remained at home, with downcast brows.
Willingly would they have accompanied him:
they wanted to live together, with all of their family.
John himself had clearly foreseen that
no one desired that he depart in such haste.

62. Thus alone he came into the desert,
and here he gives great thanks to his Lord:
"Here I will dwell by myself without fear,
living among these beasts who do me honor;

34. The sentiments of John's parents echo those of Tobias's mother when she laments his departure to Rages (see chapter 5).

they are my pleasure and my delight;
they remain with me all the hours of the day,
the bears with the wolves, the snakes and lions;
the serpents, lizards, scorpions, and poisonous snakes."

63. John dwelled with the beasts as though they were humans:
when he ate, they lingered to watch him,
and together they feel secure
and bring no harm to one another;
they treat each other with love
as though they were the purest of lambs.
These are his fathers and mothers and sons,
and none of them is ever alone.

64. As you hear, in such manner John lived there,
and much time passed. His cheeks became pale
because of the foods that he ate;
he lived all alone, his heart tender and kind,
and there he spent a great part of his life,
and he was constant and firm,
and he lived patiently in the desert
while performing harsh penitence.

65. In the fifteenth year of the reign of Tiberius,
Pilate was procurator,
sent by the imperial governor
of Rome to Judea, and here he remained.
Herod and his brother desired to
make themselves lords and increase their power,
and in Jerusalem at the time the high priests
for the tribunal were Annas and Caiaphas.[35]

66. And at this time John, son of Zechariah,
remained in the desert, and there began
to be spread about him this news:
"He is the one of whom Isaiah has spoken."

35. With this stanza, Tornabuoni returns to the account in Luke; the next fourteen stanzas draw largely from Luke 3:1–18.

He went about preaching repentance,
claiming that the reign of heaven was coming:
"I am the voice that cries out in the desert,
make straight the path of the true Lord.

67. "I say to you that every valley shall be filled,
and hearts will be led to justice;
every mountain shall be lowered,
and those who are lowly shall be raised up:
these are the things that will be seen by all.
Make yourselves ready, purify your thoughts,
and every fleshly thing will plainly
see our Lord before us, come to save us."

68. John wore a garment
made of the skins of camels, with a belt
that was wrought of neither silver nor gold;
rather it was large, of rough leather,
and it girded his loins thusly, as I hear,
and he slept on the ground in both heat and cold,
and he drank water, and ate acorns and honey
and locusts as his finest foods.[36]

69. Throughout all the region the saint was heard
to preach repentance and sanctity,
and from Jerusalem many people
departed to hear him speak.
From the district of Judea they traveled,
and they came to the Jordan to be baptized
and they confessed their sins,
returning to their homes happy and consoled.

70. But when he saw many Pharisees
and Sadducees coming to be baptized,
John hurled at them these words:
"Who has taught you to keep yourselves apart,

---

36. With some embellishments, the details on John's food and clothing are from Matt. 3:4: "But John himself had a garment of camel's hair and a leathern girdle about his loins, and his food was locusts and wild honey."

you generation of vipers? I see
that you want to stand far
from the wrath that is to come; but now repent
and surprise me with your actions!"[37]

71. "You do not wish to trust in these things,
saying 'Abraham is our father.' If God wanted to,
from these very stones, he could raise up
sons of Abraham as virtuous as those of old.
I tell you the truth, I weep greatly for your sins,
and for all that I see.
The ax is laid at the root of the tree;
it is time to humble yourselves,

72. "for every tree that does not bear good fruit
will be cut down and burned in a great conflagration."
The crowds then asked him what he meant:
"Please tell us what will happen, speak of this a little more."
John answered them, full of love:
"Who has bread and sees someone who has but little,
let him give some to him; he who has clothing,
let him do the same and let not his neighbor die."

73. The publicans came to be baptized
and they said to him: "Master, what shall we do?"
And he answered: "Do not be stingy;
each of you should be full of love,
and do not complain of what is to come.
In such a way does one serve our luminous God;
the good servant of God never ceases in his work,
and who always stands before God will remain young."[38]

74. The knights came to him and asked:
"And we, what are we to do?"

37. A difficult passage: "Fate un po' di violenza al senso." The intimation might be that John is challenging the Pharisees to change and thus to "do violence" to his own expectations about their sinfulness.

38. "Sta verde," or literally "stay green" in the Italian.

And John answered them without delay:
"You should molest no one;
do not be like the wolf who devours.
For the love of God, do not offend others,
and be content with the pay that you have
and do not ask for more."

75. Throughout the whole region it was believed
that John the Baptist was the Christ.
Orators from Judea were sent,
wanting to hear from John himself if he was the Christ,
and he answered the messengers,
confessing to them with these words: "I am not Christ."[39]
"Can you then tell us who you are? Are you Elijah?
Or are you a prophet, if you are not the Messiah?

76. "Tell us now who you are, so that we can
answer those who have sent us to you,
so that we might give witness of you
and they will know in fact that we have been here."
And he answered them humbly and plainly:
"I am a voice that cries out in all the places
of this desert: 'Prepare the way!'
as the prophet Isaiah has said before me."

77. They who had been sent to discover such things
were Pharisees, as I understand it.[40]

39. As in the translation, the second, fourth, and sixth lines of the stanza all end with
"Cristo"—reflecting Tornabuoni's Dantesque refusal to rhyme any word with "Christ" except
itself. For Dante's exemplary practice, see *Paradiso* 14:103–8 ("Qui vince la memoria mia lo
'ngegno; / ché quella croce lampeggiava Cristo, / sì ch'io non so trovare essempro degno; /
ma chi prende sua croce e segue Cristo, / ancor mi scuserà di quel ch'io lasso / vedendo in
quell'albor balenar Cristo" [And here my memory defeats my wit; / Christ's flaming from that
cross was such / that I can find no fit similitude for it. / But he who takes his cross and follows
Christ / will pardon me again for my omission— / my seeing Christ flash forth undid my
force]).

40. "Et così intendo": a phrase Tornabuoni generally inserts when she is interpreting a biblical
passage; there is no mention in Luke that such questions were planted by Pharisees ("Now
as the people were in expectation, and all were wondering in their hearts about John," Luke
3:15). The Gospel of John, on the other hand, does mention priests and Levites: "And this
is the witness of John, when the Jews sent to him from Jerusalem priests and Levites to ask
him, 'Who art thou?'" (John 1:19).

"How do you have the power to baptize
if you are not Christ? Tell us so we may know."
And without fear he answered them:
"I baptize in water and I await repentance.
I will go behind him who comes after me;
I am not worthy to unstrap his sandals.

78. "You do not know the man of whom I speak;
soon he will come and he will live with you;
you will be in the presence of the Holy Spirit
when [you will be] baptized by his hands.
If you do what he tells you, you will be
among the elect, and you will be his."
He taught them many other things,
and he beseeched them to repent.

79. These deeds of which I speak were done
in Bethany, by the river Jordan.
To see John baptizing, as was his custom,
was a marvel;
all who come before him are dissuaded
from every vice, and he shows to them the light
that illuminated a world sunk in shadows;
for which work John was sent by God.

80. Then came Jesus of Galilee
to be baptized by John.
John recused himself; he did not wish to do it,
he would not do it, and he drew away.
Jesus spoke to John, and asked him
to baptize him at once, because it was ordained for him:
"Please do not fear, and do it gladly,
for it is fitting that justice shall be fulfilled."[41]

81. There were many people who had come to be baptized,
and when they saw John refuse to baptize Jesus,

41. John's considerable reluctance to baptize Jesus is found in Matt. 3:13–17; Tornabuoni
elaborates, however, on the single protest found in 3:14: "And John was for hindering him,
and said, 'It is I who ought to be baptized by thee, and dost thou come to me?'"

they were filled with amazement,
because they had never seen him refuse anyone;
they hastened to be closer to the quarrel
to better hear and understand what was being said,
because Jesus had been reputed
to be the only son of poor Joseph.

82. When Jesus came to the Jordan
to be baptized, he was thirty years old.
Humbly and plainly, John refused,
protesting his unworthiness, and he was afraid.
But then he took some water in his humble hands
and he poured it on the head of Jesus, who waited,
attentive; and still John protested,
because Jesus should have baptized him.

83. John saw the Holy Spirit
above Jesus while he baptized him,
and the splendor of it illuminated
everything around him and his eyes were dazzled;
and he heard a sweet and solemn song
bursting from the heavens, and it comforted him,
and he saw a beautiful white dove,
more resplendent than the sun or stars.

84. When he was baptized, Jesus emerged, praying,
from the water, and the heavens were opened
and the Holy Spirit came forth:
he surrounded him, and he bathed him in light,
and a voice was heard from heaven:
"This is my son"—such were the words that issued forth—
"in whom I am greatly pleased;
honor him as I have wished!"

85. John remained in the same place as always,
with his disciples he performed baptisms,
and Jesus, our sun, would often go there,
he came to visit his John.
John turned to face him, and to his disciples
he spoke words such as these:

"Here is the lamb of our delightful God,
he will take away the sin of the world."[42]

86. And after these things of which I have spoken,
Jesus passed into Judea, where he resided
with his disciples, the chosen ones,
and there he baptized many people.
John stayed at the place where he always had been,
in Aenon, near Salim, and the country was fertile
and the water there was plentiful,
and he baptized many without ceasing.

87. The disciples did not know
which was the greater teacher, John or Jesus,
and they came to John, and they said to him:
"He to whom you paid homage at the Jordan
is baptizing too," and together they contended:
"We would like to know if he is at fault,
and if from you he has received license
to do what he does." John said to them: "Be patient."

88. John said: "No man has anything
unless it is given to him from heaven;
you yourselves should know what I answered
when they asked me
if I was the Christ. With words of faith,
I have made known the sublime secret,
and I show to you openly who I am:
I am a voice that cries out in the desert.

89. "He who has a bride is the true groom;
but the friend of the bride is all gladness;
he shows his friend a pure heart,
he esteems her as if she was his own.
His joy is great, and this is good work that he does."
John readily offered them this simile,
then added to his wise sayings:
"It is fitting that he increase and I decrease.

---

42. With the next section of six stanzas, Tornabuoni elaborates on John 1:35–36 and 3:22–
36, in which a quarrel arises between the followers of Jesus and those of John.

90. "He who comes from the earth speaks of the earth;
    he who comes from above is above all;
    he who comes from heaven is over all.
    We know the meaning of what he says,
    and his testimony does not err; in the end
    he alone will win this bitter war
    and bring peace to all who believe.
    He sent his son to be his worthy heir

91. "so that we would all do him honor
    and believe in his every word.
    He loves all without condition,
    and whoever follows his worthy teachings
    will be filled with grace and will not be hungry,
    because his life is unique in this world.[43]
    Whoever does not believe in him will have no life,
    but he will be anchored in shadows."

92. Lovingly, John taught to the people
    all the things the Holy Spirit gave him to say.
    Herod, who was lord of those lands,
    came to him because of his great fame.
    John told him what was in his heart,
    and he often reprimanded him for his failings
    and told him it was unlawful to have brought away
    the wife of his brother and married her.[44]

93. Herod listened to him, gripped with fear,
    and as he thought on this he felt he had acted wrongly;
    he returned home and spoke of these things with his wife.
    This woman whom he had taken in carnal love
    was greatly perturbed, and she began to worry:

---

43. A plausible if not entirely satisfactory translation for "perche suo vita fu nel mondo sola."
44. Tornabuoni adds this episode of Herod's going into the desert from Matthew 14 and Mark 6; as Matt. 14:3–4 recounts: "For Herod had taken John, and bound him, and put him in prison, because of Herodias, his brother's wife. For John had said to him, 'It is not lawful for thee to have her.'" Josephus constructs Herodias's genealogy in *Antiquities of the Jews*, arguing that Herod violated Mosaic law in marrying Herodias after she leaves his half-brother, Philip. In Josephus's account, Herod kills John for primarily political reasons.

"Clearly I must be shrewd in my dealings
with him; I must put my wit to work,[45]
for my plan is to have [John] killed."

94. And she began to fall into melancholy,
and nothing could make her cheerful.
Herod saw that she had become so pensive,
and he sought to know the reason:
"Tell me what troubles you, my dear wife;
tell me if there is something I might do;
I will do anything for you, O my lady,
just do not let melancholy carry you away.

95. "Let me know the reason for this suffering
that makes your beautiful face so pale:
you are not the same woman; you have so obscured your
    worth
that it seems as though you want only to die."
Then a great sigh broke forth from her heart,
and weeping, she began to speak.
"Ever since I have heard what the Baptist said,
my heart and my soul have been made most sad.

96. "In much fear have I considered
the words the Baptist told to you;
I have seen you become very concerned
that I might suffer a great blow
were I deprived of your worthy self.
I love Herod so much it is torture
not to see him, and this is the reason,
and this is why I am right to suffer and weep."

---

45. "Ogni ingegno": Tornabuoni uses the same word in her second stanza while invoking
Mary's assistance. With this reaction of Herod's wife, Tornabuoni begins elaborating on the
sparse scriptural verses that tell of John's fate, linking it explicitly to his reprimanding Herod
for his marriage. Mark 6:19 gives the most tantalizing suggestion for further developments
of the story: "But Herodias laid snares for him, and would have liked to put him to death,
but she could not. For Herod feared John, knowing that he was a just and holy man, and
protected him; and when he heard him talk, he did many things, and he liked to hear him."
Mark then proceeds to describe Herod's banquet and the dance of Herodias's daughter.

97. The king answered her and said: "O my lady,
in God's name, please cast out such thoughts.
Do you believe I would perpetrate such folly
as to desire that you go away from me?
Tear this thought right out of your head;
don't let me hear you speak of this again.
No longer be concerned about these things;
think of something else, let us seek only our pleasure.

98. "Tell me what it is that you want me to do,
regarding this or anything else, let me know."
And he gazed into that beautiful face
which had made him fear for her life.
Seeing him so happy and in such good cheer,
she looked at him again with her sweet manners,
and in this way began to speak:
"Oh, it would be best if you had him killed.

99. "Why on earth do you listen to this critic,
this barking dog who has riled up the entire nation?
See how he esteems your honor when
he has already broadcast [your sin] to all the people!
If this John really felt for you true love,
he would have advised you to take a different path,
but he loves to look like a great saint.
It looks good to have eaten nothing but acorns;

100. "it looks good to have lived in the desert:
[but] to hear him speak is to listen to a fool!
I think that the best thing would be
to have him captured as quickly as you can!"
And Herod answered: "It seems clear to me
that he will never be able to rest again:
we must think of a quick and easy way,
a way that will not weaken us, and let it happen soon."

101. Once she heard these words, that disgraceful
woman rejoiced; as I see it,
things seemed to her to have started out well,
and so she began to give some thought to a plan

and said to him: "I have already considered
a scheme, so please, be attentive to what I say:
soon your birthday will be here,
the day I want such evil to be wiped away.

102. "As you know, I have a daughter
whom I believe has no equal in the world.
I want you to see her gracious [dances],
and I will even teach her more of them;
on the day of your party you will dine
with your barons, and after you have eaten,
my daughter will come and display her new talents;
then whatever she asks of you, you must let her have."[46]

103. And he answered: "O my lovely wife,
I will certainly do whatever you want.
Don't you know, I have never discounted anything
that you have done or anything you will do?
I will always follow your subtle thoughts;
if disgrace should result, you would save me from it.
Think carefully, now, let us not rush into things,
lest the people get wind of what we are up to."

104. And she said: "Hear what I am thinking
so that you can tell me if it will succeed:
I would send for him and say that I

---

46. Tornabuoni's reasoning behind letting Herod know of Herodias's plan is obscure, suggesting some inconsistency in her treatment of the king and queen. If Herod knows ahead of time that her daughter's dancing will furnish him a means of getting rid of the prophet, why then is he so angry when she asks for John's head? On the other hand, such an inconsistency may be only apparent, arguing, as suggested in the introduction, for Tornabuoni's artistry and her familiarity with the commentary traditions synthesized and elaborated on by Jacobus de Voragine. She may also have known of plays such as *La rappresentazione di San Giovanni Battista quando fu decollato*, in which "la Femmina" likewise informs Herod beforehand what will happen at his feast day: "Santa Corona, e' ne vien la tua festa: / io manderò la tua figlia a danzare / . . . e chiederà la testa del Battista. / E tu fa vista che turbato sia / e mostra 'n atti non volerlo fare" [O my lord, your birthday is coming up; I will send in your daughter to dance . . . and she will ask you for the head of the Baptist. And you can pretend that you are greatly disturbed by her request, and with your actions show that you don't want to do it]. To which Herod responds: "Fia fatto, donna . . . i' son molto contento" [Let it be done, my wife; I'm quite content] (123–24). Is it possible that Tornabuoni is basing her *storia* on such a reading that demands Herod's complicity—a complicity that is not evident later in her poem?

would like to speak with [John] and hear what he has to
  say;
that I shall hear him willingly, and desire his presence,
and wish to follow whatever he teaches.
As soon as he arrives, you will be told,
and you should put him instantly into prison,

105. "and I would keep him guarded, not too strictly,
I would go to hear him, and that would leave people
no grounds for their base thoughts;
thus would I make all suspicion flee from their minds."
And Herod answered: "What you have told me
pleases me greatly, and I plan to follow it.
But we must be secretive about all this,
because he is esteemed as more than a prophet."

106. When it seemed timely, they sent
two of their servants to John, and they said
that their embassy was to beseech him
to come with them to Herod; he wanted
to speak with him, for there was need.
The good Baptist well knew from this
that his hour and his end had come:
he went on his way and arrived at the court.

107. And as soon as he arrived, he was put into prison
before he could speak to the king or anyone else.
This is what had been ordered: why,
he did not know, nor was anything said
except that the king sought some information
about certain things, but for the moment
he was guarded carefully, as Herodias
had ordered, if not too strictly.

108. As soon as John was put in prison,
Herodias had heard about it,
and she asked everyone the reason,
just to see what others were saying about it.
And to her question she was told
that the king wanted him arrested, at least for now;

but she, who knew everything that would happen, said:
"You have spoken too much! Now see where it's gotten
    you!"[47]

109. And she was glad, she knew great joy,
    since she had appeared to have her wish;
    and she kept after her husband at all times
    so she might encourage him in her resolve.
    Her daughter was practicing hard
    to learn new things, as I understand it,
    so she would be well prepared at the banquet
    to ask for that worthy head.

110. Calmly and humbly, John
    waits patiently in prison, and his disciples
    were not prevented from visiting him;
    all had license to do as they pleased.
    And he spoke to two of them discreetly:
    "Go to my Jesus, and go with haste,
    ask him if he is the one who is to come;
    ask whether we should obey him, or await another?"[48]

111. When those who were sent to find Jesus arrived,
    they made to him their embassy,
    and they were overcome with marvel:
    he had no rest from healing people;
    whoever he touched was made well again.
    Then he turned to them and gave them this answer:
    "Return to tell my wise John
    the things that you have heard and seen here.

112. "Say that the blind see the light of day,
    the lame go about, the lepers are made clean,
    and the deaf hear: all through that same true light

47. A complicated stanza, whose difficulties perhaps reflect the contorted nature of Herodias's plan: her "naive" question about John's capture is in fact merely a subtle attempt to obscure her role in John's eventual death.

48. See Matt. 11:2: "When John had heard in prison of the works of Christ, he sent two of his disciples to say to him, 'Art thou he who is to come, or shall we look for another?'" (also in Luke 7:18).

through which the dead are brought back to life.
Blessed is he who is shown the true light
and they who are not scandalized in me."[49]
The two returned to report what they heard,
while Jesus began to speak to the crowds

113. about John: "Whom did you go to see
in the depths of the desert?
Did you find a shaken reed?
Men who clothe themselves in delicate garments
reside in the houses of kings, and let that satisfy them.
Whom did you go to see? Tell me the truth.
Whom did you go to see with joyous face?
The prophet John is more than a prophet.

114. "He is the one of whom it is written:
'First I will send my angel into your presence
as it has been prophesied,
to make ready the way of the highest Lord.'
I have told you and affirmed the truth:
among the sons of women, there is not one
who has been born who is greater than he,
but the least in heaven is greater than he.

115. "From the days of John the Baptist
and until now, the great kingdom of heaven
is taken by force, and thus is it attained,
and the violent, who do not rest, seize it in violence;
and those with keen sight have come forward with this,
and each of them is encouraged by what he sees;
if you are willing to hear Elijah, who was to come,
then he who has ears will hear me."[50]

116. And thus he spoke such worthy things,
and many more, which I do not recount,
because neither rhyme nor prose would be sufficient,
although I have the will to tell it all.

---

49. Matt. 11:4–6; Luke 7:22–23.
50. Matt. 11:7–14; those with "buona vista" are presumably the prophets of 11:13.

I know that I have entered onto shadowy paths,
and I hope to navigate safely to the end,
through the grace of God who was there in the
  beginning,
as I pray that he alleviate my ignorance.[51]

117. In the time that John was taken,
the day of the feast was fast approaching;
Herodias, with burning heart,
nagged her husband at every turn:
"Make sure you do not forget what you promised me,
so that I will not become sad and full of grief."
Thus would she go about nagging him,
and for nothing did she ease her heart.

118. Such was her desire for John's death
that she believed the hour would never come,
and taking no comfort unless she went about
blaming him, she said to the king:
"Get him out of the way, I exhort you."
And holding on her his fixed gaze,
Herod took his leave, and he too wanted to kill John,
but he was afraid of what the people might do.

119. The day of Herod's birthday drew near,
the day the king always held a great feast.
Those who were assigned to prepare the house
began making it ready, not stopping to breathe;
with great diligence they got everything set,
because the court was to be filled
with all the princes and chiefs of state in Galilee;
every year on that same day they came.

120. Herodias was teaching her daughter
new dances, all different steps: her daughter
whom nature had gifted with beauty to make men marvel;
but this beauty would bring about misfortune.

51. As Pezzarossa and others note, with this stanza Tornabuoni embarks on one of the most original sections of her poetry; hence her reference to "shadowy paths" [vie ombrose].

Her mother devotes and sharpens every thought
to the ways she might avenge the injuries
she believed she had suffered on John's account,
and now the time and the hour were upon them.

121. How lucky for her and her mother
that she had taken on such lovely manners,
for she was full of grace and not at all vain.
She had even begun to follow
the true light of the true faith
at the time her father went to see John at the river;
she had been honest and respectful,
she feared infamy, and was not shameless.

122. She dedicated herself to singing and dance,
so talented she was in performing both;
all of the court was led to await
the dancing of which she was mistress.
Her mother spoke to her in this manner:
"My child, you have prepared yourself for this enterprise;
you know that every lord will be there.
Go before them and do yourself honor.

123. "If on the day of the feast
you dance well, with lovely measures,
you could give me no greater pleasure.
Be sure to dance so that everyone will praise you,
and I know that whatever you ask of the king,
you will obtain. Make sure that you listen and understand
    me:
if he says he will give you nothing,
return instantly to me, and I will teach you what to say."

124. Her daughter had understood her words,
and said, "Mother, I have great hope
that if my stamina endures as always,
by the time the sun begins to rise
I believe I will dance such a dance
as has never been seen before; have faith.

I am sure, mother, that I will dance so well
that the king will want to give me a bountiful reward."

125. And she spoke the truth, too, because never
     did anyone receive such a prize simply for dancing!
     Of two heads, she sought one of them,
     and she had it, and this was neither lies nor prattle.[52]
     I believe for her it would have been better
     had she been more restrained, had she kept the balance
         equal,
     and of those two heads to have bought the one
     in a manner quite different from dancing.

126. Now when the day of the great feast arrived,
     and this was the day when Herod was born,
     on behalf of the king the request was made
     that every lord be found in his court.
     All who were there were very powerful,
     and so the banquet was elegantly prepared,
     with beautiful cloths and valuable ornaments;
     and each lord came with his ministers and servants.

127. They arrived at the court with happy hearts;
     by the king they were welcomed and honored,
     and they were seated at the table to dine,
     where every sort of food was prepared in abundance.
     Thus did they feast in much delight,
     and when their appetites were satisfied,
     the queen Herodias sent in her daughter,
     gaily dressed, her beauty a marvel to behold,

---

52. "Le due teste": an obscure allusion, for which I have found no suitable explanation. One might find a rarefied allusion to the noted symmetry between John and Jesus (although it is not clear why Jesus's head would have been the better choice) or an even more esoteric reference to Esther, on which the episode with Herod and his stepdaughter is clearly based. As Roger Aus notes in *Water into Wine and the Beheading of John the Baptist*, rabbinic commentary on Esther 1 suggests that Queen Vashti's punishment is death, specifically beheading (62–64). Although it is unlikely that Tornabuoni would have been familiar with these commentaries, one might speculate that the "other head" is that of Vashti's surrogate in the Gospel text—the disobedient Herodias.

128. accompanied by women and young girls,
    pages and shield bearers and musicians.
    She seemed to be a sun surrounded by stars,
    and she came before the king and his many guests
    with graceful bows, and he made her sit with them.
    There is no need to draw out my argument;
    she arrived so beautifully adorned
    that all left off their eating to watch her.

129. The instruments were tuned, and the musicians
    began to play sweet melodies.
    This young girl got to her feet
    and gaily and joyously,
    with consummate skill, began to dance,
    first slowly, so that she hardly seemed to move;
    when she had finished her lingering steps,
    she stopped for a moment and pensively stood.

130. After she had paused a little in thought,
    she again took up the dance, this time
    in a more incontinent vein, leaving no one to guess
    whether she was suited to dancing.
    I believe that she left her audience on fire,
    and they had never felt this way before,
    so content were they to watch
    her beauty and her comely dancing.

131. She seemed as though she was sent from heaven,
    so beautifully adorned, so gentle and pretty;
    her garment was a lovely veil
    adorned with jewels, a marvelous thing,
    an incredible thing to see,
    and I conceal nothing of her beauty;
    so pretty was the garment she was wearing,
    and how perfectly it complemented her loveliness![53]

---

53. With these stanzas Tornabuoni elaborates in evocative detail on a dance that, as Françoise Meltzer has observed, is completely left to the reader's imagination in the Gospels: "As for the Salome story itself, what is singular is the reference to the famous dance, for it is totally lacking in specific description, not to mention sensuality" (*Salome and the Dance of Writing*, 33).

132. If she did not give them their full of dancing!
She left out not a single dance,
she danced all the ones she knew,
and still she knew how to invent new ones,
and to list them all would be foolishness.
With every leap you could hear their cries
as they saw her twirl about so gracefully,
and all admired her in much happiness.[54]

133. This joy would quickly turn to grief.
See the things that soon will follow
thanks to her dancing; for it
was this alone that made John die.
Be alert, listener, with ready intellect,
and you will see these pleasures turned to weeping.
How brief were the feasting and the joy!
Everyone would depart in grief and distress.

134. The music and her lovely dancing finished,
she approached the king with graceful curtsies.
Herod gazed upon her at length,
calling her to him with endearing greetings,
and thus he said: "I want to reward you
for the honor you have given me.
In the presence of these worthy lords, I swear
to give you a gift, worth up to half my kingdom."[55]

135. Hearing what the king proclaimed
she hurried with great haste to her mother.
The queen, who had been expecting this,
asked eagerly: "Did you know what to do?

---

54. Thus does Tornabuoni elaborate on a single verse in Mark: "And Herodias's own daughter having come in and danced, she pleased Herod and his guests" (Mark 6:22). The passage in Matthew is very similar: "But on Herod's birthday, the daughter of Herodias danced before them, and pleased Herod" (Matt. 14:6). The chief difference is that in Mark's account the "guests" are also delighted, guests whom Mark describes for us: "his chief officials and tribunes and chief men of Galilee" (Mark 6:21).

55. See Mark 6:22–23: "And the king said to the girl: 'Ask of me what thou willest, and I will give it to thee.' And he swore to her: 'Whatever thou dost ask, I will give thee, even though it be the half of my kingdom.'"

Tell me, quickly." She answered:
"Can you believe what happened?
I knew how to dance so beautifully
that the king wants to give me half his realm.

136. "I have come without my entourage,
so I may return quickly to the king,
for he awaits me. I want to obey you, O my mother,
I come to ask what will please you most.
The king desires only to make me happy.
What do you want me to ask him for? Tell me,
for I am in a hurry; I must return at once! Such
is my duty, before they rise up from their seats."

137. "O my daughter, now may you be blessed!
I see my efforts were not wasted;
and that now I will have my vengeance
on that dog who persecutes me.
Now go, my daughter, take the quickest way,
return to the king and tell him this:
'You would do me a great pleasure if you
served me on a plate the Baptist's head.'

138. "If he acts as though he does not wish to do this,
just be firm, and remind him he has promised you;
do not fear, do not let him send you away."
And she returned before the king
and spoke to him in this fashion:
"Make sure that I am given what I seek:
in return for my dancing at your feast,
I request the head of John the Baptist."

139. When the king heard what she had requested,
he showed himself to be disturbed and quite displeased;[56]

---

56. "Udendo il re quel che costei ha chiesto / mostrò turbarsi et haver dispiacere." It is possible that Tornabuoni's use of "mostrare" suggests dissimulation on Herod's part; hence, in possible accordance with Herodias's plan, he may be only feigning displeasure. Thus when in *The Story of Judith, Hebrew Widow,* Judith is asked by Bagoas to join Holofernes for dinner, "mostrò di rallegrarsi" [she showed that she was happy], even as we know that she is planning something sinister after the meal. On the other hand, a later use of the verb in the poem, when Herodias goes mad ("mostra chabbi molta passione," 153), carries with it no implications of pretending. It is safe to say that Herod's own role in John's death remains ambiguous at best.

he turned to her and was full of rage.
"I want you to understand me well:
you can ask me for anything but this,
for certainly from me you shall not have it!"
And she answered, her heart bold:
"You swore to make me happy."

140. "I did not think, O cursed child,
that you would have asked for flesh or blood, but
gold, silver, necklaces, brooches adorned with lovely
   gems.
Of whom were you born? A tiger or serpent?
Clearly this day will cost me dearly;
my heart within is sad and is languishing quickly;[57]
and if I swore before, now I will perjure myself.
Please, ask for something else, and you will have it."

141. "If I don't get what I have asked for,
I will be greatly displeased; I seek nothing else,
and never again will I dance for you here."
And saying this, she fell silent.
Then the lords spoke to one another,
saying: "We must help make peace here,"
and together they all began to plead
with the king not to make her sad.[58]

142. The king had his executioner called,
and he said: "Go quickly, do not delay;
go to the prison, and from there
you must bring on a trencher the head of John."
He obeyed, the master of that craft,
he went to the prison to do just that,
asking: "Where is John? This feasting will cost you:
I come to cut off your head."

---

57. "Lo core e tristo dentro et forte langue": a difficult line, which Pezzarossa misreads as
"fore langue." I have deliberately translated *tristo* [evil] as *triste* [sad], assuming scribal error.
Alternatively, however (and ungramatically), the line could refer to Herodias's daughter: "You
have the heart [of a] serpent inside you, evil and strong," in which *langue* would be read as
[*del*]*l'angue*.
58. Mark's Herod expresses no rage at the request, only grief: "And grieved as he was, the
king, because of his oath and his guests, was unwilling to displease her" (Mark 6:26).

143. John the Baptist, the meek lamb,
hearing the executioner call out, came before him,
and looked him intently in the face:
"Here I am," he said; "now do what you must."
With a wicked look, the scoundrel took
his sword in hand and brandished it before him;
he made the good prophet kneel down,
and his head is sliced from his shoulders.

144. That worthy head fell to the ground,
and he took it, and placed it on a serving plate;
thus did he carry it to the great feast
and laid it on a table before the king,
who took it in his hand, and said with downcast face:
"Now you! your dancing has cost me too much,
take this away, and don't remain here before me,
for never again do I want to see dancing."

145. She took the head and carried it away,
and with a graceful bow and a curtsy
she presented it to her mother:
"Here is the head! Now it is in your power!"
The queen took it, and gazed on it at length,
and began to speak to it, saying: "Your destiny
brought you to this terrible port.
You spoke so much that now you are dead."

146. With these and other words like it,
words full of anger, she gave vent to her wrath;
she weeps for the trials she had suffered—too many—
and she hurls the head about her, here, and there,
and did nothing else under the sun.
The king in the meantime had sent all away;
the guests who had come that day to his feast
all departed, fearful and wretched.

147. Let us leave that woman behind
who so mocked John's worthy head;
I want to return to the scene of the prison
of he who had preached the true kingdom.

Abruptly, without saying why he had come,
the executioner arrived, full of wrath and disdain;
he had sliced off John's head without fear,
whence began a deep lament.

148. Those who called him father, and those who called him
      teacher,
    were crying: "Oh, cruel fortune, oh, cruel is our fate!
    Oh, our destiny is dark for us now,
    Oh, never was there under the sun
    a king so impious and cruel!
    Our every joy is darkened and tainted."
    The news spread throughout all the land,
    and John's disciples came hurrying there.

149. They arrived at the prison, where they found
    his body on the ground, hands joined [in prayer],
    and—every eye fills with tears at the sight—
    saw his head had been severed from his shoulders,
    and the ground is drenched in blood.
    People arrive from all parts of the land,
    and they loudly lament and know no consolation:
    "This just man has died for nothing."[59]

150. And his disciples, compelled by great grief,
    began to speak with one another:
    "Let our immense love for him guide our thoughts
    as we think of the best way to honor him."
    And so together, without making noise,
    they discussed how they would bury him
    and fulfill their duty, and how they could
    let Jesus know as soon as they could.

151. With great devotion, among copious blood,
    they took that body so dismembered:
    they took that body, drenched in blood,
    and they washed it with precious water,

59. The final verse relating the story of John in Mark mentions the disciples: "His disciples, hearing of [the death], came and took away his body, and laid it in a tomb" (Mark 6:29).

and among themselves they said: "Innocent blood,
will we ever see you justly revenged?"
And they blamed the dancing and the feast:
"We must at least see the worthy head."[60]

152. And one of his disciples went up
[to the palace] to see if he could reclaim it.
When he arrived where it had been taken,
he asked some questions to learn if he could see it,
and here was the answer: "Go down there,
but there is much to-do concerning what you seek.
I speak of our lady the queen,
to whom God has sent swift punishment:

153. "she has collapsed on the ground and shows
that she is overcome by suffering;
I understand she has that severed head,
and made it the object of much derision.
Now it seems to me that God has paid her back,
and dealt with her as justice has decreed:
the king and her doctors are there to comfort her,
but we do not know if she is alive or dead.

154. "Because of what has happened, my friend,
for now no one may enter there;
but if I find the head, what should I do?
For now, I cannot return it to you,
although I would like for you to have it,
because I know you would do it honor.
If I find some stealthy means of taking it away,
so that I would be seen by no one,

155. "willingly would I bring it to you,
because it disturbs me to see her torment it so.
If I thought I could beseech the king,
and that he would render me this favor,
I promise you I would be glad to do it,

---

60. If in stanza 75 Tornabuoni had resisted using words to rhyme with "Cristo," here she does the same in regard to John's holy blood; hence lines 2, 4, and 6 all end with "sangue."

for I would like to satisfy you in this matter.
But I cannot do it without permission,
so that I beg you: be patient."

156. Hearing these words the disciple
said to himself: "Better I leave now
and return to those who await me;
it is clear there will be too much delay."
Thus he returned wretched and alone;
he went back to his friends by the quickest path,
and he said, "No longer wait to see him;
there is no way we will retrieve his head."

157. And he told them how things stood:
the queen is taken ill and lies frenzied on the ground,
and it seemed to all that she has lost her wits,
and they have not left her in peace,
and they do not know if the soul of that
cursed and daring woman has fled from her body;
but she remains mad and suffers greatly,
and her sins are the cause of it all.

158. When they learn this, the disciples are agreed
that they must lay his body in the tomb.
They rose to go and made their way
with much reverence and care,
accompanied by many devout souls
who weep as they follow them,
and they buried that blessed body,
and grieving they all returned to their homes.

159. May you, Eternal Father, be thanked,
and your Son, and the Holy Spirit;
I want to thank as well the worthy Mother,
and the prophet John in this song.
By virtue of his delightful works
and through his grace, I will be able to boast
of having told of his death and of his people,
[so that] my and others' devotion may grow!

POEMS OF PRAISE

INTRODUCTION

The *laude*, or poem of praise, probably originated with the Umbrian mystics and poets who wrote in the thirteenth century. Saint Francis's elegant "Canticle," like many *laudi*, achieves a balance between simplicity and eloquence, and Jacopone da Todi's religious poetry is the finest before Dante's. Their poems, like those of their fifteenth-century descendants, were based largely on hymns and liturgical sequences. The early *laudi* have a distinctly dramatic flair, since they often imagine an interlocutor who invokes and occasionally converses with a sacred personage: God, Mary, Christ, or a saint. In turn, popular religious movements such as that of the Bianchi, who burst onto the Italian religious landscape at the threshold of the fifteenth century, also gave the *laudi* a visibility and a basis in the common people or *popolo* that prevented them from being in any way strictly identified as an elite literary genre.[1]

Tornabuoni's nine extant *laudi* embody the metrical and thematic range of contemporary lauds. While they tend to be less innovative than her *storie sacre*, their simplicity and straightforwardness are striking. No fewer than four of her nine songs are set to the melody of a popular ballad by Angelo Poliziano, "Ben venga maggio" [Welcome to May]. In these songs, written in *settinari* or hexasyllabics and composed of six-line strophes with an AB-ABBC rhyme scheme, Tornabuoni celebrates the deity in his many aspects: as newborn babe, as Christ crucified, as resurrected king who releases the patriarchs from hell, and as Pentecostal spirit. These largely joyful and triumphant songs are marked by lilting rhythms, deliberate repetitions well suited to the ballad form, and frequent use of the vocative as the singer

---

1. See Daniel Bornstein's chapter on the *laudi* written by the Bianchi (*Bianchi of 1399*, chap. 4).

calls on "celestial souls," angels, prophets, Christ, and Mary herself in robust invitations to join in songs of praise. The invocations give to "Ecco el Messia" and "Ecco il Re forte" in particular a compelling presence, as they create for us an expansive audience that is asked to take part in the singer's festive celebrations. Especially evocative is the touching depiction in "Ecco el Messia" of the fearful rustics approaching Christ: "Shepherds shy and fearful, / You pause here in your vigil, / Linger not in trepidation, / Don't you hear the song?" Of this group of ballads, the only one that departs from an overtly triumphant mode is "Ben venga osanna," which, in at least one manuscript version, ends with the sobering image of a crucified Christ and a final address to Mary: "Oh, what a cruel thing, / Virgin daughter of Anna!"

This melancholic tone from the end of "Ben venga osanna" is more apparent in three *laudi* that depart from the ballads designed for specific liturgical celebrations. Of these more contemplative *laudi*, "O Signor mio, ben fu lamor tuo forte" [O my Lord, how strong was the love], is the most powerful. As a dialogue between the weeping sinner who gazes at Christ on the cross and Jesus who, in the final strophe, looks down and says he has opened the doors of his kingdom to her, the *laude* is a touching exchange that describes with loving detail Christ's suffering features: "your face, beaten and bloody, / Your eyes weeping and you, dead and derided, / Your head thrust back, and it finds no place to rest, / Your mouth parched and dry." The *laude* "Contempla le mie pene, o peccatore" [Contemplate my sufferings, O sinner] reverses this exchange: here Christ initiates a dialogue completed by the "peccatore," who acknowledges her own and others' failure in not accompanying him to the cross: "O sweet Jesus of mine, / you were alone at the redemption." Like "Contempla le mie pene," "Non mi curo più di te" [I concern myself with you no more], is metrically innovative with its alternating lines of eight and seven syllables. Unlike "Contempla" and "O Signor mio," it is a monologue, sung by a convert who dares her former tempter to lure her back into sin. The mocking tones of the song give it an almost sarcastic edge that is rare in Tornabuoni's work; more than the other songs, it makes considerable use of idiomatic expressions and contemporary jargon.

The final *laude* is Tornabuoni's longest and most ambitious, and in some ways her least successful. It comprises ten thirteen-line strophes that alternate lines of twelve and seven syllables and a *congedo* or farewell. This *canzone* ranges through salvation history in an attempt to unify the chief events of the Bible through an image found in Isaiah: "A shoot shall sprout from the stump of Jesse, and from his roots a bud shall blossom."[2] After beginning with an allusion to the "flower born of royal stock"—Christ himself—Tornabuoni moves into a description of Adam and Eve's sin, their enforced departure from Eden, and the unfolding of God's "gran mistero" [great mystery] on the cross. As Domenico Coppola suggests, it is perhaps in the poem's quiet and simple close that Tornabuoni is at her best. Here she asks that her song travel to those who rebel against God's law—like the satanic figure who lurked in Eden—and persuade them to turn to God: "Simple little song, go forth with fervor / comforting them, / though they are rebels," she instructs her song in the *congedo*.[3] Even if the scenes depicting Adam and Eve lamenting their loss or God's heavenly counsel are somewhat unsatisfying—the language does not quite rise to the serious level required for these symbolic events, but neither is it simple enough to convey authentic directness of feeling—the poem's format and its conscientious retelling of biblical stories look to the *storie sacre*. And its failures confirm where Tornabuoni is at her best: when she is attentive to homely nuances of setting and character, taking the time to create for her audience a sense of atmosphere and place and resisting any temptation to draw from her poetics a deeply symbolic significance. That significance is there in all of her poetry, given its reliance on biblical and liturgical materials, but it is best articulated when Tornabuoni does not strive to call attention to it.

Tornabuoni's *laudi* are preserved in twelve Italian manuscripts. Since many of her and others' *laudi* are unattributed in the *laudari*—only three of the twelve manuscripts cited note that her poems are by "Mona Lucretia de' Medici"—it is quite probable that her poems can be found in other *laudari* as well. By far the most popular of her *laudi* were the four ballads set to Poliziano's "Ben venga maggio": "Ecco il Re forte," "Viene 'l messaggio," "Ecco el Messia," and "Ben venga osanna" appear in six manuscripts.[4] Most of these manuscripts are from the mid- to late fifteenth century; Magliabechiano XXXV, 119, on which I have based several transcriptions, is dated October 1481 and thus was copied while Tornabuoni was alive.[5] Other contemporary authors included in these collections were Feo

---

2. Isa. 11:1. Coppola also calls attention to the analogue in *Poesia religiosa del secolo XV*, 68.

3. "Canzona semplicetta con ardire / Confortando va quegli / Per ben che sien rebegli." Coppola suggests that "the ending is perhaps the best part of the poem, written in simple and straightforward language" (ibid., 69).

4. For a list of the manuscripts in which Tornabuoni's *laudi* can be found, see Pezzarossa's useful appendix to *Poemetti sacri*, 251–55.

5. The three *laudi* found in this manuscript are "Ben venga osanna," "Ecco el Messia," and "Venitene pastori." This manuscript, which contains over three hundred *laudi* from the four-

Belcari, Girolamo Savonarola, Francesco d'Albizzo, and Lorenzo de' Medici; at least one manuscript, copied in the sixteenth century, includes poems by another woman, Sister Ieronima de' Malatesti. But for the most part, insofar as can be told from the *laudari* with attributions, Tornabuoni was virtually the only woman represented in these collections, in which her poetry certainly equals that of most of her prominent male peers.

POEMS OF PRAISE

1. The Song of the Nativity [Ecco el Messia]
(From Magl. VII, 1159, 54r)

This is the Messiah, and his mother Mary!

Come you souls from heaven,
Rise up from eternal choirs;
Come now and give welcome
To the Lord of lords;
And may the supreme hierarchy
Come and not delay.

This is the Messiah, and his mother Mary!

Come, you holy angels,
Come while making music;
Come everyone in heaven,
Praising Jesus Christ
And singing out his glory
With sweet harmonies.

This is the Messiah, and his mother Mary!

Patriarchs, come join us,
And come in celebration.
Dispersed are all past struggles;
He has come out of exile.
And come praising
The virginal Maria.

---

teenth and fifteenth centuries, is the best evidence we have that Tornabuoni's *laudi* circulated before her death.

This is the Messiah, and his mother Mary!

Come here, O ye prophets,
Who prophesied such riches;
Come now and be merry,
See who is born today.
For unto us is given
This little, sweet Messiah.

This is the Messiah, and his mother Mary!

Shepherds shy and fearful,
You pause here in your vigil,
Linger not in trepidation,
Don't you hear the song?
Run now to adore him,
With your minds made holy.

This is the Messiah, and his mother Mary!

You will find him born here,
Between oxen and little donkey;
Bound in sordid garments,
And he doesn't have a mantle.
On bended knee, approach him,
and the holy Mary.

This is the Messiah, and his mother Mary!

The wise men have arrived now,
Guided by the star.[6]
They bring expensive tributes,
Bowing low to earth.
They feel great consolation

6. Martelli notes that this stanza, like several others in the song, depends on the accounts of the Nativity in the New Testament; hence "E Magi son venuti, Dalla stella guidati" looks directly to Matt. 2:1: "Ecce Magi ab oriente venerunt. . . .Vidimus enim stellam eius in oriente." He makes the interesting point that Tornabuoni takes the "ecce" of Matthew and uses it for the *ritornello*, or refrain, of the song, "Ecco el Messia" [This is the Messiah] (*Letteratura fiorentina del Quattrocento*, 19–20).

Adoring the Messiah.
And his mother Mary.

This is the Messiah, and his mother Mary!

(This song is to be sung to the melody of "Ben venga maggio"
[Welcome to May] by Angelo Poliziano)[7]

2. O My Lord [O Signor mio]
(From Magl. VII, 1159, 58r)

O my Lord, how strong was the love
That led you to such a cruel death.
Who led you up there, to that cruel wood
    Where your limbs were so boldly pierced?
    It was love that led you, and not disdain.
    It was your charity that led you;
    On yourself you took no pity,
    As you straighten out our twisted works.
O my Lord, how strong was the love
That led you to such a cruel death.

When I gaze upon your sacred features,
    When I look at your face, beaten and bloody,
    Your eyes weeping and you, dead and derided,
    Your head thrust back, and it finds no place to rest,
    Your mouth parched and dry—Oh, what a cruel thing
    To see you led to such a fate.
O my Lord, how strong was the love
That led you to such a cruel death.

I gaze at the wound in your side
    From which blood and water gush forth together,
    So all the world can find itself refreshed,
    And flourish through your seed;
    O my Lord, everywhere we look
    We are comforted by your kindness and peace.

---

7. Most of Tornabuoni's *laudi* have rubrics designating the melodies to which they should be sung. This and three other of the *laudi* were to be sung to Poliziano's famous ballad "Ben venga maggio."

O my Lord, how strong was the love
That led you to such a cruel death.

I have suffered many pains, and great tortures[8]
    To save you from eternal torment;
    So that you may live, I have wanted to die;
    Else you had been a murderer of yourself.
    It remains to you now to make yourself worthy of
        heaven;
    I have opened the doors of my kingdom.
O my Lord, how strong was the love
That led you to such a cruel death.
           (No melody is indicated)

    3. *Here Comes the Messenger, and the Wise Spirit*
      [Vienel messaggio et lo spirito saggio]
        (From Magl. VII, 1159, 56v)

Here comes the messenger,[9]
    And the wise spirit!

He comes from celestial kingdoms
Where sweet new sounds are heard,
They are joyful and not discordant,
They issue from the high choirs;
He comes in the form of vapors
And rays of luminous light.

Here comes the messenger,
    And the wise spirit!

He comes as burning fire
Dispersed among speaking tongues;
The apostles have understood him,
And their souls are beautifully dressed now

---

8. Here the monologue becomes a dialogue, as Christ addresses the sinner who has been contemplating him on the cross.

9. As Pezzarossa notes, Tornabuoni uses "messaggio" to mean "messenger" in at least one other context (The Life of Saint John the Baptist, stanza 75; Pezzarossa, 174). "Messenger" seemed appropriate here as well.

In all the colorful garments
Of the world's languages.

Here comes the messenger,
    And the wise spirit!

And he comes to brighten
This world that's sunk in shadows;
He comes to save our souls
So that each of us may be freed
From that ungrateful enemy
Who journeyed to such evil.

Here comes the messenger,
    And the wise spirit!

Come, true and holy spirit,
Enter within our bosoms!
Help our souls to be made whole,
And purge us of our defects,
And keep us strong, and true to you,
And all for our great gain.

Here comes the messenger,
    And the wise spirit!

Show to us the road you take,
Show to us your virtue;
Our very souls desire
To see their own salvation,
And each one virtuously struggles
To flee from its damnation.

Here comes the messenger,
    And the wise spirit!

O gift of the highest God,
O truest majesty,
O most vehement spirit,
How great is your bounty!

With your excessive charity,
We will find good passage.

Here comes the messenger,
    And the wise spirit!

Seven flowers are the gifts
Of the Holy Spirit;
But they might be seven million,
One cannot say how many;
He has his grief turned into song
Who travels on this voyage.

Here comes the messenger,
    And the wise spirit!

Now kindle all our senses,
And confirm our hearts
In the virtue that is fitting
To make us do deeds of love.
Help us taste great sweetness,
And leave behind all outrage.

Here comes the messenger,
    And the wise spirit!

He has made us travel far
From our great enemy;
Christ has come to cancel
The sins of ancient time:
He closes off hell's gaping doors
To his disadvantage.

Here comes the messenger,
    And the wise spirit!

For you,[10] our Holy Father
Sent his son from heaven,

---

10. "Per te": here Tornabuoni is addressing a single subject, not a wide audience, thus accentuating the supposed intimacy of the exchange.

And into that blessed mother
So he might resemble us:
And as I have showed you,
This happened through divine wisdom.

Here comes the messenger,
    And the wise spirit!

Thanks be to you, Father,
And to your holy son,
And to his holy mother
And the impassioned spirit,
For which so strongly thirst
All human lineage.

    (Sung to "Ben venga maggio")

4. *I Concern Myself with You No More*
    [Non mi curo più di te]
    (From Magl. VII, 1159, 59r)[11]

I concern myself with you no more:
I have taken up strong arms against you;[12]
I do not answer when you call;
I ridicule and deride you instead.

O enemy, I now have passed
The dubious way.
My Jesus has freed me;
You gain nothing by remaining.
I have known his grace, so I will not fall;
No longer tempt me with hook and bait.
I do not answer when you call;
I ridicule and deride you instead.

You believe you have good reason
To shower me with pleasures;

11. Also found in Biblioteca Riccardiana 3112; significant variants will be noted.

12. An admittedly liberal translation of "Aggio preso forti rami"—literally, "I have strong branches" or, perhaps, "big sticks." The implication seems to be that the speaker is trying to defend herself against the onslaughts of an enemy.

But I no longer think of you
So I will not offend my Lord.
I want you to leave me be,
I no longer want to hear your cries.
I do not answer when you call;
I ridicule and deride you instead.

Who makes his way to the side of Christ,
Has little need of your words;[13]
Who takes care to stop his ears
Is not harmed by your calls.
I go to follow him who died on the cross;[14]
Do what you will, I desire you not.
I do not answer when you call;
I ridicule and deride you instead.[15]

Now I want you to leave me be,
With your threat of mortal wounds!
I will think only on my sins
And on God, whose bounty is infinite.
I want now to lead my life
So that God will love me.
I do not answer when you call;
I ridicule and deride you instead.

Now show me what you can do,
How many pleasures you know.
If you were you and of your party,
You would have from me nothing else.[16]
Consider my struggle at an end
With your false and trivial ways!
I do not answer when you call,
I ridicule and deride you instead.

13. Bib. Ricc. 3112: "pocho novo le tuo voce" (your words are hardly new to me).

14. Bib. Ricc. 3112: "vo seguire chi morì in croce" (I want to follow the one who died on the cross).

15. This stanza is not included in Giovanni Volpi's version of the *Laudi*, although he notes that he used the same manuscript (Magl. 1159) for his transcription of the poem as I did.

16. There may be some manuscript error here, even though the same line appears in both the Biblioteca Nazionale and the Riccardiana manuscripts. One possibility is that the first four lines of this stanza are spoken by the demonic figure whom the narrator "derides"; in this instance it is conceivable that the tempter is suggesting that the narrator has not truly been

You have long been quite intent
To draw me far from God.
I have made you a malcontent;
Else Christ would have died in vain.
Into his hands have I already given
The soul that he calls to himself.
I do not answer when you call;
I ridicule and deride you instead.

(*No melody is indicated*)

5. *Contemplate My Sufferings, O Sinner*
[*Contempla le mie pene, o peccatore*]

(From *Rime sacre del magnifico Lorenzo de' Medici il Vecchio,
di Maddona Lucrezia sua madre e d'altri della stessa famiglia*)

Contemplate my sufferings, O sinner,
And the martyrdom in which you find me:
See, I do not pardon even
Myself, I who hang on the cross for love of you.

Look at me: I have left the noble kingdom,
Gripped with pity for you;
And I am confined to this bitter wood
Locked in cruelty.
My charity was without measure
When I chose such martyrdom for you;
I elected this suffering,
Such was my urge,
So that you might live with me in great honor.

Contemplate my sufferings, O sinner,
And the martyrdom in which you find me:
See, I do not pardon even
Myself, I who hang on the cross for love of you.

Contemplate this carefully: gaze at my crown;
It is so sharp, and so cruel.
See how my flesh is martyred just for you.
The gall is prepared;

---

converted. The remaining four lines would return to the chief speaker, who warns her tempter
that she will still not engage him in "his false and trivial ways."

Is there no faithful follower to share this anguish?
To share in my pain?
Through five large veins
My blood gushes out, and you search for your honor.

Contemplate my sufferings, O sinner,
And the martyrdom in which you find me:
See, I do not pardon even
Myself, I who hang on the cross for love of you.

I do contemplate, Lord, your great suffering
And your bitter passion;
O sweet Jesus of mine, you were alone
At the redemption.
My soul and my heart are desolate;
[But] my hope is high
That with your mercy
You will take pity on this wretched sinner.

Contemplate my sufferings, O sinner,
And the martyrdom in which you find me:
See, I do not pardon even
Myself, I who hang on the cross for love of you.

(Sung to "O Gesu dolce, o infinito amore"
[O sweet Jesus, O infinite love])

6. *Come Away from There, Shepherds* [*Venitene pastori*]
(From Bib. Ricc. 3112, 221r)

Come away from there, shepherds,[17]
Come see Jesus, who is born,
Born naked in a stable,
More resplendent than the sun.

O shepherds, now come quickly,
To see the handsome Messiah:
There is only Joseph here, and Mary,
His glorious mother.

17. This *laude* has various opening lines depending on the manuscript version: "venite pastori" and "deh venitene pastori"; "venitene pastori" is the most metrically suitable.

Never was one so precious,
Nor will there be one again;
He has among his royal train
Only the ox and the donkey.

The Lord of lords has neither
Coat, nor cover, nor swaddling;
From the heavens come the choirs
To see the deity.

Here come the heavenly powers,
Here come the cherubim,
The virtues and the seraphim,
The celestial hierarchy.

And with sweet melody
They thank him, warm with desire:
"Glory in heaven to the high God,
Let there be peace on earth!"

O shepherds, come this way now,
To visit your noble Lord:
You will hear sweet singing
And see the king of glory.

Today is the day of victory,
Let the enemy know sorrow,
And our ancient fathers
Will happily hear the news.

A star is in the heavens,
To brighten all our world;
Come here now to thank him,
Omnipotent Jesus Christ.

All devout and pious minds
Now contemplate with sweetness
How the highest divinity
Will suffer for our sins.

(*Sung to "Quando sono in questa cittade" [When I am in this city]*)

7. Welcome, Hosanna [*Ben vengha osanna*]
(From Magl. XXXV, 119, 150v)

Welcome, Hosanna,
Welcome, Hosanna,
And the daughter of Anna!

He was born in the straw,
Between the ox and donkey;
This is the Lord of Nazareth,
As had been foretold.
Who wishes to see Jesus,
Let him come and sing Hosannas.

Welcome, Hosanna,
Welcome, Hosanna,
And the daughter of Anna!

The Magi, on their horses,
Come laden with their treasure,
And shepherds go on singing
Of the Lord of lords:
Everyone is enamored
Of singing only Hosannas!

Welcome, Hosanna,
Welcome, Hosanna,
And the daughter of Anna!

Let his pure love refresh us
And our world with peace and gladness;
The Savior descends
From the Mount of Olives,
And the people follow, crying
In loud voices, "Hosanna!"

Welcome, Hosanna,
Welcome, Hosanna,
And the daughter of Anna!

Jerusalem may rejoice now
And raise up its soul in singing.

He who will soon be weeping
Disperses olive branch and palm;
They all adore their Jesus,
And everyone cries, "Hosanna!"

Welcome, Hosanna,
Welcome, Hosanna,
And the daughter of Anna!

This is the night the Pharisees
Will experience such torment;
This is the night that Judas
Becomes enraged with Mary.[18]
He quickly left the dinner
Just to betray Hosanna.

Welcome, Hosanna,
Welcome, Hosanna,
And the daughter of Anna!

The evil man shouts, "Come now,
Take away holy Jesus."
He kissed him, and he gave the sign
For Jesus to be bound:
"O rabbi, hail!" How often
Will they cry in vain, "Hosanna!"

Welcome, Hosanna,
Welcome, Hosanna,
And the daughter of Anna!

Mary has arrived now
To find her son just taken
By men who are cruel and evil,
Who leave him whipped and beaten.
They lead him off to Calvary,
Where no one says, "Hosanna."

18. When Mary Magdalene poured precious ointment on Jesus' head, Judas accused her of wasting money that could have been given to the poor (see Matthew 26 and Mark 14).

Welcome, Hosanna,
Welcome, Hosanna,
And the daughter of Anna!

May every faithful soul turn
To God with humble voices.
May they weep for Jesus crucified
Who tasted grief for us.
Oh, what a cruel thing,
Virgin daughter of Anna!

Welcome, Hosanna, and the daughter of Anna!
(*Sung to "Ben venga maggio"*)

8. *Here Is the Strong King [Ecco il Re forte]*
(From Bib. Ricc. 3112, 156r)

Here is the strong king
Here is the strong king
Open up the gates!

O infernal prince of hell,
Do not resist his entrance:
This is the celestial king,
Who comes with almighty power:
Do him reverence instead
And open wide the gates.[19]

Here is the strong king
Here is the strong king
Open up the gates!

Who is this great one,
Who comes in victory?
He is the almighty Lord,
He is the Lord of glory.

19. See Ps. 23:7: "Lift up, O gates, your lintels: reach up, your ancient portals, that the king of glory may come in!"

The victory is his alone;
For he has conquered death.[20]

Here is the strong king
Here is the strong king
Open up the gates!

He has won the battle,
That endured for many years;
He makes the whole earth tremble
To release us from our troubles.
He seeks to replenish heaven's thrones
So he can restore his court.

Here is the strong king
Here is the strong king
Open up the gates!

He calls for the ancient father
And all his company;[21]
He wants his true friend, Abel,
And Noah to make their way,
And Moses will no longer stay.
All come! to his great court.

Here is the strong king
Here is the strong king
Open up the gates!

O Abraham, our patriarch,
Follow the great Lord;
He does not withhold his promise,
He is the Redeemer.
May the great singer come with him
To dignify his court.[22]

20. See Ps. 23:8: "Who is this king of glory? The Lord, strong and mighty, the Lord, mighty in battle."
21. An allusion to Adam and Eve.
22. A probable reference to David, singer of the Psalms.

Here is the strong king
Here is the strong king
Open up the gates!

O Saint John the Baptist,
Now come, without delay,
Keep within your holy gaze
The eternal choir above;
And Simeon comes with them
To serve them as their guide.[23]

Here is the strong king
Here is the strong king
Open up the gates!

O you innocent children,
Go now, before the others,
Now you are contented
With the wounds you have;
O gems and precious pearls,
Worship his great court.[24]

Here is the strong king
Here is the strong king
Open up the gates!

May you all come to the kingdom
That you so long desired;
Ever since, on that holy wood,
I was tortured and killed,
The wood where all human
Destiny was redeemed.[25]

23. John the Baptist's presence in Tornabuoni's *laude* probably requires little explanation; that of Simeon may. An aged prophet, he recognizes that Jesus is the Messiah when the infant is presented at the temple; he declares him "a light of revelation to the Gentiles, and a glory for thy people Israel" (Luke 2:32). Like John, then, he prophesies the coming of Christ.

24. A probable reference to the innocent children slaughtered by King Herod (father of the Herod encountered in *The Life of Saint John the Baptist*).

25. Only in this last stanza does Christ actually speak, raising the question whether he has been the voice behind the song's "vocator" throughout or whether it is only here that he replaces the narrative voice that has called "venite" all along to the worthy denizens of hell.

Here is the strong king
Here is the strong king
Open up the gates!

(*Sung to "Ben venga maggio"*)

9. *Canzone on the Flower Born of Royal Stock*
[Della stirpe regale, è nato il fiore]
(From Magl. VII, 338, 118v)[26]

The flower is born of royal stock;
    Its roots hold fast in every place,
    Whence flourishes the worthy fruit.[27]
    This alone is the one that came blessed
    In the name of exalted Savior!
    Our ancient misfortune brought together
    The Father, Son, and Spirit in counsel
    To discredit that bold one
    Who disturbed the peace
    And every hour increased his power.
    No longer did [God] want to tolerate this:
    So that devil would die,
    The plant bursts into flower. The word is made flesh![28]

The beautiful fruit gives birth to the seed,
    Which fell from the heavens through divine guidance
    And presented itself to that virginal vessel,
    And around midnight the lily flowered.
    Its perfume is everywhere redolent,
    And never for any reason will it fade.
    It blankets and overwhelms the stench
    Of the ancient serpent

---

26. Along with "Contempla le mie pene," this is the most metrically complex of Tornabuoni's short poems. Each stanza is composed of thirteen lines, with most consisting of eleven syllables and every eighth, ninth, and twelfth line consisting of seven. The short lines all rhyme, while the larger stanza obeys an AABAABB pattern. The shorter lines thus convey a somewhat truncated effect, and they generally stand out as being particularly emphatic. In the translation I have attempted to follow, albeit loosely, Tornabuoni's metrical scheme—if not her rhyme scheme—although there are occasional inconsistencies.

27. A probable allusion to Isaiah 11:1: "But a shoot shall sprout from the stump of Jesse, and from his roots a bud shall blossom."

28. "Perchel dimon sispergha / fiori la verga. El verbo si fe carne": note the internal rhyme with "spergha" and "verga"; this will be repeated in the final lines of each stanza.

Who claimed to befriend
That ambitious woman, then sent her to her ruin
With his human face and his lying words,
With his roguery.
The fool believed him, and she lost her place [in
   paradise].

They did not lose their garments or their rich raiment;
   Nor jewels from the East or magnificent treasures.
   They lost neither castles, cities, nor kingdoms:
   What they lost was delight; and thrust out of the
      choir,
   They found themselves surrounded by troubles.
   I don't think that they lived there for even an hour;
   Once they disobeyed they were instantly cast outside,
   Desolate, and naked,
   Without their sweet pastimes.
   For our first parents, it was a cursed hour
   When they protested their grief and their death,
   Chased out of the garden
   And deprived of so many good things.

Once there, they see one another anew
   And at once they conceal those parts that shame.
   And they stand still knowing not what to do:
   "What life is this? What works are now ours?
   Will we know what to do to stem his wrath?"
   They asked each other, "for we have few friends,
   Only each other with whom to lament
   How foolish desire
   Made us lose so much.
   There is nothing to do but humble ourselves
   If we want to hold our heads high or move our feet;
   Let us pray that he
   Will have mercy on all of our failings."

Seized by this thought, they both together
   Threw themselves down upon their knees,
   Beseeching God that he hear their prayers,
   And they spoke with devout words and upturned eyes

And each of them shed copious tears
As they grieved for the boundaries they had trespassed.[29]
They said, "We had license with all of the trees;
We wanted to taste them
To make ourselves equal
To our great maker, to know the lofty intellects,
And now we have learned everything, to our grief;
Now we are like God,
But trapped by the devil, through his deceit.

"Is there a remedy for us, O our Lord?
Will you ever look with favor on this our sin?
We have made ourselves ready to do penance.
This enemy made both of us sin
By showing us lies and a false disguise
And thus did he sow his evil seed.
In your prudence, O Lord, help us: let not our
Souls die with our bodies
Or our enemy triumph
Let him not have power over us."
So they uttered pious words with humble hearts.
"Lord, help us see clearly,[30]
So the venomous worm will no longer harm us."

Their humble prayers rose up to heaven,
And there they came within the hearing
Of that immense goodness, clement and just,
Who saw all of the malicious results
That had come from that presumptuous angel
Who was the first to cause trouble in heaven,
And when he lost, was quickly cast out.
The arrogant one
Turned his plaints against heaven
And made himself filthy, he who was most resplendent.

---

29. "Trapassati segni": surely an allusion to the words of Adam in Dante's *Paradiso* 26:115–17: "My sin, the cause of my long exile did not lie / within the tasting of the tree, / but solely in my trespass of the boundary" [Ma solamente il trapassar del segno] (Mandelbaum translation).

30. "Signor to vie labenda": literally, "take away the blindfold," used figuratively for "to un-deceive."

Envy led him to trick the most noble race
That God molded,
They were chased out of Eden and brought to despair.

God was not pleased that the evil one would triumph,
That the world would surrender itself to him
In obedience, and hand him the olive branch.
He found the remedy to make man live,
He offered him a way to share in his glory
And learn of his justice. Such was his intent,
And so then that divine wisdom
To charity turned;
To amend man's sin,
He chooses to suffer violence and death.
To the truly penitent he gave a sign:
They would return to him,
And he would pay for every injury with the cross.

On the wood, he wishes to suffer bitter torments,
And in exchange for the apple that was so sweet,
He will have vinegar and gall for refreshment.
He disdains no torment, no matter how cruel,
Nor does he seek to elude the shame;
All so that man may return to his kingdom
He desires to win everything back on the wood.
On the cross man was conquered,
And [God] drew and painted
The entire plan of his great mystery:
And so it was essential that he come to earth
And lift all prohibitions,
And with his meekness, he will win the war.

Simple little song, go forth with fervor;
Comforting them
Though they are rebels
So they may turn to seek God's mercy
And beseech his pardon with humble hearts
And faithful hope;
He will be their guide as they regain their gift!

BIBLIOGRAPHY

MANUSCRIPTS

Biblioteca Nazionale

Magliabechiano VII, 338. "Poesie di Lucrezia Torn[abuoni]."

Magliabechiano VII, 1083. "Laudi."

Magliabechiano VII, 1159. "La vita et morte del glorioso Giovanni Baptista"; "La storia di Giudetta giudea"; "Laudi."

Magliabechiano XXXV, 119. "Laudi."

Biblioteca Riccardiana

Biblioteca Riccardiana 2816. "Rappresentazioni, storie, e rime diverse."

Biblioteca Riccardiana 3112. "Laudi."

Biblioteca Riccardiana 3834. San Antoninus, "Regola de vivere spirituale."

PRIMARY SOURCES

Alberti, Leon Battista (1404–72). *The Family in Renaissance Florence*. Trans. Renée Neu Watkins. Columbia: University of South Carolina Press, 1969.

Alighieri, Dante. *The Divine Comedy of Dante Alighieri*. Trans. Allen Mandelbaum. Berkeley: University of California Press, 1980–82.

Ariosto, Ludovico (1474–1533). *Orlando Furioso*. Trans. Barbara Reynolds. 2 vols. New York: Penguin, 1975, 1977.

Astell, Mary (1666–1731). *The First English Feminist: "Reflections on Marriage" and Other Writings*. Ed. and introd. Bridget Hill. New York: St. Martin's Press, 1986.

Barbaro, Francesco (1390–1454). *On Wifely Duties*. Trans. Benjamin Kohl in *The Earthly Republic*, ed. Benjamin Kohl and R. G. Witt, 179–228. Philadelphia: University of Pennsylvania Press, 1978. Translation of the preface and book 2.

Bellincioni, Bernardo. *Le rime di Bernardo Bellincioni*. Ed. Pietro Fanfani. 2 vols. Bologna, 1876–78.

Biblia sacra: Iuxta latinam vulgatum versionem. Ed. Monks of the Abbey of Saint Jerome in Urbe. Rome, 1926–57.

Boccaccio, Giovanni (1313–75). *Concerning Famous Women*. Trans. Guido A. Guarino. New Brunswick, N.J.: Rutgers University Press, 1963.

———. *The Corbaccio, or The Labyrinth of Love*. Trans. and ed. Anthony K. Cassell. 2d rev. ed. Binghamton, N.Y.: Medieval and Renaissance Texts and Studies, 1993.

The Book of Tobit. Trans. Frank Zimmermann. New York: Harper, 1958.

Bruni, Leonardo (1370–1444). "On the Study of Literature (1424) to Lady Battista Malatesta of Montefeltro." In *The Humanism of Leonardo Bruni: Selected Texts*, trans. and introd. Gordon Griffiths, James Hankins, and David Thompson, 240–51. Binghamton, N.Y.: Medieval and Renaissance Texts and Studies, 1987.

Cantari religiosi senesi del Trecento. Ed. Giorgio Varanini. Bari: Laterza, 1965.

Castiglione, Baldassare (1478–1529). *The Book of the Courtier.* Trans. George Bull. New York: Penguin, 1967.

Cavalca, Domenico. *Vite dei santi padri.* Ed. Bartolomeo Sorio and A. Racheli. Trieste: Lloyd Austriaco, 1858.

Elyot, Thomas (1490–1546). *Defence of Good Women: The Feminist Controversy of the Renaissance.* Ed. Diane Bornstein. Facsimile Reproductions. New York: Delmar, 1980.

Erasmus, Desiderius (1467–1536). *Erasmus on Women.* Ed. Erika Rummel. Toronto: University of Toronto Press, 1996.

———. *The Praise of Folly.* Trans. Betty Radice, introd. and notes A. H. T. Levi. New York: Penguin, 1993.

Esther. Introd. and trans. Carey A. Moore. Anchor Bible. Garden City, N.Y.: Doubleday. 1971.

Guillaume de Lorris and Jean de Meun. *The Romance of the Rose.* Trans. Charles Dahlbert. Princeton: Princeton University Press, 1971; reprinted University Press of New England, 1983.

Holy Bible. Confraternity-Douay Version. New York: Catholic Book Publishing, 1963.

"La istoria di Susanna e Daniello, poemetto popolare antico." Ed. A. Parducci. *Romania* 42 (1913): 34–75.

Josephus, Flavius. *The Works of Flavius Josephus.* Ed. D. S. Margoliouth, trans. W. Whiston. London: Routledge, 1906.

Kempe, Margery (1373–1439). *The Book of Margery Kempe.* Trans. Barry Windeatt. New York: Viking Penguin, 1986.

King, Margaret L., and Albert Rabil Jr., eds. *Her Immaculate Hand: Selected Works by and about the Women Humanists of Quattrocento Italy.* Binghamton, N.Y.: Medieval and Renaissance Texts and Studies, 1983; 2d rev. paperback ed., 1991.

Klein, Joan Larsen, ed. *Daughters, Wives, and Widows: Writings by Men about Women and Marriage in England, 1500–1640.* Urbana: University of Illinois Press, 1992.

Knox, John (1505–72). *The Political Writings of John Knox: "The First Blast of the Trumpet against the Monstrous Regiment of Women" and Other Selected Works.* Ed. Marvin A. Breslow. Washington, D.C.: Folger Shakespeare Library, 1985.

Kors, Alan C., and Edward Peters, eds. *Witchcraft in Europe, 1100–1700: A Documentary History.* Philadelphia: University of Pennsylvania Press, 1972.

Krämer, Heinrich, and Jacob Sprenger. *Malleus Maleficarum* (ca. 1487). Trans. Montague Summers. London: Pushkin Press, 1928; reprinted New York: Dover, 1971.

Marguerite d'Angoulême, Queen of Navarre (1492–1549). *The Heptameron.* Trans. P. A. Chilton. New York: Viking Penguin, 1984.

Medici, Lorenzo de'. *Lettere di Lorenzo de' Medici.* Gen. ed. Nicolai Rubinstein. Florence: Giunti, 1977–.

————. *Selected Writings.* Ed. Corinna Salvadori. Dublin: Belfield Italian Library, 1992.

————. *Poesie.* Ed. Federico Sanguineti. Milan: Rizzoli, 1992.

Meditations on the Life of Christ. Trans. Isa Ragusa. Princeton: Princeton University Press, 1961.

Nardi, Jacopo. *Istorie della città di Firenze.* Ed. A. Gelli. Florence, 1858.

Novum Testamentum Domini nostri Jesu Christi. Ed. J. Wordsworth, J. H. White, et al. Oxford, 1889–1954.

Nuovi Testi fiorentini del Dugento. Ed. Arrigo Castellani. 2 vols. Florence: Sansoni, 1952.

Nuovo corpus di sacre rappresentazioni fiorentine del Quattrocento. Ed. Nerida Newbigin. Bologna: Commissione per i Testi di Lingua, 1983.

Petrarch, Francis. *Petrarch's Lyric Poems.* Trans. and ed. Robert M. Durling. Cambridge: Harvard University Press, 1976.

————. *Triumphi.* Ed. Marco Ariani. Milan: Mirsia, 1988.

Pizan, Christine de (1365–1431). *The Book of the City of Ladies.* Trans. Earl Jeffrey Richards, foreword Marina Warner. New York: Persea, 1982.

————. *The Treasure of the City of Ladies.* Trans. Sarah Lawson. New York: Viking Penguin, 1985. Also trans. and introd. Charity Cannon Willard, ed. and introd. Madeleine P. Cosman. New York: Persea, 1989.

Poliziano, Angelo. *Le Stanze, l'Orfeo e le rime.* Ed. G. Carducci. Florence, 1863.

Pulci, Antonia. *Florentine Drama for Convent and Festival.* Trans. James Wyatt Cook, ed. James Wyatt Cook and Barbara Collier Cook. Chicago: University of Chicago Press, 1996.

Pulci, Luigi. *Morgante e lettere.* Ed. Domenico de Robertis. Florence: Sansoni, 1962.

Il Quattrocento. Ed. G. Ponte. Bologna: Zanichelli, 1966.

Rime sacre del magnifico Lorenzo de' Medici il Vecchio, di Madonna Lucrezia sua madre e d'altri della stessa famiglia. Ed. Francesco Cionacci. Florence, 1680.

Rucellai, Giovanni. *Il Zibaldone quaresimale: Pagine scelte.* Ed. A. Perosa. London: Warburg Institute, 1960.

Scrittori di religione del Trecento: Volgarizzamenti. Ed. Don Giuseppe de Luca. Turin: Einaudi, 1977.

Spenser, Edmund (1552–1599). *The Faerie Queene.* Ed. Thomas P. Roche Jr. with the assistance of C. Patrick O'Donnell Jr. New Haven: Yale University Press, 1978.

Strozzi, Alessandra. *Selected Letters of Alessandra Strozzi.* Trans. Heather Gregory. Berkeley: University of California Press, 1997.

Teresa of Avila, Saint (1515–82). *The Life of Saint Teresa of Avila by Herself.* Trans. J. M. Cohen. New York: Viking Penguin, 1957.

Tornabuoni, Lucrezia. *La istoria della casta Susanna.* Ed. Paolo Orvieto. Bergamo: Moretti e Vitali, 1992.

————. *Le laudi di Lucrezia de' Medici.* Ed. G. Volpi. Pistoia: Flori, 1900.

————. *Lettere.* Ed. Patrizia Salvadori. Florence: Olschki, 1993.

————. *I poemetti sacri di Lucrezia Tornabuoni.* Ed. Fulvio Pezzarossa. Florence: Olschki, 1978.

Vasari, Giorgio. *Le vite de' più eccellenti pittori, scultori e architettori.* Ed. Gaetano Milanesi. Florence: Sansoni, 1906.

Voragine, Jacobus de. *The Golden Legend: Readings on the Saints.* Trans. William Granger Ryan. 2 vols. Princeton: Princeton University Press, 1993.

Weyer, Johann (1515–88). *Witches, Devils, and Doctors in the Renaissance: Johann Weyer, "De Praestigiis Daemonum."* Ed. George Mora with Benjamin G. Kohl, Erik Midelfort, and Helen Bacon, trans. John Shea. Binghamton, N.Y.: Medieval and Renaissance Texts and Studies, 1991.

Wilson, Katharina M., ed. *Medieval Women Writers.* Athens: University of Georgia Press, 1984.

———, ed. *Women Writers of the Renaissance and Reformation.* Athens: University of Georgia Press, 1987.

Wilson, Katharina M., and Frank J. Warnke, eds. *Women Writers of the Seventeenth Century.* Athens: University of Georgia Press, 1989.

Wollstonecraft, Mary. *"A Vindication of the Rights of Men" and "A Vindication of the Rights of Woman."* Ed. Sylvana Tomaselli. Cambridge: Cambridge University Press, 1995. Also in *The Vindications: The Rights of Men, the Rights of Woman,* ed. D. L. Macdonald and Kathleen Scherf. Peterborough, Ont.: Broadview Press, 1997.

Women Writers in English, 1350–1850. Series, Oxford University Press. 30 vols. projected, 15 published through 1999.

SECONDARY SOURCES

Achenbach, Gertrude M. "The Iconography of Tobias and the Angel in the Florentine Painting of the Renaissance." *Marsyas* 3 (1944): 71–86.

Akkerman, Tjitske, and Siep Sturman, eds. *Feminist Thought in European History, 1400–2000.* New York: Routledge, 1997.

Ancona, Alessandro d'. *Origini del teatro italiano.* 2 vols. Turin: Loescher, 1891.

Andres, Glenn M., John M. Hunisak, and Richard Turner. *The Art of Florence.* 2 vols. New York: Artabras, 1994.

Aus, Roger. *Water into Wine and the Beheading of John the Baptist.* Atlanta: Scholars Press, 1988.

Bach, Alice. *Women, Seduction, and Betrayal in Biblical Narrative.* Cambridge: Cambridge University Press, 1997.

Bakhtin, Mikhail. *Rabelais and His World.* Trans. Hélène Iswolsky. Bloomington: Indiana University Press, 1984.

Barriault, Anne B. *Spalliera Paintings of Renaissance Tuscany: Fables of Poets for Patrician Homes.* University Park: Pennsylvania State University Press, 1994.

Baskins, Cristelle L. *"La Festa di Susanna:* Virtue on Trial in Renaissance Sacred Drama and Painted Wedding Chests." *Art History* 14 (1991): 328–44.

Beilin, Elaine V. *Redeeming Eve: Women Writers of the English Renaissance.* Princeton: Princeton University Press, 1987.

Benson, Pamela Joseph. *The Invention of the Renaissance Woman: The Challenge of Female Independence in the Literature and Thought of Italy and England.* University Park: Pennsylvania State University Press, 1992.

Bernacchioni, Annamaria. "Filippino Lippi: 'I tre Arcangeli e Tobiolo.'" *Maestri e Botteghe: Pittura a Firenze alla fine del Quattrocento. Catalogo della mostra, Firenze 1992–93,* ed. Mina Gregori, Antonio Paolucci, and Cristina Acidini Luchinat, 76. Milan: Silvano, 1992.

Beyer, Andreas, and Bruce Boucher. *Piero de' Medici: "Il Gottoso" (1416–69).* Berlin: Akademie Verlag, 1993.

Blain, Virginia, Isobel Grundy, and Patricia Clements, eds. *The Feminist Companion to Literature in English: Women Writers from the Middle Ages to the Present.* New Haven: Yale University Press, 1990.

Bloch, R. Howard. *Medieval Misogyny and the Invention of Western Romantic Love.* Chicago: University of Chicago Press, 1991.

Bornstein, Daniel. *The Bianchi of 1399: Popular Devotion in Late Medieval Italy.* Ithaca: Cornell University Press, 1993.

Bornstein, Daniel, and Roberto Rusconi, eds. *Women and Religion in Late Medieval and Early Modern Italy.* Chicago: University of Chicago Press, 1996.

Bosanquet, Mary. *Mother of the Magnificent: A Life of Lucrezia Tornabuoni.* London: Faber and Faber, 1960.

Brant, Clare, and Diane Purkiss, eds. *Women, Texts and Histories, 1575–1760.* New York: Routledge, 1992.

Briggs, Robin. *Witches and Neighbours: The Social and Cultural Context of European Witchcraft.* HarperCollins, 1995; Viking: Penguin, 1996.

The Cambridge History of the Bible. Ed. G. W. H. Lampe. Vol. 2. Cambridge: Cambridge University Press, 1969.

Capozzi, Frank. "The Evolution and Transformation of the Judith and Holofernes Theme in Italian Drama and Art before 1627." Ph.D. diss., University of Wisconsin–Madison, 1975.

Ciletti, Elena. "Patriarchal Ideology in the Renaissance Iconography of Judith." In *Refiguring Woman: Perspectives on Gender and the Italian Renaissance,* ed. Marilyn Migiel and Juliana Schiesari, 35–70. Ithaca: Cornell University Press, 1991.

Clark, Elizabeth A. *Ascetic Piety and Women's Faith: Essays on Late Ancient Christianity.* Lewiston, N.Y.: Edwin Mellen, 1986.

Coppola, Domenico. *La poesia religiosa del secolo XV.* Florence: Olschki, 1963.

Davis, Natalie Zemon. *Society and Culture in Early Modern France.* Stanford: Stanford University Press, 1975.

———. *Women on the Margins: Three Seventeenth-Century Lives.* Cambridge: Harvard University Press, 1995.

De Erauso, Catalina. *Lieutenant Nun: Memoir of a Basque Transvestite in the New World.* Trans. Michele Stepto and Gabriel Stepto, foreword by Marjorie Garber. Boston: Beacon Press, 1995.

DeJean, Joan. *Ancients against Moderns: Culture Wars and the Making of a Fin de Siècle.* Chicago: University of Chicago Press, 1997.

———. *Tender Geographies: Women and the Origins of the Novel in France.* New York: Columbia University Press, 1991.

Dixon, Laurinda S. *Perilous Chastity: Women and Illness in Pre-Enlightenment Art and Medicine.* Ithaca: Cornell University Press, 1995.

Dixon, Suzanne. *The Roman Family.* Baltimore: Johns Hopkins University Press, 1992.

Duby, Georges, and Michelle Perrot, eds. *A History of Women in the West.* Vol. 1. *From Ancient Goddesses to Christian Saints.* Ed. Pauline Schmitt Pantel. Cambridge: Harvard University Press, 1992.

———. *A History of Women in the West.* Vol. 2. *Silences of the Middle Ages.* Ed. Christiane Klapisch-Zuber. Cambridge: Harvard University Press, 1992.

———. *A History of Women in the West.* Vol. 3: *Renaissance and Enlightenment Paradoxes.*

Ed. Natalie Zemon Davis and Arlette Farge. Cambridge: Harvard University Press, 1993.

Erickson, Amy Louise. *Women and Property in Early Modern England.* New York: Routledge, 1993.

Ferguson, Margaret W., Maureen Quilligan, and Nancy J. Vickers, eds. *Rewriting the Renaissance: The Discourses of Sexual Difference in Early Modern Europe.* Chicago: University of Chicago Press, 1987.

Fletcher, Anthony. *Gender, Sex and Subordination in England, 1500–1800.* New Haven: Yale University Press, 1995.

Foster, Kenelm. "Vernacular Scriptures in Italy." In *The Cambridge History of the Bible,* ed. G. W. H. Lampe, 2:452–64. Cambridge: Cambridge University Press, 1969.

Fubini, Riccardo. "In margine all'edizione delle *Lettere* di Lorenzo de' Medici." In *Lorenzo de' Medici: Studi,* ed. Gian Carlo Garfagnini, 167–232. Florence: Olschki, 1992.

Gallagher, Catherine. *Nobody's Story: The Vanishing Acts of Women Writers in the Marketplace, 1670–1820.* Berkeley: University of California Press, 1994.

Gardner, Jane F. *Women in Roman Law and Society.* Bloomington: Indiana University Press, 1986.

Garfagnini, Gian Carlo, ed. *Lorenzo de' Medici: Studi.* Florence: Olschki, 1992.

Gelbart, Nina Rattner. *The King's Midwife: A History and Mystery of Madame du Coudray.* Berkeley: University of California Press, 1998.

Gill, Katherine J. "Women and the Production of Religious Literature in the Vernacular, 1300–1500." In *Women and Culture in Early Modern Europe: Essays in Honor of Carolyn Walker Bynum,* 64–104. New York: Columbia University Press, 1995.

Goldsmith, Elizabeth C., and Dena Goodman, eds. *Going Public: Women and Publishing in Early Modern France.* Ithaca: Cornell University Press, 1995.

Gombrich, Ernst. "Tobias and the Angel." In *Symbolic Images and Studies in the Art of the Renaissance,* 39–45. London: Phaidon, 1972.

Groppi, Felicina. *Dante traduttore.* Rome: Orbis Catholicus, 1962.

Hardwick, Julie. *The Practice of Patriarchy: Gender and the Politics of Household Authority in Early Modern France.* University Park: Pennsylvania State University Press, 1998.

Hartt, Frederick. *History of Italian Renaissance Art.* Ed. David G. Wilkins. 4th ed. New York: Abrams, 1994.

Haselkorn, Anne M., and Betty Travitsky, eds. *The Renaissance Englishwoman in Print: Counterbalancing the Canon.* Amherst: University of Massachusetts Press, 1990.

Henderson, John. *Piety and Charity in Late Medieval Florence.* Chicago: University of Chicago Press, 1994.

Herlihy, David. "Did Women Have a Renaissance? A Reconsideration." *Medievalia et Humanistica,* n.s., 13 (1985): 1–22.

Hill, Bridget. *The Republican Virago: The Life and Times of Catharine Macaulay, Historian.* New York: Oxford University Press, 1992.

Horowitz, Maryanne Cline. "Aristotle and Women." *Journal of the History of Biology* 9 (1976): 183–213.

Hufton, Olwen H. *The Prospect before Her: A History of Women in Western Europe.* Vol. 1. *1500–1800.* New York: HarperCollins, 1996.

Hull, Suzanne W. *Chaste, Silent, and Obedient: English Books for Women, 1475–1640.* San Marino, Calif.: Huntington Library, 1982.

Janson, H. W. *The Sculpture of Donatello*. Princeton: Princeton University Press, 1963.

Jed, Stephanie H. *Chaste Thinking: The Rape of Lucretia and the Birth of Humanism*. Bloomington: Indiana University Press, 1989.

Jordan, Constance. "Listening to 'the Other Voice' in Early Modern Europe." *Renaissance Quarterly* 51 (1998): 184–92.

———. *Renaissance Feminism: Literary Texts and Political Models*. Ithaca: Cornell University Press, 1990.

Kelly, Joan. "Did Women Have a Renaissance?" In *Women, History, and Theory*, 19–50. Chicago: University of Chicago Press, 1984. Also in *Becoming Visible: Women in European History*, ed. Renate Bridenthal, Claudia Koonz, and Susan M. Stuard, 2d ed., 175–202. Boston: Houghton Mifflin, 1987.

———. "Early Feminist Theory and the *Querelle des Femmes*." In *Women, History, and Theory*, 65–109. Chicago: University of Chicago Press, 1984.

Kelso, Ruth. *Doctrine for the Lady of the Renaissance*. Foreword by Katharine M. Rogers. Urbana: University of Illinois Press, 1956, 1978.

Kent, F. W. *Household and Lineage in Renaissance Florence: The Family Life of the Capponi, Ginori, and Rucellai*. Princeton: Princeton University Press, 1977.

———. "A Proposal by Savonarola for the Self-Reform of Florentine Women (March 1496)." *Memorie Domenicane*, n.s. (1983): 335–41.

———. "Palaces, Politics and Society in Fifteenth Century Florence." *I Tatti Studies* 2 (1987): 41–70.

———. "Sainted Mother, Magnificent Son: Lucrezia Tornabuoni and Lorenzo de' Medici." *Italian History and Culture* 3 (1997): 3–34.

King, Margaret L. *Women of the Renaissance*. Foreword by Catharine R. Stimpson. Chicago: University of Chicago Press, 1991.

Klapisch-Zuber, Christiane. *Women, Family, and Ritual in Renaissance Italy*. Trans. Lydia G. Cochrane. Chicago: University of Chicago Press, 1985.

Klein, Lillian R. "Honor and Shame in Esther." In *A Feminist Companion to Esther, Judith and Susanna*, ed. Athalya Brenner, 149–75. Sheffield: Sheffield Academic Press, 1995.

Koch, Linda. "Piero de' Medici and a Chapel in San Minato del Monte." Talk given at Renaissance Society of America annual meeting, Los Angeles, March 1999.

Krontiris, Tina. *Oppositional Voices: Women as Writers and Translators of Literature in the English Renaissance*. New York: Routledge, 1992.

Kunze, Bonnelyn Young. *Margaret Fell and the Rise of Quakerism*. Stanford: Stanford University Press, 1994.

Laqueur, Thomas. *Making Sex: Body and Gender from the Greeks to Freud*. Cambridge: Harvard University Press, 1990.

Lebano, Edoardo A. "Luigi Pulci and Late Fifteenth-Century Humanism in Florence." *Renaissance Quarterly* 27 (1974): 489–98.

Lerner, Gerda. *The Creation of Feminist Consciousness: From the Middle Ages to Eighteen-Seventy*. New York: Oxford University Press, 1994.

———. *The Creation of Patriarchy*. New York: Oxford University Press, 1986.

Levantini-Pieroni, Giuseppe. *Lucrezia Tornabuoni, donna di Piero di Cosimo de' Medici*. In *Studi storici e letterari*, 1–83. Florence: Le Monnier, 1893.

Levine, Amy-Jill. "Hemmed in on Every Side." In *A Feminist Companion to Esther, Judith and Susanna*, ed. Athalya Brenner, 303–23. Sheffield: Sheffield Academic Press, 1995.

Lightbown, Ronald. *Sandro Botticelli: Life and Works.* New York: Abbeville Press, 1989.

Livorni, Ernesto. "When Death and Birth Conjoin: The Worship of St. John the Baptist in Renaissance Florence." Unpublished talk for the Renaissance Society of America annual meeting, March 2000.

Lochrie, Karma. *Margery Kempe and Translations of the Flesh.* Philadelphia: University of Pennsylvania Press, 1992.

Lowe, Katherine J. P. "A Matter of Piety or of Family Tradition and Custom? The Religious Patronage of Piero de' Medici and Lucrezia Tornabuoni." In *Piero de' Medici: "Il Gottoso" (1416–69)*, ed. Andreas Beyer and Bruce Boucher, 55–69. Berlin: Akademie Verlag, 1993.

Lungo, Isidoro del. *La donna fiorentina del buon tempo antico.* Florence: Bemporad, 1906.

Maclean, Ian. *The Renaissance Notion of Woman: A Study in the Fortunes of Scholasticism and Medical Science in European Intellectual Life.* Cambridge: Cambridge University Press, 1980.

———. *Woman Triumphant: Feminism in French Literature, 1610–1652.* Oxford: Clarendon Press, 1977.

Maguire, Yvonne. *The Women of the Medici.* London: Routledge, 1927.

Mariani, Gaetano. *Il Morgante e i cantari trecenteschi.* Florence: Le Monnier, 1953.

Martelli, Mario. *Letteratura fiorentina del Quattrocento.* Florence: Le Lettere, 1996.

———. "Lucrezia Tornabuoni." In *Les femmes écrivains en Italie au Moyen Âge et à la Renaissance*, 51–86. Aix-en-Provence: Publications de l'Université de Provence, 1994.

Matter, E. Ann, and John Coakley, eds. *Creative Women in Medieval and Early Modern Italy.* Philadelphia: University of Pennsylvania Press, 1994.

Maurri, Enzo. *Un fiorentino tra Medioevo e Rinascimento: Sant'Antonino.* Turin: Edizioni Paoline, 1989.

Meltzer, Françoise. *Salome and the Dance of Writing.* Chicago: University of Chicago Press, 1987.

Monson, Craig A., ed. *The Crannied Wall: Women, Religion, and the Arts in Early Modern Europe.* Ann Arbor: University of Michigan Press, 1992.

Newbigin, Nerida. "Politics in the *sacra rappresentazione*." In *Lorenzo the Magnificent: Culture and Politics*, ed. Michael Mallett and Nicholas Mann, 117–30. London: Warburg Institute, 1996.

Oesterley, W. O. E. *An Introduction to the Books of the Apocrypha.* London: SPCK, 1958.

Okin, Susan Moller. *Women in Western Political Thought.* Princeton: Princeton University Press, 1979.

Orvieto, Paolo. *Pulci medievale.* Rome: Salerno, 1978.

Ozment, Steven. *The Bürgermeister's Daughter: Scandal in a Sixteenth-Century German Town.* New York: St. Martin's Press, 1995.

Pagels, Elaine. *Adam, Eve, and the Serpent.* New York: HarperCollins, 1988.

Pampaloni, Guido. "I Tornaquinci poi Tornabuoni, fino ai primi del Cinquecento." *Archivio Storico Italiano* 126 (1968): 331–62.

Parducci, A. "La ystoria della devota Susanna di Lucrezia Tornabuoni." *Annali delle Università Toscane* 10 (1926): 177–201.

Pfeiffer, Robert H. *History of New Testament Times with an Introduction to the Apocrypha.* New York: Harper, 1949.

Pieraccini, Gaetano. "L'effige di Lucrezia Tornabuoni, madre di Lorenzo de' Medici." *Rivista d'Arte* 27 (1951–52): 179–84.

Pomeroy, Sarah B. *Goddesses, Whores, Wives, and Slaves: Women in Classical Antiquity.* New York: Schocken, 1976.

Riddle, John. *Contraception and Abortion from the Ancient World to the Renaissance.* Cambridge: Harvard University Press, 1992.

———. *Eve's Herbs: A History of Contraception and Abortion in the West.* Cambridge: Harvard University Press, 1997.

Rochon, André. *La jeunesse de Laurent de Médicis (1449–1478).* Paris: Belles Lettres, 1963.

Rose, Mary Beth, ed. *Women in the Middle Ages and the Renaissance: Literary and Historical Perspectives.* Syracuse: Syracuse University Press, 1986.

Rubinstein, Nicolai. "Lorenzo de' Medici: The Formation of His Statecraft." In *Lorenzo de' Medici: Studi,* ed. Gian Carlo Garfagnini, 41–66. Florence: Olschki, 1992.

Russell, Rinaldina. "Lucrezia Tornabuoni (1427–82)." In *Italian Women Writers: A Bio-bibliographical Sourcebook,* ed. Rinaldina Russell, 431–40. Westport, Conn.: Greenwood Press, 1994.

Santagata, Marco, and Stefano Carrai. *La lirica di corte nell'Italia del Quattrocento.* Milan: FrancoAngeli, 1993.

Schiebinger, Londa. *Nature's Body: Gender in the Making of Modern Science.* Boston: Beacon Press, 1993.

Scott, Karen. "St. Catherine of Siena, 'Apostola.'" *Church History* 61 (1992): 34–46.

———. "Urban Spaces, Women's Networks, and the Lay Apostolate in the Siena of Catherine Benincasa." In *Creative Women in Medieval and Early Modern Italy: A Religious and Artistic Renaissance,* ed. E. Ann Matter and John Coakley, 105–19. Philadelphia: University of Pennsylvania Press, 1995.

Sizeranne, Robert de la. *Celebrities of the Italian Renaissance in Florence and in the Louvre.* Trans. Jeffrey E. Jeffrey. London: Brentano's, 1926.

Sommerville, Margaret R. *Sex and Subjection: Attitudes to Women in Early-Modern Society.* London: Arnold, 1995.

Spencer, Jane. *The Rise of the Woman Novelist: From Aphra Behn to Jane Austen.* Oxford: Basil Blackwell, 1986.

Spender, Dale. *Mothers of the Novel: One Hundred Good Women Writers before Jane Austen.* New York: Routledge, 1986.

Steinbrugge, Lieselotte. *The Moral Sex: Woman's Nature in the French Enlightenment.* Trans. Pamela E. Selwyn. New York: Oxford University Press, 1995.

Stuard, Susan M. "The Dominion of Gender: Women's Fortunes in the High Middle Ages." In *Becoming Visible: Women in European History,* ed. Renate Bridenthal, Claudia Koonz, and Susan M. Stuard, 2d ed., 153–72. Boston: Houghton Mifflin, 1987.

Sydie, R. A. "Humanism, Patronage and the Question of Women's Artistic Genius in the Italian Renaissance." *Journal of Historical Sociology* 3 (1989): 175–205.

Tartari, V. "Il maestro della storia di Griselda e una famiglia senese di mecenati dimenticata." *Acta Historiae Artium* 25 (1979): 27–66.

Le tems revient—'l tempo si rinuova: Feste e spettacoli nella Firenze di Lorenzo il Magnifico (1449–1492). Ed. Paola Ventrone. Florence: Silvana, 1992.

Tetel, Marcel. *Marguerite de Navarre's Heptameron: Themes, Language, and Structure.* Durham, N.C.: Duke University Press, 1973.

Tomas, Natalie. *"A Positive Novelty": Women and Public Life in Renaissance Florence.* Clayton, Vic.: Monash University, Department of History, 1992.

Treggiari, Susan. *Roman Marriage: Iusti Coniuges from the Time of Cicero to the Time of Ulpian.* Oxford: Oxford University Press, 1991.

Trexler, Richard. *Public Life in Renaissance Florence.* Ithaca: Cornell University Press, 1980.

Tylus, Jane. "Caterina da Siena and the Legacy of Humanism." In *Perspectives on Early Modern and Modern Intellectual History: Essays in Honor of Nancy S. Struever,* ed. Joseph Marino and Melinda Schlitt, 116–43. Rochester: University of Rochester Press, 2000.

Walfish, Barry. *Esther in Medieval Garb: Jewish Interpretation of the Book of Esther in the Middle Ages.* Albany: State University of New York Press, 1993.

Walsh, William T. *St. Teresa of Avila: A Biography.* Rockford, Ill.: TAN, 1987.

Warner, Marina. *Alone of All Her Sex: The Myth and Cult of the Virgin Mary.* New York: Knopf, 1976.

Wiesner, Merry E. *Women and Gender in Early Modern Europe.* Cambridge: Cambridge University Press, 1993.

Willard, Charity Cannon. *Christine de Pizan: Her Life and Works.* New York: Persea, 1984.

Wilson, Katharina, ed. *An Encyclopedia of Continental Women Writers.* New York: Garland, 1991.

Zervas, Diane Finiello Zervas. "'Quos volent et eo modo quo volent': Piero de' Medici and the *Operai* of SS. Annunziata, 1445–55." In *Florence and Italy: Renaissance Studies in Honour of Nicolai Rubinstein,* ed. Peter Denley and Caroline Elam, 465–79. London: Committee for Medieval Studies, Westfield College, University of London, 1988.

Zuraw, Shelley. "The Medici Portraits of Mino da Fiesole." In *Piero de' Medici: "Il Gottoso" (1416–1469),* ed. Andreas Beyer and Bruce Boucher, 317–39. Berlin: Akademie Verlag, 1993.

INDEX